Minecraft is an open-world game that doesn't hold your hand and tell you where to travel or what to work on. You're the one in charge, and you decide what happens. This book tells you how to play the game and what you might find out there, but we're really just giving you suggestions. If you want more ideas on how to build, craft, fight, and thrive in this world, we're here to help.

This book covers every aspect of the game, so that you can quickly find whatever you're looking for. And now, we're going to go into even more detail on difficult projects: larger builds, machinery, and other tricky aspects of gameplay. This guide expands on our coverage, brings the book all the way up to date with the latest game patches, and lets you learn how to play with more Mods and Resource Packs.

Here are the chapters in this book:

WHAT'S NEW IN THIS GUIDE? tells you about all the changes we've made to this book to cover all of the new content in *Minecraft* over the last year. We also talk about the new material that we've added for higher-level gameplay!

The **ART GALLERY** chapter is an artistic addition to the guide that provides some amusing informational tidbits about major aspects of the game while showing off some dynamic, colorful illustrations inspired by *Minecraft*.

A HISTORY OF MINECRAFT goes through the years and shows when things were added to the game.

BEFORE WE START is a chapter covering *Minecraft*'s controls and the differences between various versions of the game: PC vs. consoles vs. the Pocket Edition. Beginners should go here first to find out how to move around, build, craft, and defend themselves.

LET'S BEGIN WITH THE BASICS takes your introduction to *Minecraft* a step beyond just getting started. We guide you through the first few play sessions, giving you basic goals and tips on how to survive. Once you've mastered these, it's much easier to branch out and explore the world at your leisure.

YOU CAN DO ANYTHING WITH A LITTLE PRACTICE is an advanced chapter that covers the more complex systems in *Minecraft*. We get into deeper discussions about farming, mining, special locations, achievements, enchanting, brewing, and more. When you're interested in learning all there is to learn, this is where you want to go.

PLAYING WITH YOUR FRIENDS is a brief multiplayer chapter on finding buddies to play with, running a local server, etiquette, and other social elements of the game.

TOOLS, RESOURCES, AND CONSUMABLES is a resource-heavy chapter. We give you a breakdown of every block type, item, and recipe in the game. Try this portion of the guide when you forget a crafting recipe, want to see the uses of a new item, or just feel the urge to browse through *Minecraft*'s possibilities.

CREATURES BIG AND SMALL tells you all about the monsters and animals in the Overworld, the Nether, and The End. Everything in the game is discussed, so you can see how tough enemies are, or find out how to take care of friendly creatures.

BIGGER AND BETTER PROJECTS is for veteran players who want to find more ways to explore the more challenging sides of the game. We delve much deeper into machine use, large-scale builds, and how to take your world in new directions.

MODIFYING YOUR GAME finishes the book with suggestions for taking your *Minecraft* in new directions with texture packs, special skins, mods, and more. Just when you think you've seen it all, there's always something new—that's *Minecraft* for you!

WHAT'S NEW iN THiS GUiDE?

Minecraft is a game that grows over time. Each year, more blocks, creatures, content, and options are added to the main game. This is always exciting because you never know what the future is going to bring. Because of that, we've taken the time to add more ideas, explanations, and examples to our book. Every chapter has been revised to reflect the game as it stands today. Plus we've included new chapters, so let's talk about those.

BUILD, DISCOVER, SURVIVE!
MASTERING MINECRAFT®
REVISED and EXPANDED

Written by Michael Lummis,
Christopher Burton, and Kathleen Pleet
Illustrations by Daz Tibbles

WELCOME TO MINECRAFT

Are you someone who likes to fight monsters, adventure through strange worlds, and come back laden with gold, riches, and glory? Or are you the type of person who wants to explore, build great castles, mine the depths of the world, and see all there is to see in the universe?

Either way, you should be very happy because we have an entire book devoted to talking about *Minecraft*! Whether you're a fighter, explorer, builder, or dreamer, this game has something special for you.

ART GALLERY

In this edition of the guide, we've included original artwork inspired by the characters, creatures, items, and worlds of *Minecraft*. Visit this artistic section of the guide for dynamic, colorful depictions of some of your favorite characters and creatures, along with some amusing tidbits of information. See, Creepers don't have to be scary. They can be cute. From a distance.

A HISTORY OF MINECRAFT

We wanted to show off the changes from more recent patches to the game, but in the middle of doing that, we thought, "Why not go through the history of *Minecraft* and talk about when all of the game systems were added—it's pretty cool stuff." So that's exactly what we did. You won't have to read this if you're looking for purely mechanical help with playing the game, but if you're interested in the legacy of *Minecraft*, this chapter is right up your alley.

BIGGER AND BETTER PROJECTS

This chapter is our primary focus for new ideas and fun in this version of the book. Last year, we gave everyone a solid foundation to build on for a wide variety of *Minecraft* structures, traps, and machines. Now that people have had time to practice, they should be ready for the next step. We take you through creating dungeons, group projects, and other wild ideas. If you haven't read the rest of the guide yet, hold off on this chapter; we're going to forge ahead without taking as long to explain the fundamentals. This is for players who've already mastered the basics and want to try entirely new challenges.

STEVE

STATUS:
Friendly

REGION:
Anywhere

APPEARS:
When People
Want to Play

ITEM DROPS:
Whatever
He's Carrying

HEALTH:
20

**ATTACK
DAMAGE:**
Weapon
Dependent

**EXPERIENCE
VALUE:**
Varies

TAMEABLE:
No

RIDEABLE:
No

QUOTATION:
"Did you hear
something?"

Steve is the epitome of miners. He's worked hard to find a place for himself in the Overworld, and it's been a long struggle to discover how to survive in such a rugged wilderness. Sometimes alone, other times joined by others, he's made a niche for himself.

PiG

STATUS:
Passive

REGION:
The Overworld

APPEARS:
In Small Groups

ITEM DROPS:
Raw Porkchop

HEALTH:
10

ATTACK DAMAGE:
None

EXPERIENCE VALUE:
1-3

TAMEABLE:
No

RIDEABLE:
Yes

QUOTATION:
"Carrots are delicious!"

Horses are wonderful, but Pigs are clearly the ultimate mount in *Minecraft*. They're easy to find and can be ridden anywhere. Also, if you're desperate, pigs can be eaten. If you haven't taken the time to hug your friendly Pigs today, try and do so.

SHEEP

STATUS:
Passive

REGION:
The Overworld

APPEARS:
In Small Herds

ITEM DROPS:
Wool,
Raw Mutton

HEALTH:
8

ATTACK DAMAGE:
None

EXPERIENCE VALUE:
1-3

TAMEABLE:
No

RIDEABLE:
No

QUOTATION:
"Shears get you more Wool. I'm not tasty at all! Put that Sword away."

Sheep are your source of Wool, and that should never be underestimated. Wool provides Beds and decorative blocks that can be turned into any color with the appropriate dyes. This makes Sheep the finest resource for decorations in all of *Minecraft*. It's possible to make your house look like almost anything with enough Sheep around.

CREEPER

STATUS:
Aggressive

REGION:
The Overworld

APPEARS:
When It's Dark

ITEM DROPS:
Gunpowder,
Music Discs

HEALTH:
20

**ATTACK
DAMAGE:**
49-97

**EXPERIENCE
VALUE:**
5

TAMEABLE:
No

RIDEABLE:
No

QUOTATION:
"Tsssssssssssss."

Creepers are the best known and most feared enemy throughout the Overworld. While some watch the night in terror of Endermen, the stealthy Creepers are the more common danger. Silent until it's too late, these horrors are patient and brutal in their effectiveness. Even in broad daylight, they persist and hunt their victims. Get distracted for one minute and the last thing you hear may very well be that dreaded hiss.

SKELETON

STATUS:
Aggressive

REGION:
The Overworld

APPEARS:
When It's Dark

ITEM DROPS:
Arrow, Bone

HEALTH:
20

ATTACK DAMAGE:
3 at Range,
2 in Melee

EXPERIENCE VALUE:
5

TAMEABLE:
No

RIDEABLE:
No

QUOTATION:
"Twang."

Skeletons are easy to kill once they are nearby, but these nightly hunters shoot well and can badly hurt anyone who doesn't find cover quickly. The sound of a bow firing in the distance is your cue to sprint toward shelter.

ENDERMAN

STATUS:
Neutral

REGION:
The Overworld
or The End

APPEARS:
In the Dark

ITEM DROPS:
Ender Pearls

HEALTH:
40

**ATTACK
DAMAGE:**
7

**EXPERIENCE
VALUE:**
5

TAMEABLE:
No

RIDEABLE:
No

QUOTATION:
"I don't like
    when people
    look at me!!!"

Endermen are like ink moving in the shadows. Docile at first, they become enraged if you dare to look them in the eyes. Keep a submissive gaze on the floor to avoid their wrath, or arm yourself with the best weapons and armor and grin triumphantly while staring them down.

ZOMBiE

STATUS:
Aggressive

REGION:
The Overworld

APPEARS:
In the Dark

ITEM DROPS:
Rotten Flesh

HEALTH:
20

ATTACK DAMAGE:
1-6

EXPERIENCE VALUE:
5

TAMEABLE:
No

RIDEABLE:
No

QUOTATION:
"Brains."

Zombies are a humble threat, but they're also a constant danger. Lurking in the night, they can strike at any time. Whether banging around outside your house or wandering through the forest, they ensure that nighttime is rarely the right time to go wandering alone. Hunt Zombies for experience, their flesh—edible in only the most desperate cases—or for rare drops. For some reason, Zombies sometimes like to carry Potatoes and Carrots. Maybe they were farmers in their past lives.

ZOMBiE PiGMAN

STATUS:
Neutral

REGION:
The Nether

APPEARS:
All Over
the Place

ITEM DROPS:
Rotten Flesh,
Gold Nugget,
Gold Ingot

HEALTH:
20

**ATTACK
DAMAGE:**
9

**EXPERIENCE
VALUE:**
5

TAMEABLE:
No

RIDEABLE:
No

QUOTATION:
"If you hurt
one of us,
all of us are
going to hurt
you more."

Zombie Pigmen live in small communities throughout the Nether. They don't attack on sight, but become very aggressive if anything hurts one of their members. Be careful not to attack any Pigmen unless you're ready to fight all of them in the area. Flee if a Ghast manages to set any Pigmen on fire; the Pigmen get a bit stabby about that, even if it's not directly your fault.

WITCH

STATUS:
Aggressive

REGION:
The Overworld

APPEARS:
In the Dark

ITEM DROPS:
Glass Bottle,
Glowstone Dust,
Gunpowder,
Redstone,
Spider Eye,
Stick, Sugar

HEALTH:
26

ATTACK DAMAGE:
Poison and
Harming

EXPERIENCE VALUE:
5

TAMEABLE:
No

RIDEABLE:
No

QUOTATION:
"Here, drink
this. It's good
for you."

Witches are alchemists who have mastered the art of potion brewing. Instead of attacking with melee weapons, they hurl potions, causing either Poison or Harm effects. Neither are good news, so stay behind cover and ambush Witches if they come around the corner. Kill them quickly and escape to heal from any of their potions' effects.

GHAST

STATUS:
Aggressive

REGION:
The Nether

APPEARS:
All the Time

ITEM DROPS:
Gunpowder,
Ghast Tears

HEALTH:
10

**ATTACK
DAMAGE:**
17

**EXPERIENCE
VALUE:**
5

TAMEABLE:
No

RIDEABLE:
No

QUOTATION:
"Where
aaarrrreeee
you?"

Ghasts are flying beasts of the Nether. They unleash fireballs once you're spotted, and they have amazing range. Run to get away from these projectiles, and then find a good spot to return fire using a Bow. In a pinch, brave warriors can reflect Ghast fireballs by striking them at the last minute. Returning a fireball and scoring a kill against a Ghast is a sight to see!

STATUS:
Aggressive

REGION:
Anywhere

APPEARS:
When
Summoned

ITEM DROPS:
Nether Star

HEALTH:
300

**ATTACK
DAMAGE:**
8

**EXPERIENCE
VALUE:**
50

TAMEABLE:
No

RIDEABLE:
No

QUOTATION:
"Black is my
favorite color.
I like writing
sad poetry
and hunting
miners."

The Wither is a boss many people will never see. It takes serious dedication to summon one of these monsters—the ritual requires Wither Skeleton skulls. These skulls don't drop often, and the Wither Skeletons that spawn them are only found in Nether Fortresses (and not even all of those have them). With the necessary materials, find a very out-of-the-way location to summon the Wither and get ready to see half of the landscape obliterated. Whenever possible, bring friends. It's dangerous to go alone.

THE ENDERDRAGON

STATUS:
Aggressive

REGION:
The End

APPEARS:
There Until
Killed

ITEM DROPS:
Overworld
Portal,
Dragon Egg

HEALTH:
200

**ATTACK
DAMAGE:**
10

**EXPERIENCE
VALUE:**
12,000

TAMEABLE:
No

RIDEABLE:
You Wish

QUOTATION:
"Ender Crystals
heal me. You
cannot defeat
me unless you
destroy them.
Why did I tell
you that?"

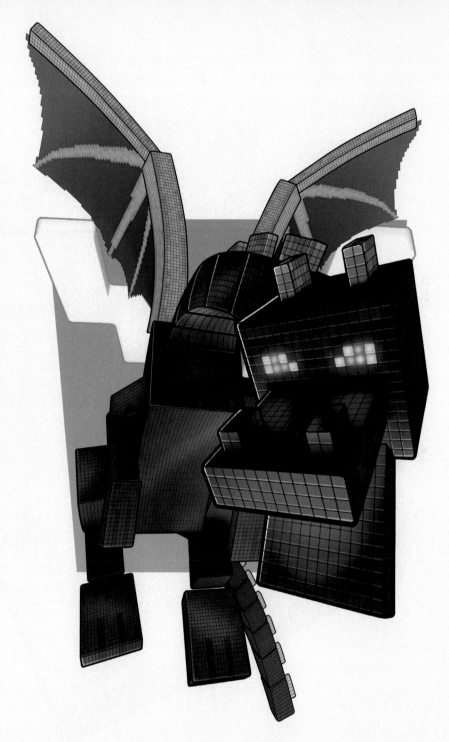

The Enderdragon is the greatest test of mettle in all of *Minecraft*. Even harder to kill than the Wither, this boss of bosses has many layers of protection. First off, it's hard to find The Enderdragon's home. It lives in a world called The End, and it can only be reached through extensive toil and questing. Even if you find the way to The End, you must destroy the creature's Ender Crystals and then take the battle directly to the Enderdragon. All of this is easier said than done!

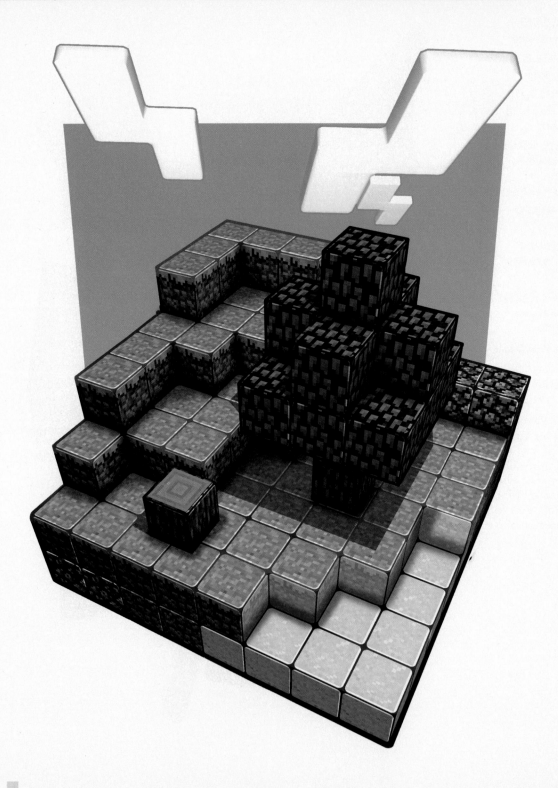

The Overworld is where all miners begin their journey. This land is filled with many biomes that encompass forests, oceans, plains, desert, and beyond. There are mountains to climb, chasms to spelunk, and monsters to battle. This land is your home for most of the journey, though there are other places to explore for the truly daring.

THE NETHER

In a world far beyond the Overworld lies a land of fire and ruin. This is the Nether. It has the deadliest monsters, the harshest environment, and a few treasures not seen anywhere else in the universe. Come here to master crafting, find materials to summon the Wither, or simply to test yourself against a realm of flame.

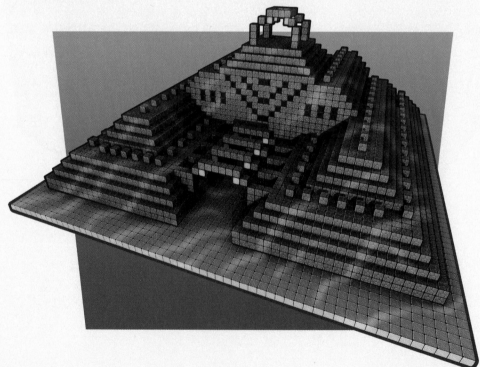

The Overworld has special places created by people long ago. These monuments live on in testament to the creativity of others. Find them in deserts and jungles, and even under the waves of the oceans. Search carefully, for these monuments have rare treasures, but also be wary of their traps and guards.

Miners are nothing without their tools. If you're going to shape the surrounding world, it's a requirement to have weapons, armor, light, food, and a wealth of additional toys. *Minecraft* is all about exploration and creation, so combine things and try new recipes and materials to make whatever you desire.

A HiSTORY OF MiNECRAFT

Minecraft, as we write this book, is the third best-selling video game of all time. It's sold over 65 million registered copies across many platforms, and continues to grow and expand. It has spawned its own convention (Minecon), and has fans all over the world. But where did it come from?

Minecraft started its alpha testing in 2009, and it was released in full during 2011's holiday season. It's been several years since then, and several rounds of improvements have been made to the base game. If you've ever wondered about the timeline for this, read on. We've catalogued everything that's come and gone in the last six years. Let's see where it takes us.

PRE-ALPHA MINECRAFT
(May 2009 – June 2010)

Minecraft was in heavy development during 2009. Players followed the introduction of a huge range of items into *Minecraft*. This is called *Minecraft Classic*. Not many games were picked up by players during development at that time. This has changed quite a bit in the last few years, and *Minecraft*'s success likely played a critical factor in that.

The first official version of *Minecraft* that we know of was 0.0.9a. This was a time when you'd see new types of blocks added constantly. Many of the items became core elements of gameplay that are still here today (e.g., Lava, Trees, and Sand).

Indev and Infdev came next. During late 2009 and the first half of 2010, players saw the introduction of far more complex items. Signs, Ladders, and Doors came into use. Cave systems became more complex. Minecarts, Spawners, and Dungeons were all added as well. Things got a lot more dangerous out there in the night. Luckily, daylight hours were increased, so players had more time to build shelter before the nasties started knocking on doors.

Survival Mode helped *Minecraft* grow from a building and exploration simulator into a full-fledged game of life or death. The burning hiss of Creepers continues to live on in players' nightmares.

ALPHA
(June 2010 – December 2010)

Alpha took up the second half of 2010. Machinery was a major focus at this time. To power the machinery, Levers, Buttons, Plates, and Redstone were provided. These made the game much more intricate. It wasn't just a survival game with cool buildings; you could suddenly make the game do things that didn't even seem possible without some serious forethought and planning. Automated systems started with doors that you didn't need to open manually, basic traps, and so forth. Soon, they grew into automated farms, monster harvesting rooms, and even storage systems. Players have made "hard drives" within *Minecraft* and created computers that let you play *Minecraft*—while you're playing *Minecraft*.

BETA
(December 2010 – November 2011)

Leading up to release, players got to fill out the world. Weather added some considerable ambience, and also held a few surprises (what happens when various things are struck by lightning?).

Even more machinery was added, but there was also a large push for better player mechanics. Combat improved with critical strikes, the need to keep yourself properly fed for healing, and superior bow fighting. The sluggish heroes finally learned how to sprint and get around the world much faster.

Villages, Strongholds, and other rare locations also began to appear. *Minecraft* had more toys in its sandbox, which made exploration even more fun.

RELEASE
(November 2011)

The game released with a few new features that hadn't been part of the Beta (they were in the Beta 1.9 release that never came to be because they were rolled into the main game). This included Hardcore Mode, for people who wanted to really challenge themselves.

Negative and positive status effects appeared, such as Strength boosting, Poison, and so forth. Brewing was introduced, as well as Breeding. The End was added, along with Nether Fortresses, so players had quite a huge amount of new things to try and accomplish.

1.1 (January 2012)

Players didn't have to wait long for a substantial patch. Major language support was added (try playing the game in Pirate Speak or Klingon sometime!). There were also quite a few tweaks and adjustments made to improve general gameplay, but not too many major overhauls were done at that time.

1.2 (March 2012)

NPC Villages weren't too happy about this patch—it came with Zombie sieges. At night, villagers had to contend with heavy monster attacks as long as there were players anywhere in the same chunk. This sometimes led to entire depopulations of the towns. Pretty nifty, actually. Fallen villagers become Zombies themselves, further adding to the chaos and destruction. Good times!

Biomes continued to expand, so world generation improved a decent bit after 1.2 was added.

1.3 (August 2012)

This was the first patch where Adventure Mode was available. Players could craft specific challenges and structures for others to explore, and this was possible because creating buildings was disabled. Fire and bucket use were also restricted, so adventurers couldn't simply tunnel or burn their way through everything.

Villages continued to improve as well. Trading was introduced, so villagers had a bit more purpose besides simply being cool to find and protect (or slaughter if you weren't such a nice person).

1.4 "The Pretty Scary Update" (October 2012)

Beacons and Anvils were added. Beacons were especially cool because they are so hard to create, so they serve as yet another type of late-game goal for serious players to focus on. Speaking of endgame stuff, the Wither was included in this update. Being one of the nastiest things in the game, this boss is hard to summon and can be quite tough to kill.

Players also got to meet Witches, Wither Skeletons, and Bats. This made for a really cool Halloween in *Minecraft* history.

1.5 "The Redstone Update" (March 2013)

Even more machines came into play with 1.5. Activator Rails, Daylight Sensors, Droppers, Hoppers, Redstone Blocks, Comparators, and Weighted Pressure Plates were introduced. *Minecraft* machinery was always cool, but many more automations were possible after this.

1.6 "The Horse Update" (July 2013)

Wolves and Ocelots were already in the game, but Horses were an absolutely necessary inclusion for many players. Exploration was even cooler now that you could take your animal friend along for the ride.

1.7 "The Update That Changed the World" (October 2013)

Our personal favorite was patch 1.7. The improvement to world generation was extreme; biome additions and improvements made the world richer, so regions felt like they had much better differentiation.

1.8 "The Bountiful Update" (September 2014)

Mapmaking and Survival Mode both received updates and improvements in 1.8. There were also quite a few new types of blocks added to the world, which greatly enhanced the feeling that the underground wasn't just a huge slab of rock and special resources. New varieties of stones and ores added visual appeal to the underground areas, and also improved the ability to build interesting structures that had more stylish decorations.

Villages also became more robust. Villagers could be encouraged to breed through gifts of food, and adult villagers gained distinct professions for trading.

The rest of the world became slightly happier and cuter with the inclusion of Rabbits. To balance all things good and evil, Guardians and Endermites were also included.

1.9 "The Combat Update" (Unreleased)

Shields, Quivers, and left-handed items are all planned inclusions in the next major update. We can't wait to try them all out!

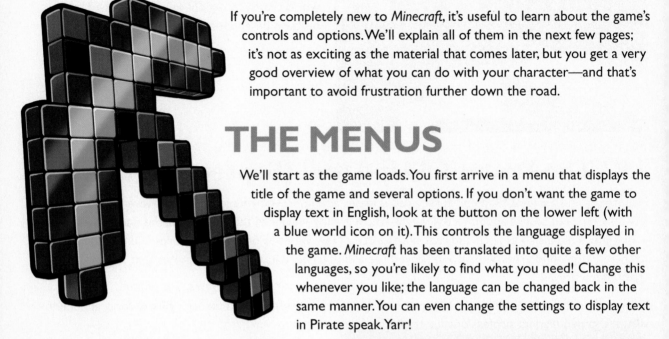

If you're completely new to *Minecraft*, it's useful to learn about the game's controls and options. We'll explain all of them in the next few pages; it's not as exciting as the material that comes later, but you get a very good overview of what you can do with your character—and that's important to avoid frustration further down the road.

THE MENUS

We'll start as the game loads. You first arrive in a menu that displays the title of the game and several options. If you don't want the game to display text in English, look at the button on the lower left (with a blue world icon on it). This controls the language displayed in the game. *Minecraft* has been translated into quite a few other languages, so you're likely to find what you need! Change this whenever you like; the language can be changed back in the same manner. You can even change the settings to display text in Pirate speak. Yarr!

Next, look at the Options menu, toward the bottom. You can access this menu while you're playing or when you're just sitting in the menu. There are quite a few controls here, so we have a few things to cover. Some are mentioned elsewhere in the guide because of their relevance to different subjects, but we'll also talk about all of the options right now.

FOV

FOV stands for Field of View. This determines how much of the game world your character sees at a given time. Set this really high if you'd like to see a huge amount of the world around your character. Set it low if you want to look closely at things that are directly in front of you.

Because this isn't a game with much shooting, the default FOV works really well. It's a good balance of vision around your character.

Difficulty

Choose between Peaceful, Easy, Normal, and Hard difficulties. These settings control the damage output of monsters and a number of additional factors as well. Peaceful Difficulty turns off monster damage entirely. After that, raising the Difficulty meter makes the game harder and harder. Damage on Hard is sometimes more than twice what it is on Easy.

- Chance for Villagers to turn into Zombies when slain by Zombies

- How often monsters appear with weapons (and if those weapons are enchanted)

- If monsters attempt to pick up dropped items

- If Spider attacks have status effects

- The rate at which Zombie Pigmen come out of Nether Portals

- Whether Zombies appear with additional Zombie allies

Music and Sounds

Use this submenu to control the volume of various game elements. If you want music to be off (or quieter), come here. The same is true for weather noises, monsters, other players, blocks, the environment, and so forth.

If anything bothers you, slide these bars around to find out how to silence the sound that you don't like. Otherwise, you don't need to mess with this submenu.

Super Secret Settings

This odd button in the Options menu lets you influence how the game is displayed. Most of the possibilities are strange-looking and make *Minecraft* somewhat harder to play, but it's fun to mess around with them.

Broadcast Settings

This submenu lets you link your game account with a Twitch account, so you can stream *Minecraft* online. This is a somewhat advanced thing to do, so you don't have to try it when you're a beginner. We'll talk more about that later.

Video Settings

Come to Video Settings if you want to tweak how much detail is rendered in *Minecraft*. You can control whether the game looks as pretty as possible or runs as quickly as you'd like. Very strong systems can run everything in *Minecraft* without sacrificing any quality, but people run this game on a wide range of computers.

If the game doesn't feel like it's running quickly, turn down settings like Anisotropic Filter or Particles, and switch Graphics to Fast. You should also lower the Render Distance.

If your computer is running *Minecraft* wonderfully, then turn everything up and see if the game still runs fine. Go ahead and enjoy the game even more!

If your system can handle it, adjust the Graphics and Render Distance settings to see the in-game world at its best.

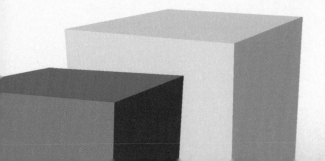

Controls

The Control submenu is the most involved menu in the group. It lets you influence how you move your character, break blocks, build things, and so forth. You can flip the mouse so that it acts more like a joystick; turn on/off Touchscreen Mode; or switch the keys that control your character.

Because our book handles all versions of *Minecraft*, we don't know how you'll assign your keyboard controls, or if you're even going to use a keyboard! Therefore, we won't say things like, "Press Left Control to do this." Instead, we'll talk about the game's actual commands, like this:

"Sprint to get away from the Creeper."

"Break three blocks of Stone and look in your inventory after you pick them up."

"Stack blocks together until you're happy with how they look."

Because of this, it's very important that you learn what the commands are before going deeper into the book. Here they are!

MINECRAFT COMMANDS

COMMAND NAME	WHAT IT DOES
Attack/Destroy	Uses your hands or the object you're holding to hit anything in front of your character.
Drop Item	Drops the item that you are currently holding.
Pick Block	If you're looking at a type of block, this switches so that your character holds any blocks of that type that are in your inventory.
Sprint	Move at higher speed, but causes you to get hungry much faster.
Use Item/Place Block	Places a block that you're holding on the ground where you are looking. Or tries to activate any Doors, Levers, or controllable objects in front of your character.
Hotbar Slot (1-9)	Switches what you're holding to the item that is located on your hotbar at the bottom of the screen. There are nine of these slots.
Inventory	Opens your inventory and shows you what your character is holding. Your hotbar slots are also shown there.
Take Screenshot	Grabs a picture of the game.
Toggle Cinematic Camera	Makes the camera move in a slower, panning fashion.
Toggle Fullscreen	Switches between a windowed view of the game and a full-screen display.
Toggle Perspective	Lets you decide whether to look at the world from a first-person perspective or from one of two third-person perspectives.
Jump	Causes you to jump; this also causes your character to get hungry faster.
Sneak	Lets you move quietly and slowly, preventing your character from falling off of ledges. Very useful!
Strafe Left	Walk to the left.
Strafe Right	Walk to the right.
Walk Forward	Go forward.
Walk Backward	Go backward.
List Players	See a list of the people who are playing on the same server.
Open Chat	Lets you type in anything you want and then shows the message to everyone on the server. "Hi guys!"
Open Command	Lets you type in a command to control the game world.
Pause Stream	Stops showing your game on Twitch; press the button again to resume your stream.
Push to Talk	Use this to broadcast what you're saying to people on your stream.
Show Stream Commercials	Starts commercials on your stream, if that is set up.
Start/Stop Stream	Begin or end sessions with this command.

Language

This opens the same menu that you accessed from the world icon back in the game's front menu.

Multiplayer Settings

This submenu is primarily focused on the way text displays when you join multiplayer servers. To make the screen easier to read on those servers, you can always turn off Colors, Web Links, or even the entire Chat system.

Resource Packs

Resource Packs modify the game in a variety of ways. We'll go over these at the end of the book, so you'll know what they do and how to set them up.

Snooper Settings

Turn this off if you don't want the game to send information about your play to Mojang. Or, turn this back on if you're cool with that. Leaving the Snooper mode on does not influence gameplay in a major way, so there isn't a substantial downside to turning it on or off.

SINGLE PLAYER

This menu lets you create a new world or return to one that you've already made. We'll walk you through that in the next chapter, and it's a very intuitive process.

MULTIPLAYER

When you first open the Multiplayer menu, there won't be any servers available. Instead, you have to go online and look up places to join. Search the internet with your browser, and use "Minecraft Servers" to find lists of them. When you go, copy their IP addresses, and come back to the Multiplayer menu.

Now that you're here with an IP address, press "Add Server" and paste the IP you found into the empty bar. Press "Done," and then you can enter that server from the Multiplayer menu in the future without having to do anything special. The game even searches ahead of time to tell you how many people are already playing on that server.

You're free to add as many or as few servers as you like. We'll talk about multiplayer servers and etiquette in a later chapter, "Playing with Your Friends."

MINECRAFT REALMS

This is a paid service that lets you set up multiplayer servers more easily. If you don't know much about multiplayer servers but still really want to have a world of your own for others to play in, this is an option. Just know that it costs money to use.

CONTROLLING YOUR CHARACTER

Once you're in game, put the commands to good use by wandering around the world and messing with everything you find. Let's quickly explain what everything on the screen means and how to control your character.

Understanding the Interface

Minecraft has a fairly simple display, so it doesn't take long to understand it. Most of the screen is taken up by a view of the game world itself. You can see what's in front of your character, and that's how you decide where to go and what to do. Easy enough.

At the very bottom of the screen are nine grey boxes. These represent your hotbar slots! Pressing the keyboard keys that are bound to those hotbar slots lets you switch between items quickly once you assign objects to the slots. For example, you can put a Pickaxe in "1," a Shovel in "2," an Axe in "3," and so forth. Doing this makes it easy to use all of your tools quickly and efficiently.

By default, consider anything that you use the most. We suggest Pickaxe, Shovel, Axe, Sword, Torches, some type of food, a construction material (Dirt or Stone), and whatever else you need.

To change your hotbar assignments, go into your inventory and drag items to the bottom row. That's where your hotbar slots are located. Move items around so that similar tools are together and can be accessed without delay.

Above your hotbar is an experience bar. This fills as your character gets orbs of experience. These are gained by killing creatures, breeding animals, refining metals in a Furnace, gathering certain minerals, and so forth.

When the bar completely fills, your character gains a level. This doesn't raise any stats, like it would in some role-playing games. Instead, levels are there so you can enchant objects later on. That's more advanced play, so we'll talk about that in the "You Can Do Anything with a Little Practice" chapter.

There are three sets of icons above your experience bar. The red hearts display your character's health. As you take damage from fire, falls, monster attacks, poison, or hunger, the hearts disappear. If all of them go away, your character dies and then respawns at either your starting point or the last Bed that you used. In Hardcore mode, even a single death is permanent, so you're gone forever.

The meat and bone icons represent your hunger meter. They deplete over time, as well as when you heal from damage or exert yourself by jumping and sprinting. Refill hunger by eating food. Characters regenerate health when only their hunger meter is nearly full, so it's wise to keep your meter at nine or ten pips as often as possible.

The last icon set shows a number of shirts. They depict your armor. The more shirts there are the better protection from monster attacks your character possesses. Craft leather or metal armor

when possible, and wear it to protect yourself. If any of those shirts suddenly disappear, it likely means that a piece of your armor just broke. Replace it!

Movement

Now that you know the interface, try moving around. Walk forward, backward, left, and right. These commands are as basic as they come, so it shouldn't take long to understand them.

Double-tap the movement keys (i.e., press them twice in the same direction as quickly as you can). This tells your character to sprint in that direction. It burns through your food quickly, but sprinting can save your life when a Creeper is about to explode or when you just need to get somewhere quickly. When night is falling and you're away from home, sprinting is often a good idea.

When you've mastered basic movement and sprinting, try jumping. Your character can hop up a single block's worth of height. If you have to go any higher than that, either dig through blocks that are more than one space above you, or build a ladder with Sticks to climb up vertical faces of mountains, trees, or whatever.

Breaking and Gathering Blocks

Once you're moving around the world, it's time to gather materials. Do this by hitting things until they break. The most basic gathering action is to walk up to a tree and attack it with your bare hands until the block of Wood breaks and falls to the ground in front of you. Collect these resources by walking directly over them; your character even picks up items automatically if they're on the ground nearby. This creates a happy "pop" sound to let you know you grabbed something.

Use your hands to break easier materials, like Dirt, Grass, Flowers, Wood, and whatnot. It's not especially fast, but it works well enough. Once you do a little bit of crafting, you get to make tools that allow faster resource gathering.

Whether you're using tools or your fists, the basics of gathering never change. Approach the block that you want to gather, attack it with your hands or tools, and keep hitting the block until it breaks. Rinse and repeat. When objects are damaged by your attacks but not destroyed, they'll almost immediately heal. That's why you have to hold the Attack button until the job is done. Test this by hitting a tree for a couple seconds and then stopping. Notice that the cracks in the Wood disappear almost immediately. The same is true for Stone and other minerals.

If you try to break blocks that are really hard, you might not even be able to break them. Or, you won't be able to gather anything even when you succeed. For example, it's possible to break Stone with your bare hands. This takes a very long time, and then when the Stone breaks, no resources fall to the ground. That's because you need a Pickaxe to break Stone. You might even need specific types of Pickaxes to harvest certain resources. More advanced metals and minerals can't be gathered without Iron or even Diamond Pickaxes!

Placing Blocks

After gathering materials, such as Wood, the items appear in your inventory. Place them in a hotbar slot to make them easier to work with. Then switch to the hotbar slot in question by pressing the shortcut key that you bound in the Options menu.

Selecting a hotbar slot with an item essentially equips that item. If it's a tool or weapon, your character holds it up and gets ready to attack with it. Other objects are held but still act like regular fists if you attack anything.

Some materials can be placed back into the game world. Blocks of Wood, Stone, Planks, and metals all fall into this category. Select these items on your hotbar and use the "Place Block" command to put the object directly in front of your character. This command is how you place furniture and building materials in the world.

Put Wood blocks down in front of your character. Look! You can make a basic wall like this. But that takes a long time. There must be a better way to get building materials, right? Let's talk about that.

Basic Crafting

You can now jump, sprint, move around, break blocks, look through your inventory, and place blocks around the world. Let's finish this puzzle. Crafting gives you the power to change materials and do thousands of interesting things. The Console and Pocket versions of *Minecraft* simplify crafting, so we'll teach you the PC method because it's the hardest version to learn. If you can craft on the PC version of *Minecraft*, you can handle any of the other versions without difficulty.

In the PC version of *Minecraft*, you have a 2 x 2 space in your inventory. It says "Crafting" above it, so you know exactly where to look. To the right of the four crafting spaces is a single square where the output from your crafting appears.

To make an item, put materials into the crafting boxes and find the right recipes to produce what you need. Experiment as much as you want, but don't get worried. Our item chapter, "Tools, Resources, and Consumables," lists everything you need to build all of the items in the game.

Also, we list common recipes again in some sections of the guide where they're especially important.

As a quick test of crafting, put a block of Wood into the crafting squares. It doesn't matter which of the four spaces you use. Just put a piece of Wood into one of them. Behold! A Wood Plank icon appears on the right. Your regular Wood block is turned into four Wooden Planks by this very simple crafting recipe. Highlight and grab the Wood Planks to put them in your inventory, and then use them as you see fit.

You can convert multiple items at the same time by stacking them on top of each other. For example, put ten blocks of Wood into the same crafting square. As before, the Wood Planks appear as a result. Click on them again and again to retrieve as many of the Wood Planks as you need.

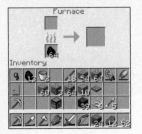

Press Shift and click on the results to craft as many items as possible instantly. Shortcuts like this allow you to craft quickly and efficiently when making huge stacks of specific items.

DIFFERENT VERSIONS OF MINECRAFT

We try very hard to talk about *Minecraft* in all of its flavors throughout this book. *Minecraft* has already been released on a huge range of platforms, including PC, tablets, and a sizable group of consoles. Using generic commands instead of specific hardware controls helps with that a fair bit, but there are other differences between the game versions as well. Some of these differences are addressed when needed as we talk about the game, but others are more global. Let's mention those now, so you know a bit more about version differences!

In effect, there are three major versions of *Minecraft*: PC, Console, and Pocket. We use the PC version as a default because that was the first *Minecraft* to hit the market. Also, in most cases, it's the most detailed version. So, if you learn the PC method for doing something, the other versions are usually a piece of cake. Throughout this book, we'll talk as if the PC version is the default, and mention changes for the other versions when they're important.

Major Console Version Changes

(Xbox 360, Xbox One, PlayStation 3, PlayStation 4, and PlayStation Vita)

- Achievements are slightly different.

- Crafting is simplified and doesn't require you to memorize patterns.

- Creatures are sometimes version-specific, so not all monsters are present in the Console versions.

- Difficulty is chosen before you enter the game world.

- LAN play is not possible, but splitscreen play is available instead (except on the PS Vita).

- There is a game tutorial to start you off and teach you the basics of the game.

- There is an "end" to the world, which you cannot pass.

- Worlds are smaller, but they can still be quite impressive.

- You start games with a Map.

Major Pocket Version Changes

(Android, iOS, Windows Phone)

- Crafting is simplified.

- Monsters behave differently.

- Multiplayer can be run in LAN mode, on Minecraft Realms, or through multiplayer servers.

- Some creatures aren't available compared with the PC version of Minecraft.

- Some flowers and crops are available only in the Pocket version.

- There is an "end" to the world.

- There isn't a world called The Nether. Instead, there is a subsection of the game involving a Nether Reactor.

Major Pi Edition Changes

(Raspberry Pi)

- This is a practice version of the game for developers/programmers to play around with.

- Combat is disabled, so exploration and construction are the primary features of the game.

LET'S BEGIN WITH THE BASICS

Minecraft is easy to play once you've gotten used to it. But, it takes a little while to get through the first part of the game without running into trouble. When you don't know how to create a safe home, grow food, or build the items you need, life can be harder!

This chapter takes you through the first 30 minutes of the game, after you've created a new world. Although you normally have a different starting point every time you play, there are common techniques that are essential for survival against monsters, starvation, and other hazards.

We'll talk about these survival techniques and give you goals to work toward, so you can use each minute as productively as possible until you've mastered the basics that are so important to your life in *Minecraft*.

If you have any trouble getting things done as quickly as you'd like, don't be afraid to start over and try again. Your first time going through these techniques will be *much* harder than the second time. So have fun and keep trying these tricks until they become second nature to you.

CREATING YOUR FIRST WORLD

Log into the game using whatever version you own, and enjoy. Select Single-Player from the main menu, and then pick "Create New World" from the menu that appears.

You arrive in a new menu. Name your world anything you'd like here; we've chosen to name ours "Minecraft 101!"

Next, choose a Game Mode: Creative, Survival, or Hardcore.

WHAT DO GAME MODES MEAN?

Creative	No risks, easy building, fly around, and do whatever you want
Survival	There are monsters, resources are limited
Hardcore	Monsters are more dangerous, and death is permanent!

We suggest that you try Survival from the very beginning. Creative mode is fun for making massive projects to show off to other people, but the challenges of Survival are quite fun. They keep you invested in the game even more than playing without a specific goal in mind.

Hardcore mode is an even better challenge, but it's probably better to wait on that until you're more experienced with the game. Dying and losing everything can be frustrating if you don't have the basics down pat.

More World Options

If you want even more power when creating your new world, select "More World Options" and toggle some of the settings in there.

Generate Structures is turned on by default. This lets the game world have villages, dungeons, abandoned mine shafts, and other cool features.

World Type lets you try out extreme biome conditions. In other words, you can have your world create larger biomes—this makes it harder to gather multiple resource types as quickly, because travel is a greater investment. Amplified biomes make your regions more extreme. It's pretty wild, but that's another option that we don't recommend for beginners.

Allow Cheats if you want to use various commands to make the game easier, or to test out specific things. You can see monsters that are normally restricted to specific places, or just goof around.

The Bonus Chest is a feature that *is* beginner-friendly. If you're having any trouble with the game, go ahead and turn this on to begin your journey with a few extra items.

WHAT'S IN THE BOX?

The Bonus Chest has a few Torches surrounding it. The chest itself has a little bit of food and some wood. This gets you started on your construction even faster than usual.

When you set the options exactly the way you like, create the world and wait a moment while the game puts it together. Soon, you'll begin your journey.

IS THIS WHERE YOU WANT TO LIVE?

As soon as the screen clears and you can look around, see what's near your character. Let's create a checklist to see if you have what you need to survive!

CHECKLIST FOR SURVIVAL

- Are there trees in your line of sight?

- Do you see or hear any animals?

- Can you find a location that would be safe for building a house or a cave?

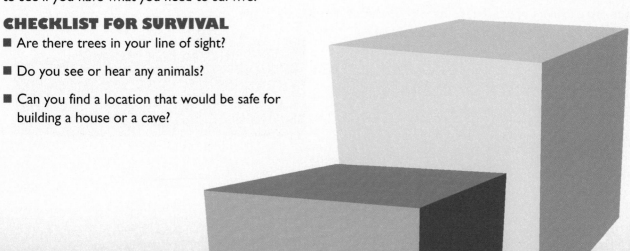

WOOD

The three items in the preceding checklist are your immediate priorities. You need trees for Wood. That's essential for your survival, because you need Wood for construction, basic tools, and for fire. It's your lifeblood during the earliest parts of the game. If you can't see any trees at all, either restart or move quickly in any direction to find an area that does have trees. You can survive without Wood, but it'll be much tougher because you won't be able to use any tools.

ANIMALS

Many animals that you can see and hear during the day are useful. These creatures provide food, Wool, Leather, and other nice items for crafting. In the early game, edible animals are the best because they get you food much sooner than farming. We've sorted the common animals in the following list from most useful to least useful for a starting hero.

Cows	Drop multiple pieces of meat and can be milked once you find a bit of Iron
Chickens	Easy to raise, drop meat when killed
Pigs	Drop meat when killed
Sheep	Drop Mutton when killed and have Wool for Beds
Horses	Not very useful in the early game

SAFE HOUSING

You can build a house darn near anywhere, but some locations are easier and faster to work with. Open, flat ground is nice if you want to have a free-standing house that looks nice. If you're just interested in survival, you're even better off scanning the area for a hill or mountain. Building into existing Dirt or Stone lets you create a defensive location very quickly, because you won't need to put down many blocks of Wood or Stone to secure yourself. Instead, hollow out a small space and you'll be good to go in almost no time at all.

Now that you know what to look for—is your area a good enough starting point? For a total beginner, we recommend you demand at least trees and either a safe area or animals. You don't need to have all three right there in front of you, but going for two out of the three starting items is a good compromise.

WHAT ABOUT US?

We thought you'd like to see where we started and what we did with our first 30 minutes.

While looking around our starting point, we saw Pigs and a good forest nearby. The cliffs in the distance are too far away to use on the first day, but they could be nice to explore later on. This is absolutely a good starting point, so we're happy to be here!

YOU HAVE 10 MINUTES TO WORK SAFELY

The sun is up for about 10 minutes each day, and nighttime lasts just as long. Because the freaks come out at night, you need to have someplace safe to stay once it gets dark. That leaves only a short time to get everything done!

Goal #1: Harvest Three Blocks of Wood

Run toward the nearest tree and attack it. You have only your hands to work with, so breaking

through the bark will take a few seconds. Hold down the Attack command the entire time. If you stop at any point, the damage to the Wood disappears and you'll have to start again.

ATTACKING

```
Your hands, tools, and weapons are
all used with the same controls.
Anything that you currently hold
in your hand is used to interact
with objects when using the Attack
command. This command is used when
punching trees for Wood, attacking
animals for food, defending
yourself, or mining for minerals.
```

Attack the tree in a single spot and watch the Wood break. Eventually, the block disappears and a small piece of Wood falls to the ground. Move over the piece to pick up the Wood. A faint popping noise lets you know that your character grabbed the item, and it goes into your inventory. Yay! Success.

Do this again for two more pieces of Wood, so you have three total pieces to work with.

Goal #2: Make an Axe for Yourself

Go into your inventory and put the three pieces of Wood into your crafting area. Notice that a new item appears on the right side of the screen. The displayed item represents the results if you choose to craft those pieces of Wood. Every piece turns into four Planks of Wood. Turn your three pieces of Wood into 12 Planks.

You then need to craft several items with your new Planks. Fill the entire crafting box with Planks (one in each slot, as shown). These four Planks are turned into a Crafting Table. Put that into one of your hotbar slots at the bottom of the inventory screen.

Leave that screen and use your appropriate quickslot command to put the Crafting Table down somewhere close. These tables allow you to work with a far greater variety of items. When you interact with a Crafting Table, it brings up a larger interface, so you can put up to nine ingredients into your crafting. Other versions of the game simplify this, but they still require you to use a Crafting Table to make most of the items.

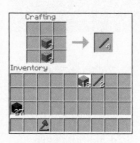

Next, put two Planks into your crafting slots (while using use the Crafting Table or your normal inventory interface for crafting). Putting two Planks together, one above the other, lets you make Sticks. Sticks are required for a huge number of tools.

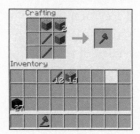

Look at the next picture to see how to make a Wooden Axe. Two Sticks and three Planks go together to make this happen. Now that you have a Wooden Axe, it's much easier to chop Wood. Get several more pieces of Wood now.

Goal #3: Make a Pickaxe and a Shovel

Many tools are made almost exactly the same way, so use your new supply of Wood to make a Pickaxe and a Shovel. They require a similar setup, with two Sticks to form a handle, and then one or two pieces of Wood to complete the tool, depending on what you're making.

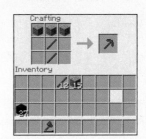
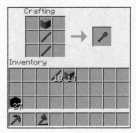

Once you have a Wooden Pickaxe, Shovel, and Axe, put all three of them on your hotbar. You can then start the next phase of your project. We're going to hunt for Stone!

Goal #4: Find a Source of Stone and Harvest at Least Six Pieces

Select your Shovel and dig into the Dirt until you find Stone (usually a few spaces down). If there are deposits of Stone nearby—in a cliff or wherever—then go ahead and rush over to those instead. The general rule is that if you can't find Stone, just start digging downward. It'll be there.

Once you hit Stone, stop using your Shovel. Switch to your Pickaxe and hit the Stone just like you hit the trees with your Axe and the Dirt with your Shovel. Harvest at least six pieces of Stone as soon as possible, and then return to your Crafting Table.

If you dug down into the earth to get your Stone, you might not be able to get directly back to the surface. If that happens, then carve a crude set of steps out of the blocks around you. Your character can jump as high as a single block, so cut the blocks around you until you can jump up one block in front of your character. Then cut until you can do that again and again until you're back on the surface. There are ways to make nicer steps that don't require these big jumps, but you're on a schedule and don't need to worry about that just yet.

Goal #5: Switch to Stone Tools

Use your Crafting Table and recreate your Pickaxe, Shovel, and Axe. This time, use Stone and Sticks instead of Wood and Sticks. The final products are Stone tools. These last longer and are faster at their tasks compared to Wooden tools, so this is a very big upgrade without having spent much of your time. After this point, you can stop using Wooden Tools entirely; they have practically no value to you. However, hang onto yours for the moment—you'll use them for fuel in the furnace you're about to build.

Goal #6: Make Shelter for the Evening

Use the remaining time in your day to build shelter for yourself. Dig into a rockface, a hill, or use a tunnel into the ground at the base for your evening's home. Or, if you have more time than that, build a Stone or Wood structure around yourself. This takes more resources and time, but it's 100% possible if you work quickly before nightfall.

Once you have your shelter, make a Crafting Table to put in there, so you can keep making items during the evening. It's possible to chop down your old table with an Axe and bring it inside, but that often takes more time.

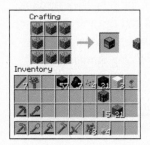

Using a full box of Cobblestone (as shown in our picture), you should also make a Furnace. These are major items to help keep you alive. You can cook food in them (such as any Raw Chicken, Beef, or Pork gathered from animals in your area). Furnaces also get you Charcoal. If there isn't Coal Ore mixed in with the Stone in your area, you'll need some Charcoal tonight. So let's talk about how to get some!

> **PUT A ROOF ON THAT!**
>
> If you build a shelter outside, *always* remember to put a roof on it either three or four blocks high. If you leave your house open to the sky, Spiders can climb into your home at night and attack. You do not want this to happen.

Goal #7: Setting Up Your Furnace, Door, and Light

Place your Furnace near the Crafting Table, and throw your old Wooden Tools into the lower slot of the Furnace. That's your fuel. The tools won't burn for long, but they'll get the job done. Use Wooden Blocks in the Furnace's upper box. That's the item that you're trying to cook. Burn through several pieces of Wood (using your tools as fuel), and collect the Charcoal that is created. Charcoal is very efficient fuel for your Furnace, so you can now cook plenty of other items during the late afternoon and evening. Burn Wood when more Charcoal is needed. Also, cook any meat that you harvested today. Don't eat raw meat because it's not as filling for your character, and sometimes it's even dangerous (raw meat can poison your character).

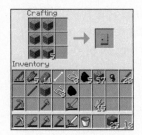

Furnaces light the area while they're cooking, so you can see in the dark or even underground while this is going on. Take six Planks of Wood to make a Door for your house. Block off the rest of the entryway, so there is only a narrow space one block wide and two blocks high leading into your shelter. Put the Door there to keep enemies from entering.

The finishing touch is to use Sticks and Charcoal to craft a few Torches. Once you make them, these simple devices keep your home and area well lit. That's important for getting around, but it's also great for keeping monsters off your back. Monsters only appear in dark areas. As long as you keep your home lit, nothing horrible will appear there, even when your character is away. Monsters can still come after you, or walk through open doors, but they can't magically appear anywhere that's properly lit.

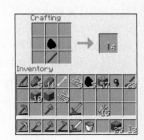

Put Torches on your hotbar, and hang them on walls inside and around your house. Don't worry; they won't burn anything down! They also won't need to be replaced or reset. Torches burn forever.

PROGRESS ON OUR END

In our world, things are going pretty well. Like you, we've rushed to get Stone tools as soon as we could. Running with a full set, we've burrowed into the earth and made a small room for ourselves below ground level. Just before night fell, we also hunted several Pigs for food and Sheep for Wool. Some Porkchops are roasting in the Furnace now, and we used spare Wood to make Charcoal, since there wasn't any Coal in the area where we started mining. All is well!

Our house is smaller than usual, but we have Torches, plenty of tools, spare materials, food, and even a bed (luxury for the first evening). If we wanted to, we could sleep now and immediately skip to the morning of day two, but we won't. There's too much work yet to be done.

Tssssssssssss, BOOM!

There's a thin line between brave and reckless in *Minecraft*. If you go outside at night, accept the possibility that you could die. Quickly. And even if you don't, a Creeper explosion has the potential to tear the wall out of your home if you're standing close by. Be extremely alert.

Also, watch your back in the morning when going outside. Sunlight kills many monsters, but not all of them. Don't be surprised by late-partying monsters that may still be near your home.

SURVIVING THE NIGHT

Once the sun goes down, the light levels fall dramatically. It's hard to see if you walk around outside, and monsters can spawn almost anywhere. Zombies are the most common, and they're easy to outrun. They moan frequently and are easy to hear or spot. But Creepers are quiet and very deadly. They explode if they sneak up on you, dealing potentially lethal damage and destroying anything nearby. Until you have weapons, armor, and more practice, you're better off hiding during the nighttime hours.

If you check your clock, the evening lasts 10 minutes. Later, you can craft a Clock in-game to tell time more accurately.

As evening passes, be productive. Carve down into the earth and gather more Stone. You're going to need many, many pieces throughout your career. And while mining, you might find Coal, Flint (in Gravel), or Iron. Iron is the best of the resources to find in the earth's upper layers. To spot this metal, look for Stone blocks that have a lightish metal embedded inside them. Once mined, refine these in your Furnace to get Iron Ingots, which are quite useful. Make Pickaxes with them so you can harvest Gold, Redstone, Diamond, and other rare materials in the deeper levels of the world.

Goal #8: Forging a Sword

Take a break from your mining at some point during the night. Use your Crafting Table to make a weapon for yourself. One Stick and two pieces of Wood, Stone, or Metal make a Sword. For now, a Stone Sword is perfectly adequate, but an Iron Sword will be much better later on. Always keep your Sword in the same slot on your hotbar so you get used to switching to it quickly. Monsters can jump you while you're wandering outside, mining, or whenever. Even when you think you're safe, there are sometimes moments when you get surprised. Practice switching to your blade quickly and comfortably. The better you get with it, the longer you'll live.

Expand your home and your mines until morning. Look through the holes in your Door to see if it's light outside, or gently wander outside if you're feeling brave. Just be ready to head back through the door if you see trouble coming.

FINDING SOME FOOD

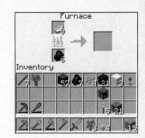

As time passes and you get ready for the next day, you may notice that your hunger meter is falling—that's the series of drumsticks on the lower-right portion of the screen. Your character can't heal from injuries unless your hunger meter is almost full. And if it ever goes down to zero, you lose almost all of your health. Hunger won't kill your character in Survival mode, but it can take you down to half a heart, and that's barely anything. You can't even survive a three-block fall with that!

Goal #9: Gather Enough Food to Keep Yourself Full

Eating is a good thing. It'll take days to get a good farm ready, so you need something to snack on before then. You can hunt Chickens, Pigs, and Cows, and then cook their raw meat. That's a great way to survive in the early days, and it's good later when you breed these animals as well.

But there are many options.

WAYS TO STAY FED

- Cook raw meat from nearby animals.

- Leave your local area and wander around until you find more distant cattle or livestock to eat.

- Make a Fishing Rod with Sticks and String, and then fish in any body of water.

- Plant Seeds for a Wheat farm, and hide somewhere safe for about half an hour while it grows.

- Spiders and Zombies drop Spider Eyes and Rotten Flesh; these aren't good for your health, but they can be eaten.

- Chop down leaves from trees and hope to find Apples—this is not very effective.

MINE, EXPAND, AND THRIVE

Once you have enough food to get by, it's sensible to expand your mining operation. Gather more Stone and keep searching for more Iron. If you have enough Iron, it's possible to make armor for your character. This makes it much harder for monsters to hurt you. Leather and Iron are both used for armor, so hunting enough Cows early on can get you decent armor long before you can spare the Iron for defensive purposes.

Goal #10: Make a Tunnel Down to the Bottom of the World

When you're digging down into the earth, don't go randomly in any direction. Instead, make a single path that leads down into the depths. On the PC, you can press F3 to see how deep you are. About 30 blocks up from the bottom, you start getting a chance to find Gold. 15 Blocks from the bottom, you can find Diamond—the real prize!

You won't want to spend minutes getting to these lower levels every time you go down there. One way to keep this process fast and efficient is to mine a set of steps that leads from your house all the way to the bottom. The straighter your tunnel, the less time you waste getting down there.

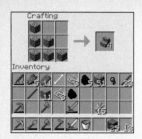

Next, make Stone or Wooden steps. Adding these to your downward tunnel makes getting around faster, especially during the climb back to the surface. Also, stairs reduce the amount of hunger you incur from this trip. Jumping back to the surface takes a great deal of energy; climbing the stairs isn't nearly as bad. So the sooner you make real steps, the better off you are. Here is a picture of the recipe for stairs—use whatever material you like, depending on whether you have more Wood or Stone.

As you grow more comfortable with the game, start to read our next chapter about more advanced techniques. You can build water systems, railways, and other transportation routes to improve your mining efficiency.

For now, though, it's fine to simply dig deep and start making tunnels until you find good ore. Just remember a few rules.

MINING TIPS AND WARNINGS

- Most good minerals are found in veins; if you see one piece of Iron, Coal, Gold, or other good materials, there are probably more! Dig out the entire area around each special mineral to make sure you get everything.

- Always bring food, Wood, Torches, and tools on your mining expeditions.

- If you hear bubbling lava or monster noises, you are likely getting close to a dangerous cavern; proceed slowly and carefully.

- Never dig straight down unless you have a death wish; one day, you will fall to your death or drop into lava.

- Don't dig out huge caverns to find ore. Make lots of narrow tunnels to maximize your search area.

- Leave precious ores and materials in chests that you keep inside your home. Don't carry everything with you, or you might lose it all if your character dies.

- Once you have a Bucket, keep some water with you at all times (for putting out fires, cooling lava, etc.).

- Always put Torches on the same side of a new tunnel. If you get turned around, you'll always know which direction leads toward home.

KNOW WHERE YOU ARE

Start to get a feel for the resources in your current biome. If there aren't animals, specific flowers, plants, or other goodies that you need, look up these items and find out where they naturally spawn. For example, if you want Sugar Cane, look it up to learn that Sugar Cane is common in sandy areas, near rivers or deserts. Make sure you gather all the valuable items in your area, and start to steal useful items that are anywhere within close range of your base.

LOOK AROUND

Goal #11: Make a Landmark So You Can Find Your Home from a Distance

It's nice and safe to stay near your home, but you can't always thrive by remaining in one place. Make landmarks so you can see your house from a good distance away. A massive tower of Dirt is one of the fastest, cheapest ways to accomplish this task. We talk about ways to create more landmarks in the next chapter.

Once you've made it easier to find your way back, start to explore the surface. There are other biomes within easy reach if you're brave enough to walk a minute or two in any direction. This opens the way toward more animals, plants, and blocks.

Always secure your rare items in chests at home before venturing too far. If you die and can't make it back to your body, you don't want to lose anything important!

MOVING ON

Goal #12: Survive and Build!

As you get better and better at the game, you should add new tricks to your exploration and mining. The next chapter talks about many ways to improve your play: enchanting, brewing, combat techniques, using The Nether and The End, and so forth. There is still so much to learn. But you now have enough information to survive your first few days in *Minecraft*. With that, it's not much harder to build a house and use it as a base of operations for everything else. It all gets easier from here.

YOU CAN DO ANYTHING WITH A LITTLE PRACTICE

By the time you read this chapter, you should understand how to control your character and survive in the wild, while crafting basic tools and structures. This chapter takes those minimal goals and extends them considerably. By the end, you should know how to build large structures, harvest any type of material, defeat monsters in all three of *Minecraft*'s worlds, and so on. All major concepts are dealt with here in detail.

HOW TO CRAFT

We've already talked about the very basics of crafting in *Minecraft,* but now we'll delve all the way into the heart of the matter. Crafting is an important skill for any player. You can't do much of anything without it, so knowing how to access all recipes in the game is vital.

Your basic character can always craft any recipe that only requires the 2x2 crafting grid. This is accessed from your inventory at any time. To use more complex recipes, you need a Crafting Table. This is made by putting a Wooden Plank into each slot of the 2x2 crafting grid. You then deploy your Crafting Table somewhere nearby and start working.

For this reason, we always suggest that players carry around either a Crafting Table or at least a decent number of Wooden Planks so they can make a table without much delay. Having Wooden Planks is great for many reasons and they're also vital for Sticks, which are key components of almost every tool. So you'd be crazy not to keep spare Wood around.

With access to a Crafting Table, you can work on any recipe that you have the correct ingredients to make. Learn which ingredients you need by searching through the "Tools, Resources, and Collectibles" chapter.

Certain basic ingredients are so common that they're great to keep at hand. We already mentioned Wood, but you also want to have some Cobblestone and perhaps a bit of Steel as well. A supply of these base materials can yield quite a bit of what you need. With just Wooden Planks and Cobblestone, you can set up a convenient, safe base anywhere in the world. Make a Crafting Table, Furnace, block yourself into a room, and add a Door, and you can work in peace for as long as you like. Add Chests as needed to store things there for the future.

It's often smart to place Chests near your Furnaces and Crafting Tables because these three household features work together. Keep ingredients in the Chests, smelt them in the Furnace, and use your Crafting Tables to make more advanced products. You don't want to run around your house wasting time going to each station. Having these things in the same area is extremely convenient!

Consider placing Signs near your Chests once you have more than a few of them. Organize the contents of these Chests to make sure you know where your items are located. That way, you can access them quickly without having to look around for minutes each time.

Several shortcuts allow you to craft more comfortably. If you put enough crafting ingredients in their slots to make multiple items, hold down the Shift key and click on the final product to make as many as possible instantly.

Another trick is to grab a stack of items you're working with and to slide them over several slots in your inventory. Do this when you need to divide items into several stacks. For example, if you want to divide your Wood Planks in half for making Sticks, just roll your stack across two spaces while holding the button. Release the button when you have the proper number of stacks, and watch the items divide evenly. Quite nice! This is so wonderful when making Bread.

SOMETIMES THINGS BREAK (I.E., DURABILITY)

Consumable items are those used only once before they're depleted. You eat a piece of Bread and it's gone. You blow up your TNT, and that's that. Certain items are reusable but can't be used forever. This is usually the case for tools, such as Axes, Shovels, armor, and so on. Items that rely on durability break when they've been used too many times. Armor loses durability when you take hits, and tools lose durability when they finish either dealing damage to a target or harvesting a block. You don't lose anything for swinging tools in midair or just carrying them around.

Watch the bars that appear underneath items after you use them. Those bars reflect the items' remaining durability. Once they get really low, you know that the item in question will soon break (and be completely destroyed). Before that happens, you have the option of repairing the object with an Anvil or simply preparing a substitute tool, so you still have something to work with when your primary one breaks.

We strongly advise that you carry multiple tools of your favorite types. In the early game, this is a lifesaver because Wood and Stone tools break very quickly. You need to have two or even three Pickaxes and Shovels so your digging isn't disrupted for long.

Tools that get less use aren't as big of a deal. You certainly don't need three Hoes every time you head out; one is more than enough. Or you could even leave the Hoe at home and grab it only when you're in the mood to farm.

NUMBER OF USES FOR TOOLS, BY MATERIAL

Wood	60
Stone	132
Iron	251
Gold	33
Diamond	1562

BREAKING TOO QUICKLY

If you use tools for the wrong function, they break much faster. Each improper use of a tool costs two or even three points of their durability.

Using Pickaxes, Axes, and Shovels as weapons costs twice the durability. Using a Sword to break blocks works the same way. Using your Fishing Rod against monsters, to pull them around, costs triple durability.

GENERAL GUIDELINE FOR TOOLS

TOOL	NUMBER OF TOOLS TO CARRY
Pickaxe	2-3 (very important)
Shovel	2
Axe	1-2
Hoe	0-1
Sword	2
Shears	1

If you know you're about to focus on a specific activity, like chopping more Wood, then adjust your tool count accordingly. Go ahead and make a few extra Axes before you go to harvest Wood. The same is true for Shears if you're chopping through heavy forest.

Each time you leave your base of operations, think about the activities you have planned. Take what you need the most, and do what you can to maximize your free inventory space so your character isn't loaded down with crud you won't even use. The more free space you have, the more treasure you'll return with!

Anvils and Enchanting

When you get further into the game, it's sometimes useful to save tools that are especially valuable. Enchanting lets you turn your character's levels into special properties for weapons, armor, and tools. Imagine a Pickaxe that can harvest multiple minerals per block and mines faster and lasts longer. You'll get one of those at some point! If it's a Diamond Pickaxe with those traits, you'll be so happy every time you use it. This means you won't ever want it to break.

Repairing items is possible, though it's costly. Don't repair standard tools that aren't enchanted. It's not that important, because you can make replacements quickly and without much cost anyway. Save repair jobs for things you love.

To start a repair, make an Anvil. These expensive items take a pile of Iron to complete, but you won't need to make many of them. Keep an Anvil in your primary base, and leave it at that. Your smaller bases and mining stations won't require something this impressive.

Once you have an Anvil, interact with it to bring up the repair interface. Use the item's base material to restore its durability. Thus, Diamond tools require Diamonds to repair (ouch).

Items cost more to repair if they have extremely high durability (e.g., Diamond tools). They also cost more to repair if they're enchanted, and if you've already worked on them previously. At some point, you have to give up on even the best items, because they cost way too much to repair.

Don't Rely on Damaged Tools

Tools that are almost out of durability should be treated as trash. Bring an extra tool of that type when you leave base to account for the imminent destruction of your current tool. Or simply throw the badly damaged item into your garbage bin and stop worrying about it.

Do not keep damaged tools in Chests for the rest of your game. It's annoying to have a backlog of useless, damaged tools that you're never going to mess with again. Use them until they're destroyed or throw them away.

FARMING

Once you have a few supplies and the basics squared away, farming is the way to go for food. You can hunt for meat, but eventually all the nearby animals will be gone. So why not spend some time learning how to plant and harvest fruits, grains, and vegetables? They're easy to grow, can be replanted, and fill up your hunger bar. Some of them can even be used later in things like potions. So let's play in the dirt!

Setting Up Your Field

At the most basic level, farming is about planting seeds in wet dirt with access to lots of light. You can start a farm on the shoreline of a lake, by the sea, or you can get a Bucket and make your own little puddle surrounded by dirt blocks. One water block can keep four dirt blocks in any direction damp, so you can create a trench for the water to flow through with dirt on either side, or dig a pit in the middle of the field for the water. You can even get fancy and create terraces of dirt with a waterfall!

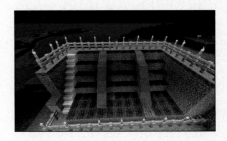

Seeds and Edible Plants

- Wheat: the staple of the farm
- Carrots: pointy, orange, delicious
- Potatoes: nutritious, but sometimes produce Poisonous Potatoes
- Watermelons: the long-term crop
- Pumpkins: gourd of many uses
- Sugar Cane: used in making Paper and Sugar
- Cocoa Beans: used in baking and dyes

WHEAT

You can get Wheat Seeds from any tall grass, so chop away at nearby patches. Don't worry too much if you don't find many, or if you start your game in an area without much in the way of grassy fields. Not every patch of grass drops Seeds, but harvested Wheat usually drops more than one Seed in addition to the Wheat itself, so you can replant and grow your farm from even the smallest beginnings. If you have plains nearby, you're in Wheat heaven; the large amount of tall grass there helps you gather Seeds by the handful.

Ripe Wheat is a golden brown color. When harvested, the crop produces one Wheat and zero to three Seeds. If you harvest too early, you get only Seeds and no Wheat.

Wheat Seeds can be used to lure Chickens and fed to them so they breed. Ripe Wheat can lure Cows and Sheep into following you, or fed to a pair of Cows or a pair of Sheep to make them breed. You can pack nine Wheat together to make a Bale of Hay for Horses, or use three Wheat to make Bread for feeding yourself. Wheat is useful stuff!

CARROTS

You can find Carrots growing in Villager farms, so be sure and dig them up if you get the chance. Zombies also occasionally drop Carrots. Once planted, a single Carrot grows into as many as four more when ripe. You will know when Carrots are ready to be harvested when you see four of them poking out from the ground.

Carrots can be eaten directly out of the ground or replanted. They can also be used to attract Pigs and Rabbits or make them breed. If you have a Saddle and want to ride a Pig around, make a Carrot on a Stick to get the Pig to go wherever you want!

POTATOES

Like Carrots, you can find Potatoes growing in Villager farms, and you can harvest them. Zombies also rarely drop Potatoes, so it may take a while before you can start enjoying delicious Baked Potatoes. A raw Potato planted in the ground grows into a group of Potatoes. You know that they're ripe when the tops pop out of the ground.

Potatoes can be replanted immediately to increase your farm. Once you have enough that you can cook some, stick them in a Furnace to make Baked Potatoes, which are very good for satisfying hunger. You can eat them raw, but they won't fill you up nearly as much.

THE POISON POTATO

When you harvest potatoes, there is a tiny chance that some of them will be Poisonous Potatoes, which can't be cooked or planted. You can eat them, but you probably shouldn't (because of the poison).

WATERMELONS

Watermelons are found growing wild in jungle biomes. Break them into slices and turn those slices into seeds! You can also find Melon Seeds in Chests in abandoned mineshafts, or you can trade for them if you find a Farmer Villager.

Once planted, a Melon Seed turns into a stem. Once the stem has matured, it tries to grow a Melon next to itself. The Melon will grow only if there is a free space for it, so

Glistering Melons

Melon Slices can be combined with Gold Nuggets to make Glistering Melons. These are a key ingredient in making health potions, which you learn about later in this chapter.

don't crowd them with other crops. Once the Melon bears fruit, harvest it, but save the stem! If you leave the stem, a new Melon will soon grow, saving you the need to replant. Melons can be broken into numerous slices. Each one fills the hunger bar only a tiny bit, so they are good for keeping your bar topped off.

PUMPKINS

Pumpkins grow naturally on grassland and can be crafted into Pumpkin Seeds. Like Melons, Pumpkin Seeds require some spacing as they grow into a stem. Once the stem matures, it needs an adjacent free block to grow a Pumpkin. Ripe Pumpkins can be harvested whole, leaving the stem behind to continue the cycle of growth.

If you're hungry, use some Eggs and Sugar with a Pumpkin to make a tasty Pumpkin Pie!

The Amazing Pumpkin

Pumpkins have lots of uses! They can be worn as helmets to keep Endermen from attacking when you look at them. They can be crafted into Jack o' Lanterns, which are brighter than torches and even work

underwater. Want a Golem? Put a pumpkin on top of some Snow or Iron blocks to make a defensive Golem.

YOU CAN DO ANYTHING WITH A LITTLE PRACTICE

SUGAR CANE

Sugar Cane can't be eaten by itself, but it's still a useful crop. Search river areas and deserts for this tall plant, and chop it down. A full-sized plant of Sugar Cane is three blocks tall and thus gets you three pieces of Sugar Cane to plant.

Create a full line of Sand or regular Dirt, and then dig a ditch beside it to fill with water. Sugar Cane is very thirsty and needs to have access to water just to take root.

Give Sugar Cane time to grow. Harvest it by cutting down the upper two blocks of each plant. Leave the base of the Sugar Cane untouched so it can continue to grow for as long as you like. In this way, you can get a huge amount of Sugar Cane without much effort after the initial planting.

COCOA BEANS

Cocoa Beans are found only in jungle biomes, where they grow as pods on the side of small jungle trees. Unripe pods are green, but they turn a golden brown when they are ready to harvest.

Making a Cocoa Bean farm is slightly more challenging than some other types of farms. It's more of an orchard. Cocoa Beans don't require water, but they do need Wood, and only Wood from jungle trees will do. As you go through the jungle gathering Cocoa pods, chop down a few jungle trees. Take the Wood from the trees back to your farm, set it down where you want your orchard, and put the pods on the Wood. A fully harvested Cocoa pod gives two to three Cocoa Beans.

Two pieces of Wheat and one Cocoa Bean makes eight Cookies. Delicious! Cocoa Beans can also be used to dye items brown, which is an extra benefit.

Time to Dig in the Dirt!

You've got Dirt, Seeds, and Water. Now you need to prepare the ground for planting. This is the job for the Hoe. A Wood or Stone one will work just fine, so you don't have to use any of your precious Iron, Gold, or Diamonds unless you really want to dig in style.

Use the Hoe on the ground to change the Dirt into tilled land (a Farmland block), ready for planting. If you look closely, you can see the blocks of tilled land nearest the water start to get darker, which means that they're getting nice and damp. You might also see them going back to normal Dirt, which means they are too far away from the water and are drying out. This also happens if you jump on your tilled land, so don't hop around in your garden.

SAVING SPACE

Because you need only a single block of Water to irrigate a large area, it's possible to plant a 9x9 farm with only one block of Water in the center. If you're measuring ahead of time and want to wall off the area, make an 11x11 set of walls, and put your water pit in the center of that hollow space.

PLANTING

Now that the ground is prepared, use your Seeds (Potatoes, Carrots, and so forth) on the Farmland. Look! Tiny green shoots appear. That lets you know that the plants are growing. Give them time and light, and soon they'll be ready for harvest.

Light makes your plants grow and ripen. Sunlight works just fine, but Torches are a great addition because they keep monsters from spawning in your garden. They also let the plants keep growing at night. You can even make an underground farm by using Torches! If you don't have any Torches handy, be sure to sleep as soon as it starts getting dark. The plants don't grow if there is no light, and sleeping prevents monsters from spawning and trampling your nice farm.

PROTECTING YOUR CROP

Creepers are a big threat to growing plants. If they explode, they'll blow up hours of hard work in a single moment, destroying lots of Seeds in the process. Torches help keep Creepers from spawning in the middle of the garden, but they can still wander in at night unless you protect your farmland. Fences or Stone Walls are a great way to keep the plants safe, but you can also make a complete building with a nice Glass roof to let in the light. If you want to work in the garden at night, a building can be a great way to protect yourself from Spiders and Skeletons. That way, you don't have to watch your back constantly.

MAKING PLANTS GROW

The easiest way to make plants grow is to do nothing and wait for them to ripen. As long as they have light and water available, they'll continue growing until they're ready to harvest. If you want things to move faster, add Torches so they grow at night.

You can break Bones down into Bone Meal, which can be used on plants to make them grow faster. Each use on a plant causes it to grow, sometimes all the way to maturity with just a single application. This can be extremely useful when starting with only one Seed, Carrot, or Potato, as you get a lot more crops for replanting very quickly. It can also be good when you need some food right away!

Bone Meal isn't restricted to farm crops. You can use it on Grass to make flowers. Use it on tree Saplings to make them shoot up, fully grown and ready to be chopped down. You can even use it on Mushrooms to turn them gigantic!

HARVESTING

Finally, it's time to reap the benefits of farming. You know that Wheat is ready when it turns brown. Potatoes and Carrots poke out of the ground. Pumpkins and Melons grow fruit. Hit ripe crops to pop them out of the ground. Walk over them to collect these goodies. Use an Axe to break Pumpkins and Melons, because they're tougher to smash.

Often, ripe Wheat gets you more Seeds than it took to plant, but there is no guarantee. Potatoes and Carrots get you anywhere from one to four plants when harvested, and you can choose whether to eat or replant them. It's generally a good idea to plant a new crop as you harvest the old one, so you can keep the cycle going without accidentally eating all your future produce.

If you've enclosed your farm with walls, a fun trick when harvesting is to take a Bucket of Water and flood your field. Then use the Bucket to pick up the Water source block. The ripple of water uproots all your crops at once and pushes them to the walls. This makes it super easy to pick up everything at once. Flooding a field will always uproot Seeds, so it's useful when everything is ripe at the same time. However, it can be annoying if some of your crops aren't ready yet (once they get uprooted, they lose any progress they made). Make sure to let everything fully ripen to get the greatest benefit from this method. If only half your field is ready, either wait longer or pick the ripened crops by hand.

CREATING MINES

Once you've survived the first night and started to get established, it's time to think about going deeper. Having some Iron and a small supply of Cobblestone is nice, but there's treasure to be found in the depths. Maybe you can find some Diamonds!

Bring What You Need

Before doing any kind of deep mining, you should take a few basic supplies with you.

The Essentials

- **Iron Pickaxe** for mining

- **Shovel** for patches of Dirt or Gravel

- **Bucket of Water** for putting out fires or Lava

- **Torches** for seeing and reducing monster spawns

- **Ladders** for climbing out

- **Crafting Table** for building a base

- **Chest** for storing useful things

- **Wood Planks and Sticks** for replacements

- **Food** because everyone gets hungry

IRON PICKAXE AND STONE SHOVEL

Stone pickaxes are great when you're starting out, but Iron is extremely useful once you start any sort of large-scale digging. You have to use resources to get resources, because you can't get Gold, Redstone, and Diamond without using an Iron Pickaxe or better. Take one along so you don't leave behind a cluster of Diamonds.

Take a Stone Shovel or two as well, so you can clear Dirt and Gravel without wasting any time.

BUCKET OF WATER

As you go deeper into the earth, Lava starts to be a concern. Lava pools can be a real challenge! You might see some great resources on the walls and ceiling around a Lava pool, but going after them is a risk; you or the materials could fall into the Lava, losing everything. We'll cover how to get resources around Lava a bit later, in a section titled "Lava Mining."

There is usually a way around the Lava, but if you don't feel like walking around, you can use your trusty Bucket of Water to turn large swathes of it into Obsidian. Simply pour the water out near the edge and then immediately pick up the source block. The ripple of water turns all the nearby Lava into Obsidian. Lava is so hot that you can also catch on fire just by being near it. The Bucket of Water is also great for putting yourself out if that happens. Just pour it out and hop in!

You can also use Water when you're faced with a ravine or giant cave. If you tunnel out in the middle of a cave wall with empty space below, use the water to create a waterfall and swim down. It's much better than jumping, and you can swim back up the waterfall when you want to get out.

TORCHES

The world's deep places tend to be very dark. Torches keep your mines illuminated, so monsters don't spawn and you don't miss patches of resources. Also, use them to track your exploration in cave systems to see where you've been and where you came from.

Gravel can be an annoyance in any sort of large-scale mining work. Blocks of it drop down and get in the way when you mine the block supporting them. When confronting a wall of Gravel, dig underneath the supporting block and put a Torch on the ground underneath the stack. Then mine away the block supporting them; instead of falling down, the Gravel hits the Torch and breaks.

LADDERS

What goes down eventually wants to come up again. Ladders create an easy way to get from your central base to the bottom of your mineshaft, without having to risk jumping or building stairs. Take Ladders with you when creating the original shaft to set up a quick way home.

Exploring caves can be risky, especially large ones with sharp drops and high ledges. You can use mined blocks of Stone and Dirt to create pillars, but Ladders are more useful and quicker to use. They also make very handy landmarks to important places!

CRAFTING TABLE

The very first thing you should do when creating a large underground mine is set up a secondary base camp. This is where you can go to drop off resources or pick up something you need, like food or a new tool, without having to go all the way back up.

Taking a Crafting Table ensures you can adapt to any changes or difficulties. If you break a tool, you can make another quickly. Build Furnaces to smelt your raw materials. You can also make things like Signs, Doors, and Chests to organize your resources and keep from getting lost.

If you need to save inventory space, just bring tons of spare Wood Planks and make a Crafting Table on the fly. They're cheap and quick.

CHEST

Storage is always a priority when creating a mine. The last thing you want is to have all your precious things on you when a Creeper sneaks up and defeats you, or a gang of Zombies overpowers you, or you fall into Lava. It's heartbreaking when the last thing you see is a dozen Diamonds burning in a puddle of Lava, or when you realize you have no idea where you (and all of your stuff) were when those Skeletons came and took you out.

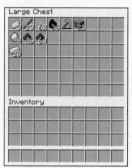

Accidents happen to even the most careful miners. Avoid pain and mental anguish. Put spare items into your Chests, and leave those Chests by your secondary bases. Don't collect the goods until you're ready to head back to the surface!

WOOD PLANKS

Spare Wood is essential. Unless you've created an underground tree farm (and if you have, that's fantastic!), there won't be any trees in your mine. Wood is useful for Torches, new tools, Signs, and plenty of other essential goods. Don't go down into the mines without a substantial supply of Wood Planks.

Doors and Signs are great additions to an extensive mining operation. Use Doors as barriers to keep monsters from wandering into your safer areas or as visual cues that you're close to places you've already developed. Signs can point the way home, warn you (or others) about hazards or particularly rich areas, or label Chests when your storage increases. When you find yourself rummaging through all of your Chests to find a single item, then it's time to make a few Signs and do some sorting!

FOOD

The last essential when you start a mining operation is food. Returning home every time you get hungry slows everything down. It's also dangerous to be hungry and unable to run when you encounter a group of monsters. You need to keep your health at max, because there are falls and hazards everywhere. A single heart can make the difference between surviving and losing all of your hard work.

Don't just avoid starvation, either. Keep your hunger bar maxed out so your character heals quickly from wounds. Don't be stingy with your food while exploring caverns; too much can go wrong.

Types of Mining Operations

After you gather your essentials, it's time to mine. Now you have to decide what kind of mine to make. Will you explore a cave? Dig down to the very bedrock? Follow a pool of Lava? You might find yourself doing all three, or coming up with a new system!

CAVE EXPLORATION

Caves are great access points into deeper areas. They can spare you from having to create your own mineshaft. They can be ideal mining locations, especially if you start near one. The main challenges in cave mining are getting lost, fighting monsters, and getting to the resources you want.

Caves can be really big, in some cases going from the surface all the way down to bedrock. They sometimes branch off in multiple directions, at multiple heights. You can easily get lost if you don't take care to mark your exits and keep a trail of Torches. Signs, Doors, and Torches are essential to track your progress and find the way out.

CROUCHING ON THE EDGE

Crouching keeps you from falling off edges and lets you reach really far without fear of suddenly dropping. When you make a bridge to a patch of resources or across a chasm, crouch and walk backward. You won't fall, and you can place a block, then walk to the edge of that block and place another. Before you know it, you're safely across.

Navigating Caves

You have to think in three dimensions with big cave systems because you often go up and down. Signs are very helpful; even something as simple as an arrow pointing the way back to base camp can save your time and energy. Use Torch patterns to mark out special places, like putting triple Torches around the corridor that leads home, or to the cave that you are currently exploring. For the big ravines with lots of vertical height, consider making pillars or intentionally creating Lava flows by carving out a hole high up and putting in a Lava source block. Lava flows make nasty puddles on the floor, so plan them out carefully and surround them with a wall of Dirt or Stone. Lava pillars provide light, landmarks, and a trap for monsters!

Illuminate everything you can so monsters don't constantly surprise you. Use Cobblestone walls to partition large caves and ravines. Smaller areas prevent you from being overwhelmed with monsters. You might even want to seal up areas that are just too big and dangerous to deal with. Caves are full of nasty ambush spots, with Skeletons shooting you off ledges or attacking from places where you can't reach. You also face Zombies and Spiders dropping from higher ledges, and Creepers sneaking up on you in the darkness. If you find yourself dying and getting frustrated, seal off the entire area. Make a giant wall with an iron door that monsters can't get past. Be careful, get armor as soon as you have the resources for it, and always be ready to cut and run. You can always explore a tough cave again later, when you have more food and armor!

DEEP MINING

Mineshafts are great for getting down to the lower levels. These are different from exploring a surface cave, as you are going deep into the earth and creating your own tunnels. You may run into caves or Lava pools, but sometimes it's very quiet down there. You might go a long time without seeing any hazards or monsters.

The easiest way to start is to dig a 4x4 hole in the ground. You may even want create a separate room or special area for the dig, so you don't fall into it by accident, and so you can find it again later. Take your essentials with you and start digging downward. *Never* mine the block directly beneath you. That's a certain way to fall into unexpected caves or Lava pools. Mine around yourself first, and move onto the newly revealed blocks to keep accidents from happening. Place Torches on the wall and use Ladders to get back to the surface.

If you keep going straight down and don't break into a cave, you eventually hit bedrock. Though you can start mining near this level, it's easy to break into Lava pools. It can actually be safer to build back up 10 blocks or so from the bedrock. Staying at this level (roughly "Y" 10-12) lets you come in above most Lava caverns.

Once the mineshaft is finished, make a temporary base and store everything you don't want to take with. Consider using some of the Cobblestone that you've mined on the way down to build a few Furnaces. Smelt any Iron found on the way to make spare tools. Dig out the area to give yourself room for future expansion.

Quick Trip Down

You need your Ladders for the way back to the surface, but a little pocket of Water makes your downward trips very fast. Put a hole at the bottom of your shaft and fill it with Water. In the future, leap down the shaft and land in the water to safely shorten your ride to the bottom. As long as you don't have dangerous ledges in your shaft, this method is safe and fun.

From the bottom of your shaft, pick a direction and start mining. Go as far as you want, but be sure to keep Torches at regular intervals. As always, you don't want to mine the ground directly beneath you; falling into Lava is a terrible way to lose everything. Keep the corridors straight so you don't get lost.

Once you've made a central corridor, start creating branches at regular intervals to the left and right. These can also be as long as you want and should be well lit. As long as you don't go up or down, you don't have to worry about Lava suddenly coming from the ceiling or falling into it. If you happen to break into a Lava pool, you can explore or seal it off. If you find a patch of resources, mine them fully!

Navigating Your Corridors

Because everything in the corridor contains right angles, telling which corridor leads back to your base can get confusing. You can solve this by using Doors to the branches and Signs pointing the way home. A little preparation and organization keeps you from getting confused and wandering your own system in circles.

YOU CAN DO ANYTHING WITH A LITTLE PRACTICE

LAVA MINING

Because Lava pools form deep underground, Lava mining often comes into play at some point. To brave the danger, follow the Lava pools and mine the edges and ceiling. Let the Lava be your light source, and let the caves it creates reveal Gold, Redstone, Lapis Lazuli, Iron, Coal, and Diamonds. Large Lava lakes also tend to lead to other large lakes, letting you repeat the process. It's a useful technique when you don't want to spend much time in little corridors, but you also don't want to deal with huge caverns full of monsters.

Lava mining has one big danger: the Lava itself. Just standing near it can set you on fire, and actually falling in can be deadly and burn up all your stuff. So respect the Lava and learn how to handle it with a degree of safety.

Everyone Falls In

At some point, everyone falls into Lava. It can be by surprise when mining a block beneath you, or when rushing ahead while mining and walking straight off the edge. Maybe you'll break through a wall or ceiling and it flows on top of you; that's common in The Nether. It might even happen when a Skeleton shoots you off a cliff's edge!

So why not get it over with? Leave all your stuff in a Chest, make sure you've slept, and then hop right in! You'll get to see firsthand what happens, at a time of your choosing. Try getting out to see how difficult it is.

This is the best way to practice surviving a fall into Lava. You don't have to try this if you don't want to. But it's a great way to learn just how nasty Lava is without the stress of trying to save your resources from burning up!

Lava Safety Tips

There are three types of Lava to watch out for: the flowing kind, the surprise kind, and the kind that sits around in pools. Small Lava streams are common in caves. The large pools tend to occur deep underground, close to the bedrock. You may see some Lava pools on the surface as well, particularly in mountain biomes.

When you come across a small Lava flow, the first question to ask is, "Can this help me?" Caves and ravines are really dark, and having a large light source is helpful. Lava pools are also nice to have around as navigation aids. It might be better to put up a wall around the Lava's edges and keep it around!

If you want the Lava gone, you can remove it by taking away the source block. A Bucket will do the trick, or you can just put Dirt or Stone into the source to block it off. Dunking water over the Lava flow also works, though this creates Obsidian (which is hard to mine).

Lava, like Coal, can be fuel for a Furnace. If you need to smelt a lot of raw ore, why not put a Bucket of Lava to good use? It burns for a very long time! And you get your Bucket back immediately, so there's no loss of resources.

If you mine a wall, ceiling, or floor, and suddenly find a Lava flow that you weren't expecting, then Congratulations! You've found surprise Lava!

Act quickly. Grab a Stone block and swiftly fill the hole you just mined. This blocks the Lava and cuts off the flow before it starts. You can also back away, let the Lava spill out, and then carefully brick it up again.

This type of surprise Lava is more frequent in The Nether, which is filled with all sorts of fire. Lava also flows more quickly there, so it's easy for surprise Lava to spill out and cover an area. It's often easiest to retreat, set down a Cobblestone wall to block the incoming flow, and then work your way back to the hole from which the Lava originated to stop it up. Working carefully here means working safely.

If you mined a block underneath you and fell into Lava, you might be able to knock out a block beside you and get out of it. But there's a good chance you'll burn up and lose all your stuff. Never, ever, ever mine directly beneath yourself! We may have mentioned that once or twice already. And you know what? You'll still do it at least once and regret it. Almost everyone does.

Some telltale signs of surprise Lava are glowing drips from the ceiling. They indicate that Lava is directly above you, separated by only one block. Unless you really want Lava, don't mine when you see those drips! You can also hear it bubbling when it's nearby, so be extra careful until you locate the source.

Keep a Bucket of Water handy to extinguish yourself if you catch on fire or manage to escape the Lava. Speed is always essential, because Lava takes away huge chunks of your health! Use the Bucket above the Lava so the water flows over your character *and* the Lava below, turning it to Obsidian.

Large pools are safer than flows or surprise Lava because they don't go anywhere. The dangerous part comes from falling directly into them, as they tend to be several blocks deep, making it almost impossible to escape.

Making Lava Work for You

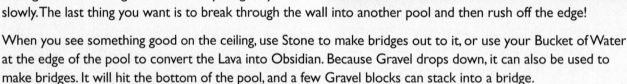

Lava is really bright—this means that Lava pools don't spawn monsters, and mining nearby doesn't require much in the way of Torches. The caves that the pools create reveal all sorts of resources. The largest Lava lakes can create gigantic, interconnected caves that are brightly lit and full of precious things. If you're careful, you can make this work for you with Lava mining!

Start at the nearest edge and make it safer by mining out a two- or three-block ledge to stand on. Keep mining around the edge, but take everything very slowly. The last thing you want is to break through the wall into another pool and then rush off the edge!

When you see something good on the ceiling, use Stone to make bridges out to it, or use your Bucket of Water at the edge of the pool to convert the Lava into Obsidian. Because Gravel drops down, it can also be used to make bridges. It will hit the bottom of the pool, and a few Gravel blocks can stack into a bridge.

As you go, look at the bottom edges of the blocks at the Lava lake's edge. Some of them have an orange strip at the bottom, which means there is more Lava underneath them. Even if a Lava cave seems entirely cut off and isolated, you can sometimes follow the small channels that go under the walls to find even more caves.

Don't rush for valuable minerals. Always stay calm and go slowly when mining around Lava. Excited miners often become dead miners.

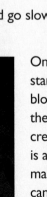

One key to safety is to mine blocks while you're standing still. Go to the wall and start mining. When the block breaks, keep holding the Attack button to mine the next block, and the one after that, and so on. This creates a small hole you can look into to see if there is another big Lava lake on the other side. Once you make your small hole, widen it into a corridor that you can pass through. Keep Water handy, and take a trip back to your Chests to drop off resources when you get them. Respect the danger!

Navigating the Pools

One of Lava mining's benefits is that the large pools are easier to navigate than a giant cave system or branching corridors. There is plenty of light, the lines of sight are nice and clear, and you can get from point to point around the Lava's edges or create Obsidian or Stone pathways straight across. Mark the exits toward base camp to avoid confusion. An easy way to do this is to set up a Cobblestone archway around the corridor and then line it with Torches. Signs are also useful to point out the way to a fresh pool, but keep them away from the very edge of the Lava, or they'll burn up.

BUILDING UP AND OUT

Not all of *Minecraft* is about going down to the inky deeps. There are plenty of occasions where going up is the answer! Learning to build up and out is an essential skill, whether you want to build a new level for your house, cross a ravine to get to some fresh resources, or you come across a giant tree and really want to build a fort up high. Just because you start on the ground doesn't mean you need to stay there!

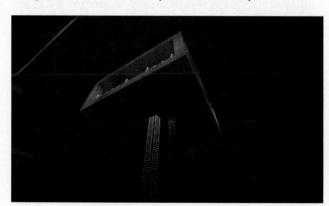

To the Sky!

Take a look at your house. Wouldn't it look better with a second story? You could put an Enchanting Table up there! You could make a storeroom to organize all the resources you've mined! Maybe put a Nether Portal on the roof! It's time to build up and learn how to make things taller.

The first thing to do is bring all the resources you need, plus a little extra Dirt to get yourself into position. In the case of building a new level on your house, you need tools to dismantle the roof and turn it into a floor, unless you built a flat roof in the first place. You also need material to make new walls, stairs or ladders to connect the upper floor with the bottom level, and a brand new roof. Bring all of this with you, so you don't have to go back for it later. In the case of building your house, getting more stacks of Wood or Stone is pretty easy. However, when you build a larger project farther away (like building up to some Diamonds high on the wall of a cave), running out of building material halfway can be very inconvenient!

Expanding your house upward uses the same basic principal of putting one block on top of another to get you where you need to be, and then making a new structure there. The easiest way to start climbing is to make a basic pillar at the base of the thing you want to modify: in this case, your house. Put down a Dirt block and hop on top of it. Then, while standing on the Dirt block, look down at your feet, jump, and place a block at the same time. It's easier than it sounds, because you can just hold down the buttons! You wind up on top of the newly placed block, higher off the ground. Keep jumping and placing blocks until the pillar of Dirt reaches the top of your house. Because you built the pillar next to your house, you can step straight off onto the roof!

GET LOW FOR SAFETY!

Crouching keeps you from falling off ledges and lets you safely go way out to the edges. It's not perfect, because monsters can still knock you off, but it really helps for construction!

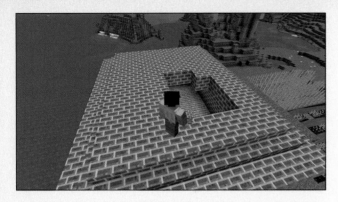

Dismantle the roof or flatten it out, since you'll use it as flooring for your new level. When you start placing blocks for the walls, crouch and move to the edge to avoid falling off. Lay down the wall's lowest blocks around the edge to give yourself a pattern to follow. Once the new wall's base is laid out, hop on top, crouch down, and work around the perimeter. Place new wall blocks and hop on top when it is nearly complete to finish placing the last few blocks. Keep repeating this until the wall is high enough to accommodate whatever needs to fit in the new room. Now that you're standing on top of your newly built wall, you can jump into the room and make a ceiling, or you can do it from the top of the wall by building outward.

Building Bridges

Building out is the technique of building into empty space. Crossing a chasm with a bridge is an example of building out. Another example is starting from a small ledge high up and turning it into a larger structure. If you want to make things up in the air, you have to get comfortable working on the edges!

First things first. Crouch! Always crouch when building out. A very simple experiment shows the reason why. If you're still on the roof of your house, you might want to come down first via your Dirt pillar. Now place a block on the ground. Hop on top of it and see how close to the edge you can go before falling off. It's pretty easy to fall! Next get back on top of the block and crouch down. Now see how far you can get. Not only can you reach much farther, but you actually stop when you reach the very edge, even if you keep trying to move off the block. Stay crouched, look down at your feet, and turn around. By doing this, it looks like you're standing on empty space! You can see the edge of the block that you're standing on. For some real fun, you can place a new block at the edge while crouching and walking backward. You can place a block, walk onto it, and then move to the very edge again!

This technique is the heart of building out. You ride the very edge, placing new blocks that you can then use to reach even farther. In the case of a bridge, crouch-walk backward, placing new blocks as you go. You'll be across that chasm in no time! If you want to build a ledge, crouch at the edge and walk side to side, laying new blocks to make the ledge wider. Then move to the edge of the new blocks and go back the other way. In the case of your newly expanded house, get back on top of the wall and then crouch-walk your way toward the center, filling in the roof layer as you go.

This method is ideal for crossing lakes, Lava, and ravines, and for building sky bridges to anywhere you'd like to go.

Putting It All Together

There are times when you find a giant tree while exploring and think, "That would make a great tree house!" Let's get some supplies and make it happen!

TREE HOUSE CHECK LIST

- **Really big tree:** Jungle trees are certainly tall enough, but you have to do some landscaping to clear out the leaves. Mega taiga spruces are ideal, as they are very tall and thick, and the leaves are really high up. But any big tree will do!

- **Wood Planks:** You can easily find these in the nearby woods or bring them from another base camp.

- **Dirt blocks:** You can find these all around the tree.

- **Fences:** These are assembled from Sticks and serve as railings for your fort.

- **Ladders:** Once you've built the tree house, you want an easy way to get up and down.

- **Trapdoor:** This keeps you from falling down through the ladder hole!

- **Torches:** You need these to light everything!

- **Bed:** This comes in handy for sleeping when it gets dark. You'll be too high for most monsters, but an arrow can still knock you off.

Build a Dirt pillar beside the tree, and stop at the tree's upper section. This doesn't have to be precise. Now use the Wooden Planks against the bark of the tree to create a small ledge. Walk onto it when the ledge is complete and crouch down. While crouching, walk around the tree in a spiral, building a ledge that completely circles the tree trunk. Continue circling until the ledge is several blocks wide. This will be your tree house's floor, so make it as wide as you want! Once you're satisfied with the floor, set up the Bed and sleep if it's dark.

Now it's time for walls. Because monsters can't reach you, have some fun with this. Place wooden Fences all around the edges to act as railings, but leave the corners bare. These bare corners will become small pillars to support the roof. You may be under the leaves, but it's always nice to have something more solid overhead. Make Wood Plank pillars three or four blocks tall. When you're finished, crouch and build inward to start making a flat roof. Maybe later, you can convert it into a small storage space!

WHEN TO RISK IT ALL

It's best to start high-altitude construction projects when you've just lost a huge amount of experience, either to death or to some enchanting work. Don't risk a deadly fall when your character has 50 levels sitting there, ready to spend. It's better to try these large projects when you don't have much to lose!

Once you've made a Ladder, your fort is almost complete. Place Torches along the Fence posts for light, and add more by the Ladder to serve as markers. Go ahead and knock down the remaining Dirt, since you don't need it anymore, or move it and make it even bigger to serve as a landmark. Maybe later, you can make a bridge over to the other trees and create a network of forts connected by bridges.

We're almost finished. Now it's time to make a Trapdoor and Ladder leading back to the ground. Go ahead and knock out one of the Wooden Planks on the floor against the tree. Then place your Trapdoor in the open space. Open it and look down. It's a pretty big drop, but you can survive the fall if you are at full health. Place some Ladders against the tree and start working your way down to the ground. If you fall, no problem— that's what the Bed was for! Your spawn point is up in the tree, so if worse comes to worst, you start over and continue building down.

LANDSCAPING

Landscaping is the act of shaping the world around you. These acts range from tiny actions, like digging holes in the ground and clearing out trees, or they can be as grand as blowing up a mountain with TNT or reshaping an island in Creative mode. If it changes the way the world looks, it's landscaping!

Groundskeeping

One of your earliest experiences with landscaping is clearing the area around your house. You can do all sorts of landscaping projects to make your region safer and more convenient.

Trees are useful, but having them close to the house is dangerous. The shade they provide allows Skeletons and Zombies to survive the sunlight, so they can attack during the day. Clear the trees to make sure you can watch the monsters burn when the dawn comes.

Now that you've made the immediate area safer, it's time to flatten out some space to prepare for farms and animal pens. You might not do any farming or animal raising until much later, but flattening the area also makes it easier for you to get around and see incoming enemies. This is a great opportunity to evaluate the area and decide what to do with irregular holes and random cave entrances. You can seal cave entrances with Doors, widen the openings into proper mines, or even remove the top layer of dirt and rock to expose them to sunlight for easier mining. If you have any small water holes nearby, flatten the area around them for later farming, or start planting crops right away around the edges!

Moving Mountains

You can clear the area around your house quickly, but some projects require more effort. Mountainous terrain, for instance, is very annoying to navigate; it tends to be full of sudden drops, sheer cliffs, and lots of climbing. This can result in complex paths as you move from place to place. Winding through the landscape is a good way to get lost, so why not change it?

Tunnel through large obstacles to reduce travel time. This is useful in exploring, as it reduces the need for excessive landmarks. If you expect to return to a certain place, such as a Village, make a more permanent roadway. Trails of landmarks are great for exploring new territory, but sometimes you want something more permanent. A roadway lets you follow an obvious path instead of playing hide and seek with Signs!

With hand tools and time, you can make any tunnel you want. Pickaxes and Shovels are fine for most situations, but if you want to go through a really large obstacle, like a mountain, there are other options. Try blasting through heavy blocks with TNT—it lets you blow stuff up! Hissing like a Creeper is optional but highly recommended.

Getting Gunpowder can be dangerous, as it involves killing Creepers before they explode. Once you get a good Sword (Iron or Diamond), killing Creepers becomes much easier, and you get Gunpowder more frequently. If you have Gunpowder stockpiled in a Chest, why not put it to use?

Gunpowder forms an explosive block called TNT when mixed with Sand. You can place TNT like normal blocks, and then ignite them to produce violent explosions. Place a string of TNT blocks to make a chain reaction and blow large craters into the landscape, or place them one at a time to gradually blow through walls. No mountain can stand up to explosives!

ISLAND OF DOOM, AN EXAMPLE IN WORLD SHAPING

Some starting locations are very tough for beginners: for example, tiny desert islands. They don't provide many resources to start with or easy terrain to manipulate.

We've talked about landscaping in terms of making your world nicer, but now it's time to think big. Make a copy of the world in Creative mode, and let your imagination run wild! It's time to break out the Obsidian and Lava, and turn this pretty little island into a fortress of doom!

In Creative mode, you have unlimited access to every material in the game, you can break blocks with a single touch, and you can fly. When you work with Obsidian, you can correct mistakes in a second instead of having to bring out the Diamond Pickaxe and spend time breaking a misplaced block. Grab an Obsidian block (in the Building Materials tab, or you can search for it) and go to work turning the island's Sand and Dirt into Obsidian.

Turning the island into an Obsidian reflection involves replacing every Dirt or Sand surface block with an Obsidian one. Work around the edges at the water line, and then move steadily up. You can replace large, flat patches quickly, but the small hills and contours require more patience. While you're flying, look for places that would make interesting locations for a tower, a pool of bubbling Lava, or anything else you can imagine!

Monsters don't attack in Creative mode and you never get hungry. You can work through the night, or save the eyestrain of placing black blocks at night by grabbing a Bed from the Decorations tab and sleeping. In the morning, jump twice rapidly to start flying. Get an aerial view of the island and see the progress you've made. Holding the Jump button makes you go higher, and double-jumping again makes you fall like a stone—you don't take damage! Once the island is coated with Obsidian, make some holes and fill the nooks and crannies with Lava for some splashes of color (and evil). Remember that flowing Lava makes Stone blocks when it hits the water. So if you make a mistake, it might take some cleaning! Use a Bucket to remove a Lava source block until everything is clear, and then break the Stone. The sea rushes back in to fix itself, but if there are any problems, use a Water Bucket to bring the sea back to normal.

Once the island is fitted with pools of fiery death, it's time to build your fortress. Nether Bricks are a traditionally evil fortress construction material, but they'll be dark against the Obsidian. Besides, if you want to see a standard evil fortress, you can go to the Nether! Experiment with available blocks to find one that contrasts well with the black of the Obsidian, the blue of the water, and the orange of the Lava. In this case, Iron blocks go well as neutral gray. Iron also happens to be a very traditional tower material for evil types.

Build up and away! Placing Glowstone at regular intervals keeps the tower illuminated and makes it look good. Flying and jumping let you build up very quickly. Falling has no effect, so dust yourself off and return to the air if you happen to plummet.

Once you complete the central tower, add embellishments like Iron Doors, crenellations on the roof, and channels for Lava to flow to the ground below. A prison at the tower's base shows the monsters who is in charge of the island. Use Monster Eggs to spawn Skeletons and other creatures inside the prison to serve as examples to the others. Be sure to mock them mercilessly when the sun comes up! For the final touches, add secondary towers for your nefarious activities. Be sure to build plenty of space for gloating, cackling maniacally, and reading ancient scrolls of power!

Now that your doom tower is complete, rule the island with an iron fist!

FORMING AND USING LANDMARKS

Let's explore the world! *Minecraft* worlds are big places, and eventually you'll venture out into one. The problem is that it's easy to get lost. How can you find your way back home? How can you remember the way to the new places you find?

Picture this: You've been walking around for 10 minutes, filling your inventory with things like Sugar Cane, Clay, Coal, and Iron, and you finally see a Village on the horizon just as it gets dark. You make your way over, but before you get inside, you hear the telltale hiss of a Creeper and the world explodes around you. Now you spawn back at home! How will you ever find your way back?

This is what landmarks are for. You can create distinctive features visible from far away when traveling or even large-scale projects that are visible on a map. That way, you can find your way around without getting lost, as well as lead other people to the incredible discoveries you've made.

Visual Landmarks

Visual landmarks are anything you can see while you're walking around. They can be quick projects, like a pillar of Dirt; large-scale ones, like giant sky arrows; writing on the side of a mountain; or anything in between. If you can see it from far away, you've made a visual landmark!

PILLARS AND TORCHES

Quick, place a Torch! Congratulations! You've made a landmark. Torches are visible from far away, they create pools of light, and they occur naturally in only a few places (Villages, strongholds, and abandoned mineshafts). When you see a Torch, you know that a person placed it, or that you've come across something special! When you explore the Overworld, use Torches to leave a trail for yourself. Take a few stacks of Torches with you and regularly put one on the ground, on a tree, or on some other feature of the landscape. If you don't find anything interesting on your trip, turn around and recollect the Torches on your return, or leave them for later exploration.

If you find something you really want to return to, dig Dirt blocks (or take some with you) and make a pillar. You don't have to go all the way up to the clouds, but you definitely want it higher than the trees, preferably 10-20 blocks above the highest one. Be careful, because you don't want to fall! You may be able to find your way back, but it can be a long walk. Build the pillar two blocks wide as you go up, and then just mine one of them downward, leaving a one-block-wide pillar to guide your future travels. Another method is to carry two Buckets of Water. With these, make a pool three blocks wide and filled at each end with Water from your Buckets. Refill the Buckets with the

Water block in the middle of the stream, and you're still left with a pool to jump into from the top of the Dirt pillar that you're about to build.

Making a pillar is one of the very first things you should do when starting a long-term base, so you can find your way back to it after hunting or gathering wood.

DISTINCTIVE LANDMARKS

As time goes on, you collect more and more resources and continue to explore. With more time and energy, you should create larger markers that are even more distinctive. Pillars and Torch trails are great when you're starting, but they can get confusing later on when you have multiple trails and many pillars marking different locations. It's time to make things more distinctive.

The Pillar of Fire

Lava is a great way to make a landmark visually stand out. Simply taking a Bucket of Lava to the top of a pillar and letting it flow down creates a very distinctive, bright, and dangerous landmark. Be sure to wall off the base so Lava doesn't spill everywhere!

Regular wayposts with Signs attached are a simple and effective way to mark the world around you. Leave a message describing where a trail of Torches leads and how long you have to travel to get there. This is an extremely useful way to remind yourself where all the neat things are located. But why be satisfied with small things? Take some time to carve an arrow into a nearby cliff!

Because you can leave blocks floating in midair, make a floating arrow pointing at your house! Convert some of the Redstone you've mined into blocks. Redstone is one of the easiest resources to get when deep mining, so there should be plenty to spare. These bright red blocks show up extremely well, so they make excellent landmarks. Make at least 10 Redstone blocks, preferably more, before you scout an entirely new region.

Cobblestone is abundant, so grab stacks of that as well. Bring Ladders, because some climbing is in your future. A Pickaxe and Shovel are essential as well!

You've already made a Dirt pillar near your house as one of your first landmarks, so use the Ladders to ascend it. Once you get to the top, mine halfway down and make a small platform. This is where you'll start building the point of your arrow.

Crouch at the edge of the platform and place a Redstone block. This block will be the tip of the arrow pointing down. Now, place a Stone block beside the Redstone on either side. Then another Redstone block on top of each of the stone squares. You can leave the Stone block, but your arrow will look pointier if you mine it out, so stand on the Redstone, stay crouched, and mine away. Leave it with three Redstone blocks making a glowing marker, or go as big as you want. Make a giant point if you're motivated!

Once you have a sufficiently pointy arrow, make a tail for it out of Stone by creating a pillar on top of the Redstone center block. Add Redstone blocks as you go up to make it even more distinctive.

Map Landmarks

Map landmarks are all about making places stand out visually when you look at them on a map.

Maps show a top-down view of the world, so when you think about making a landmark big enough to be visible on a map, you have to think in top-down terms. It helps to have a *very* clear idea before you start. It's even better to have a piece of paper with the pattern drawn on it. Go into these projects knowing that they will take a *long* time to perfect.

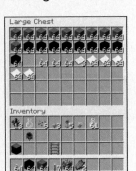

Like all big projects in *Minecraft*, it really helps to have a friend! Get your buddies involved in the project and watch the hours melt away.

THE COLLECTION

You really need two things to get started. The first are some Maps. Maps come in different scales, so having several of them lets you see how the project is progressing on each scale. On the lowest scale, a shape doesn't have to be thousands of blocks long to show up, but at the largest scale you really need to think *big*.

Next you need lots and lots of colorful resources. Maps are all about showing off the land, and color plays a large role. So if you're in a green field,

think about collecting red Wool to make your marker pop out. If you are in a desert, think about something dark. Wool is easy to work with because you can get multiple pieces from a Sheep by using the Shears, and it can be dyed all sorts of colors.

If you're playing in Survival mode, start shearing any Sheep you find, breeding more by using Wheat, and coming back to them again and again until you have a full chest of Wool stacks.

Next you need to make dye, so you have to collect flowers and plant them to harvest for the dye materials. Lapis Lazuli is used to make blue dye, and you find it in abundance when mining. Red dye is easy due to all the flowers you can grow with Bone Meal.

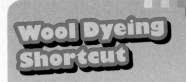
Wool Dyeing Shortcut

Dye your Sheep before shearing them to make dyed materials. Instead of having to use a piece of dye for every unit of Wool, you can get several dyed units of Wool per Sheep shearing. It's also funny to do this because your Sheep briefly take on an odd color.

SCALE PROGRESSION

Find a flat area of land, or make one. Then start with a 30x30 square of red Wool and see how it shows up on a Map. Track your progress on the small-scale Map to see how it's starting to look. If it looks pretty distinctive on the small scale, see how it shows up on larger scales. Be sure to sleep, and keep the area well lit with Torches. The last thing you want is for a Creeper to undo hours and hours of careful work. Once you make a marker that shows up, the rest is all in how big you want to go!

BIOMES

What Are Biomes?

Biomes are often referred to as "ecosystems." They're large areas separated from each other by climate and geography. In *Minecraft*, just like the real world, each biome has its own set of geographical features, elevations of natural formations, plants and animals, temperatures, humidity ratings, weather, and sky and foliage colors.

The mixture of different biomes creates the world you explore in *Minecraft*. The specific set of biomes used to generate a world is called a "seed." When you first create your *Minecraft* world, you have the option to use a randomly generated world (a random seed) or enter a known seed. Although you may be familiar with some features available in a known seed, your experience in the world will still be unique; the only difference is that you may be more experienced with nearby environments or interesting locations.

Looking Up Seeds

You can search online to find fun seeds that other people have discovered; you can also share exciting seeds of your own. Some worlds have especially awesome landmarks or rare temples. Whatever you're looking for, feel free to search through other people's listings and try out their worlds.

Biome Categories

Regardless of how your world is created, you soon find yourself in one of several possible biomes. You can tell which biome you're in simply by looking around and examining the terrain's color, the number of mountains and hills, and the kinds of trees. The types of blocks that are immediately available to you also provide a good indication.

If you don't like the biome in your starting location, you have two options. First, you can restart and generate a different world. Each time you create a world, you start in a different location (you may not get a different biome; some biomes are more common than others). The second option is to pick a direction and run as fast and as far as possible. If you're still in a region you don't like by the time night falls, dig a hole three blocks deep, cap it off with a ceiling block, and wait inside for day to break. Either way, you'll eventually arrive at a biome with your preferred conditions.

The biome types in *Minecraft* are divided by temperature. There are five categories: snowy, cold, medium, dry/warm, and neutral. The temperature ranges prevent biomes with large differences from being next to each other; for example, deserts aren't found next to ice plains.

Weather

A biome's temperature range also determines its weather. Depending on where you are, your biome may have snow, rain, both, or neither. In game terms, both snow and rain are considered the same weather effect, but whether you get snow or rain varies according to biome type. If a non-snowy biome touches a snowy biome, there can be both rain and snow. The required values for different weather conditions are <0.15 for snow, 0.15-0.95 for rain, and >1.0 for none.

Elevation also plays a role in weather. An area with hills or mountains has a greater chance to have snow over rain. In the same way, a low, hot region of desert has no rain or snow at all.

Noteworthy weather can occur during the day or night. Usually, weather occurs every seven *Minecraft* days and continues for 15 minutes. If you don't like the weather, you can use a Bed to sleep through it during evenings or thunderstorms.

Both rain and snow have a chance to form thunderstorms. Thunderstorms are relatively rare occurrences, but their dark conditions and potential for lightning make them more dangerous than other weather. Even if it's daytime during a thunderstorm, the low light causes monsters to spawn. There's also the potential for lightning to strike enemies. Creepers that are struck by lightning do a *huge* amount of damage, so be on the lookout at all times.

Possible Effects of Lightning

- Starts fires
- Turns Pigs into Zombie Pigmen
- Supercharges Creepers (watch out!)
- Damages players
- Turns Villagers into Witches (requires Version 1.8)

Biome Types

There are 61 total biomes. Some are quite similar to others, but each has a few distinct elements. Your current biome determines the availability of various blocks, plants, and creatures.

FREE IRRIGATION!

Storms bring water into a region, causing crops to grow faster for a little while. This offers the same effect as irrigating your crops.

SNOWY BIOMES

Common Features	Snow at any elevation
Grass and Foliage	Blue/Green

BIOME	ID	FEATURES
Cold Beach	26	Desolate, cold beaches
Cold Taiga	30	More trees are here, making this an easier snowy biome to start
Cold Taiga (M)	158	Cold taiga with much taller mountains
Frozen River	11	Fairly clear area, few features, ice on all water
Ice Plains	12	Flat, snowy; has icy water, limited wood
Ice Plains Spikes	140	Lovely fields of frozen spikes

COLD BIOMES

Common Features	Snow at higher elevation, rain at lower elevation
Grass and Foliage	Blue/Green

BIOME	ID	FEATURES
Extreme Hills	3	High peaks and low valleys
Extreme Hills (M)	131	Less plant growth, even higher mountains
Extreme Hills+	34	Adds some much needed tree growth to the biome
Extreme Hills+ (M)	162	Again, adds more trees to the extreme hills (M) biome
Mega Spruce Taiga	160	Thick forests are here, limiting movement and visibility
Mega Taiga	32	Huge spruce trees dominate this area
Stone Beach	25	Raised beaches with stone drop-offs into the water
Taiga	5	Spruce trees, Wolves, and cold temperatures are key features here
Taiga (M)	133	Makes the taiga terrain more mountainous

MEDIUM BIOMES

Common Features	Snow only at extreme elevations, rain anywhere lower
Grass and Foliage	Green

BIOME	ID	FEATURES
Beach	16	Sandy lowlands that lead into the ocean
Birch Forest	27	A forest of birch trees
Birch Forest (M)	155	A forest of tall, impressive birch trees
Birch Forest Hills (M)	156	A forest of birch trees with large hills and taller trees
Flower Forest	132	A forest with slightly fewer trees and many more flowers
Forest	4	Simple biome with a strong mix of resources and few downsides; wood and food are prevalent
Jungle	21	Dense wooded areas with heavy foliage; it's hard to move quickly through these areas, so they can be dangerous if you're caught by monsters
Jungle (M)	149	Add mountainous terrain to the usual jungle biomes
Jungle Edge	23	Jungles thin out near their borders with other major biomes
Jungle Edge (M)	151	Greater elevation changes are present in this version
Mushroom Island	14	Has Mycelium instead of Dirt; Mushrooms are found in great quantities, and Mooshrooms are the only animals that appear in this area
Mushroom Island Shore	15	Provides a border between Mushroom Islands and the sea
Plains	1	Simple grasslands, not much wood access; you can find Horses here
River	7	Clay blocks, fairly shallow water
Roofed Forest	29	Oak forest with a heavy canopy and little light
Roofed Forest (M)	157	Has cliffs and valleys to make the roofed forest even more daunting
Sunflower Plains	129	Similar to plains but with many more flowers in the area
Swampland	6	Movement is hampered by many pools of Water; increased danger from unusual monster spawns (including Witches)

DRY/WARM BIOMES

Common Features	No rain or snow
Grass and Foliage	Yellow/Brown

BIOME	ID	FEATURES
Desert	2	Sandy, dry area with Cacti
Desert (M)	130	There are occasional oases here
Mesa	37	Dry, Clay-filled hills
Plateau	36, 38, 39	Wide, open hills with livable areas up top
Plateau (M)	164, 166, 167	Very high plateaus
Savanna	35	Open grasslands with the potential for Horses
Savanna (M)	163	Mountainous grasslands

NEUTRAL BIOMES

Common Features	Mid-range temperature
Grass and Foliage	Varies

BIOME	ID	FEATURES
Deep Ocean	24	Especially deep Water
Hills	17, 18, 19, 22, 28, 31, 33, 156, 161	These hill sections are often embedded in other biomes
Ocean	0	Large swaths of Water tiles

SPECIAL AREAS

Some interesting locations in *Minecraft* aren't common parts of their biomes. These places aren't 100% unique, but they're pretty close. You might go days or weeks without finding some of these, so they're awesome treats when you uncover them.

Abandoned Mineshafts

These pre-existing tunnels are found underground in the Overworld. They're useful because they often let you travel quickly through an area, finding spare Railways, Coal, Iron, perhaps Cobwebs, and such. Chests of both common and rare treasures are located in these shafts, so search them thoroughly. You might find Diamonds, special Seeds, Saddles, Horse Armor, or Enchanted Books.

While you search, remember to keep all Torches on one specific side of the shaft. This ensures that you know how to get back to the entrance when you decide to leave.

Monster Spawners in these shafts create Cave Spiders—they're poisonous, so be careful when you fight them. Keep your health high, and bring Milk if at all possible. It's nice to have as a backup after a close fight.

Dungeons

Huge cave complexes often have a small Cobblestone room with a Monster Spawner inside them. These rooms are called dungeons. They contain Chests of treasure, so they're excellent to find, and you can build deadly trap rooms to farm experience from the Monster Spawners if you have the inclination to do so.

Dungeons are found in the Overworld, and the best way to raise your chances of seeing them is to dig through areas until you find ravines or caverns. Follow these all the way to their end, while looking for high concentrations of monsters; that's sometimes a tipoff that a Monster Spawner is there. If you dig in an area and hear monsters, always search for the cavern that houses the beasts, and you may find a dungeon.

Dungeon Chests can hold Golden Apples, high-quality Horse Armor, Name Tags, Music Discs, Saddles, and other decent goodies. It's always good to loot these locations!

Nether Fortresses

These monster bastions are located in the Nether. They're made of Nether Bricks and are well defended by Blazes, Wither Skeletons, Magma Cubes, and a Monster Spawner (which makes even more Blazes). You can't find Nether Wart anywhere else in *Minecraft*, so that alone is a good reason to search for a Nether Fortress. Nether Wart is required for any real brewing, so finding a source of this rare herb is amazingly good news.

If you find a Nether Fortress and don't get everything you want out of it, search directly north or south from there to find more fortresses. They're always aligned in this way, so looking east or west will get you off track. On the other hand, if you can't find *any* fortresses, travel east or west in the hopes of finding your first one.

As with most special locations, Nether Fortresses have Chests of loot as well as rare resources. Diamonds, metal, Golden equipment, Saddles, Horse Armor, and Nether Wart are all possible rewards here.

Don't assume you've seen all of a Nether Fortress once you've explored the areas above ground. These massive complexes can be buried in the ground, requiring some serious excavation to dig out.

Villages

Happy towns of peaceful Villagers exist in the Overworld. Search plains, desert, and savanna biomes to find them. Once you do, talk to the Villagers by approaching them and interacting with each person. They have different professions and items to trade. They request specific items and give Emeralds as payment. These Emeralds can then be traded for items that the Villagers create.

Look for rare items in town. Chainmail armor, Bottles of Enchanting, and a few other fun toys are available this way.

If you cause too much trouble in a Village, the Iron Golems that defend it become aggressive toward your character.

THINGS THAT INFLUENCE YOUR POPULARITY IN A VILLAGE

Attacking a Villager	-1
Killing a Villager	-2
Attacking a Child	-3
Killing an Iron Golem	-5
Trading the Last Item on a Villager's List	+1

If you want to trade and walk safely around town, avoid hitting any Villagers, and run away from them if you get into any trouble. Don't fight your way out, and don't attack the Iron Golems even if they come after you.

Village Blacksmiths often have cool loot. Search their buildings for Chests, and trade with the Blacksmiths to see if they have anything fun to offer.

If you'd like to expand a Village, add Doors to its buildings. This causes even more Villagers to spawn. You're also free to add physical defenses so fewer Zombies can reach and attack the Villagers. Zombies are a major threat to towns. Wall off remote areas to provide some defense. Zombies spawn within town limits, so there's only so much you can do, but building good walls is a start, and they make Villages look even more exciting.

Also, use Iron Golems for additional Village defenders. Either fight aggressively to protect townsfolk during the evening, or run away before sunset and keep your distance from town to prevent it from being attacked. Zombies won't siege a Village unless you're nearby.

Strongholds

These large, dangerous complexes are major features in the Overworld. They can appear in any biome, and they're always somewhat closer to your starting point. In other words, you won't find them hours away from home. They're a critical part of the game's progression, because you can only reach The End and face the Ender Dragon by finding a Stronghold and activating its portal.

Use Eyes of Ender to locate strongholds. These special items give you a direction to the nearest stronghold. They're often deep underground, but they may bump into ravines or other special terrain features.

Once you find a stronghold, be careful. Monster Eggs are common, so Silverfish are major threats. They attack in large groups if you trigger them, and strongholds contain Monster Spawners that deploy even more Silverfish to hassle you.

Once you find the heart of the stronghold, destroy its Monster Spawner and look for the End Portal. Activate these with more Eyes of Ender and explore The End.

Treasure Chests in strongholds feature a huge range of rewards. Storage rooms have Chests with a chance to yield metal, food, and an Enchanted Book. Rooms with Slabs may have Ender Pearls, metal, food, Iron equipment, Golden Apples, Saddles, Enchanted Books, or Horse Armor. Library rooms can have Books, Paper, Maps, Compasses, or Enchanted Books.

Temples

Desert, Ocean, and jungle biomes have the potential to host temples. These neat land features are normally found at ground level and are quite fun to explore. They often hold considerable treasure, so everyone loves to look for them.

Don't relax while you wander through these structures. They often have traps, and you don't want to get yourself killed and lose so much potential treasure in the process.

Explore carefully and look for traps before triggering them. Be willing to dig around hallways and come in from the side or rear of each chamber to avoid trouble. Or disarm traps by finding their Tripwires/Pressure Plates; break those to disable the traps.

SECRETS REVEALED

Jungle Temples have a hidden Chest that is revealed if you find the proper settings for three Levers inside the temple.

Desert Temples have a hidden room under the floor. That room is trapped to explode, so dig down to it carefully and avoid the Pressure Plate while looting the place.

Witch Huts

Most often located in swamp or plains areas, Witch Huts are small residences that may have Witches in them—Witches don't spawn there forever, so any that have fallen out, left, or been killed won't reappear.

HOW TIME PASSES

It's smart to understand the day/night cycles in *Minecraft* because getting caught out in the darkness is dangerous. Let's deal with time for a moment.

There are 20 minutes in each day/night cycle in *Minecraft*. You get 10 minutes of sunshine and 10 minutes of shadow (including dawn and dusk). Many of the dangerous creatures are limited to nighttime, so you're much, much safer playing outside during the day.

POCKET EDITION CHANGE

The *Minecraft Pocket Edition* goes on a 12-minute cycle instead. Thus, day and night are each six minutes long for players of that version.

You can track the progress of the day by watching the sun—as long as you're outside! Watch as the sun travels through the sky, eventually setting and bringing on dusk. Before you have the resources to make a Clock, the sun is your best way to tell time.

That said, you can also use your own watch or clock in real life. Look at the time when dawn breaks and remember that the evening will come in 10 minutes. Apart from the exception that we noted about the Pocket Edition, the duration of the day/night cycle varies only if you are playing in single-player mode and pause the game by pressing Escape; this stops the clock until you return to normal gameplay.

During the Day

Your first day begins at dawn. That's a good thing because you have plenty to do in those short 10 minutes. Make the most of them so Zombies don't eat your character when night falls.

Daylight prevents most monsters from spawning, helps crops to grow quickly, and is brighter than a Torch even when it's up close. In fact, it's so bright that some monsters aren't merely driven into hiding. Zombies and Skeletons are killed by direct sunlight. Endermen teleport to a safe, dark area. Spiders don't leave, but they become docile and don't attack until they are attacked or placed in shadow.

As the Moon Rises

Enjoy the pretty view while you can. Sunset is lovely, but danger grows with each passing second. When the light starts to dim, sprint back toward your home or dig an emergency shelter and lock yourself into a makeshift cave. The moon rises in the evening, and dusk lasts for a short time. Light levels diminish during the next minute and a half.

It's quite possible to stay outside all night, working as you wish. Fighting Creepers, Zombies, and Skeletons is dangerous work, but someone with a Sword, armor, and experience fighting these monsters should be okay. This doesn't mean that you should do it; using resources, risking your life, and killing enemies is fun but not always productive.

The best reason to stay outside and fight is if you're gathering specific resources: Bone, String, and Arrows from Skeletons; Gunpowder from Creepers; Ender Pearls from Endermen; and Carrots or Potatoes from Zombies. Once you get enough of these items, nighttime becomes even less appealing.

Telling Time

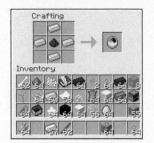

If you aren't using a real-world clock to tell time, make a Clock inside *Minecraft*. They are quite helpful when you're deciding whether to risk a long-range scouting expedition. They let you know how much daylight remains. They're even better underground, when you want to figure out whether it's a good time to return to the surface.

Getting Some Sleep

Night passes instantly if your character rests in a Bed. This does not advance time—at least, not exactly. Crops don't grow, your Furnaces won't cook any faster, and so forth. Beds simply advance your character to morning. Rain or snow that's falling can end thanks to "skipping ahead," but this is the only effect aside from getting you quickly through the night.

Beds save your position when you rest. If your character dies (anywhere, in any world), you return to the last place where your character slept. Always put your Bed somewhere safe, so you don't get attacked while you're trying to get your bearings. Keep a Bed inside your base, where there are resources to arm yourself. If you die, grab new tools, weapons, armor, food, and Torches, and then head out to retrieve any items that fell. You won't want to run back out there empty handed!

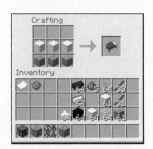

Beds are handy to bring with you on long-distance exploration expeditions. If you want to see the Overworld, take a Bed in your inventory and use it as night falls. You get to sleep through the nighttime monster spawns and pick up your journey where you left off. If you die, you wake up where you last slept instead of back at home. It's a good way to save time and stay safe, while getting the most out of your exploration. It's also a potential lifesaver if you're the type who gets lost easily whenever you step outside your house.

THE WAY MONSTERS ARE BORN

Minecraft wouldn't be complete without monsters! They provide an extra level of excitement and danger: a challenge or obstacle to overcome. We'll now explain how monsters appear so you can protect your home from various bad guys!

Some Facts About Monsters

Most monsters start to notice your presence when you're roughly 16 blocks away. Monsters that immediately move to attack are called hostile or aggressive. Some monsters can see you through rocks, and others can climb or fall to reach you.

Monsters are usually affected by the environment in the same ways as you. Thus, they take falling damage, can suffocate or drown under water, and they can be set on fire, too. Additionally, and most importantly, monsters take damage from weapon attacks.

Monsters can also ride in Minecarts, and you can transport them around this way. And although monsters can't open Doors, they can break them down under the right conditions.

When a monster is killed, it may drop an item. Some monsters can pick up blocks or equipment and use it against you, or simply carry things around. Other monsters wear armor or use creatures as mounts.

Born in the Darkness

Night is the time of monsters. As the sun sets, monsters appear. The sudden appearance of a monster into the world is called "spawning." Some monsters spawn more often than others—Zombies are the most common.

Light level is usually what determines monster spawning. The following table shows which monsters appear at a given illumination level:

LIGHT LEVEL	MONSTERS	ADDITIONAL DETAILS
7	Zombies, Skeletons, Wither Skeletons, Creepers, Witches, Endermen, Spiders, Spider Jockeys, Chicken Jockeys	Spiders are no longer hostile once the light level is 12 (they attack if you hit them, though).
8	Slimes	Only in Swamps; if below layer 40 underground, Slimes spawn at any light level.
11	Silverfish, Blazes	Silverfish are found deep in the Overworld, inside blocks that break a little too quickly; Blazes are Nether creatures that fly around, shooting fire at anyone who gets too close to their fortresses.
Any	Zombie Pigment, Ghasts, Magma Cubes, Endermites	Zombie Pigmen are found in the Nether but can appear in the Overworld under very rare conditions; very rarely, Endermites are formed after an Enderman teleports.

When the sun rises, most of the monsters outside start to catch fire. Zombies and Skeletons, which are the most common monsters to spawn, can't deal with bright light and quickly become walking torches! If you attack them at close range while they're on fire, be careful; you can catch fire as well. However, if there's enough shade or a storm outside, monsters can survive the daytime. They might also wear protective armor (a helmet helps) to shield them from the sun's deadly rays.

Some monsters don't care about daylight; Witches, Creepers, and Spiders can all be found while the sun's out. Endermen often teleport away from the light to find more comfortable areas.

YOU CAN DO ANYTHING WITH A LITTLE PRACTICE

Monster Hideouts

Because monsters spawn anywhere the light isn't too bright, naturally occurring caves are monster playgrounds. Dark pits in the ground, large openings into mountains, or deep underground pockets make wonderful monster homes.

If you're mining underground and break into a natural cave, it's a sure bet that monsters are in it somewhere. **Go through the cave cautiously, and keep your ears open for the sounds of creatures. As you move through, put Torches on the walls at regular intervals. This keeps monsters from spawning after you leave. If you come to an area that you can't illuminate, or if you want to grab a lot of material at your own pace without monster interference, wall off a section. You can always come back and explore later; your safety is more precious than Gold.**

Strongholds, fortresses, temples, dungeons, and abandoned mineshafts are all places where monsters live. There are wonderful treasures to be found in these locations, but it's dangerous to go there unprepared.

Monster Spawners

Monster Spawners are bluish-black, cage-like blocks found in special locations: fortresses, dungeons, abandoned mineshafts, and strongholds. Within the block, there are flames and a small, spinning monster soon to be spawned. Generally, Monster Spawners create only Zombies, Skeletons, Spiders, Blazes, and Silverfish, but they can make animals as well.

A Monster Spawner activates when you are 16 blocks away and immediately begins spawning a random monster within an 8x2x8 block area (8 blocks wide, 2 blocks high, and 8 blocks long). As long as the light level is appropriate and any other conditions are met, monsters appear anywhere in this zone. They can even spawn midair.

You can stop Monster Spawners by surrounding their area with Torches (i.e., raising the light level) or attacking them with weapons. They drop 15-43 experience when you break them. Some people create traps of various types around Monster Spawners; when the monster appears, it finds itself falling into a large pit, for example. You can set up the traps to be instantly lethal as a means to gather certain items. Or you can use this as a way to corral monsters if you want to slaughter them at your leisure. Any experience or items gained from the monster's destruction can then be gathered later.

Spawn Eggs

In Creative mode, monsters come from eggs, called Spawn Eggs. In total, there are 25 Spawn Eggs, but this includes animals (neutral creatures) and Villagers. Hostile monsters still appear during the evening in Creative mode, but they never attack the player. But what if you want to decorate using monsters or have them wander around your house? Who wouldn't want a pet Creeper!

Select the Spawn Egg, put it on your hotbar, and use it; the creature immediately appears. Unlike Chicken Eggs, Spawn Eggs are not thrown; you have to be within range on an appropriate block. After that, the creature moves on its own. If you want, put Spawn Eggs in Dispensers; for example, you can surprise someone with an instantly appearing buddy!

Withers

You can summon a special boss monster, a Wither, in game. It's very dangerous! This monster is found only in the PC game; you must be in the Overworld, and you cannot be in Creative mode. To create a Wither in the crafting interface, put Soul Sand in a T-shape, with the T's horizontal bar going across the middle section. Then add three Wither Skeleton Skulls on top. The Wither Skeleton Skulls must be added last. The sky immediately turns darker, and the Wither appears. As the Wither grows, it begins to flash blue. It doesn't move or attack at this point, and it can't take any damage. Don't stay close to it. Once the Wither reaches its full size, it explodes, blasting anything within range!

The Wither considers every living thing to be its enemy (especially you), and it attacks anything that isn't considered undead.

THREATS TO YOUR SURVIVAL

We've talked about health and mentioned that certain things can hurt your character: fire, falls, monsters, poison, etc. Now it's time to discuss these specific dangers and how you can avoid, counter, or fall prey to them!

Your Health

Characters in *Minecraft* have 10 Hearts worth of health. Each Heart is split in half and is worth two points of damage, so it's possible to withstand up to 20 points of damage before dying.

Your health is restored naturally as long as you have nine points on your hunger meter. Keep yourself well fed so you're always at nine or 10 hunger. This way, you regenerate soon after suffering any damage.

Restoring lost health drains your hunger meter quickly, so remember to eat soon after healing from damage. You can use potions and special foods, such as Golden Apples, to give your character extra health to help with dangerous battles.

Attack Damage
Armor reduces attack damage.

Other players and monsters inflict damage if they attack with their bodies or weapons. Some of these foes have ranged weapons and can shoot you from far away. Others have to walk up to your character and attack directly to deal any damage.

Incoming attack damage is reduced if you're wearing armor. The stronger your armor, the greater the damage reduction. You're always better off wearing at least some protection when you fight. Avoid attack damage by dodging enemies or backing away from them. You can also raise Swords in a defensive position. This reduces incoming damage by half if you don't think you have a way to avoid the attack entirely.

Starvation
Armor does not affect starvation damage.

If your hunger bar depletes entirely, starvation begins. Your character loses health somewhat quickly, and this continues until you're almost dead or you find something to eat.

The best way to avoid starvation is to keep your hunger bar high at all times. This isn't just good for regenerating health. Your hunger bar doesn't deplete unless your food saturation falls to zero; this is a hidden stat, so you can't tell exactly where it is. In a simple way, your saturation can be as high as your current hunger level. This means that recently eaten food "stays with" your character longer if you're already well fed and high up on the hunger bar. When you're almost starving, it's easier to lose points on the hunger bar, even with relatively little exertion.

So you're better off eating several pieces of food to fill your bar completely. Having one snack here and there isn't as effective, and it leaves you much more vulnerable to damage.

Some items trigger a hunger effect that forces your hunger meter to fall even faster than usual. Rotten Flesh, Raw Chicken, and Pufferfish all have a chance to do this. Avoid eating these foods unless you're already about to starve. In that circumstance, eat as much Rotten Flesh as you need to fill your hunger bar. The effect of this hunger is not cumulative, so you pay the price only once instead of dealing with extra hunger for every piece you just ate.

Have Milk for Dessert

If you're forced to dine on foods that cause poison or hunger, drink Milk at the end of your foul feast. This cures your status effect and ensures that you hold onto as much health/ food as possible.

Explosions
Armor reduces explosion damage.

TNT and Creepers have something in common: They love to explode. Explosive damage is very high if your character stands too close to any detonation. Set off TNT carefully, and give Creepers a wide berth. In fact, it's usually better to shoot Creepers with Arrows or sprint away from them entirely until you're really good at killing them with hit-and-run melee attacks.

Explosions hurt everything in the area, so other monsters and even blocks take damage from these blasts. Use this as a way to break through tunnels quickly with TNT, or to kill groups of enemies by luring Creepers into their midst.

Falling
Armor does not reduce falling damage.

Falling downward more than three blocks damages your character. You take one point of damage for every block after the third. Landing in Water negates this, so aim for a Water landing any time you jump off a high ledge.

Your character can also catch Ladders or Vines in mid-fall, and this instantly stops your descent without causing any damage. Gutsy players often use this to jump down mine tunnels without getting hurt— don't miss!

An armor enchantment called Feather Falling reduces damage from falling. Long falls can still kill you, but this enchantment gives you a larger survival window.

Fire
Armor does not reduce fire damage.

Your character catches fire if you touch Lava, get hit by a Ghast's fireball, or if you bump into anything that is already burning, such as Zombies, your house, and so forth. As a rule of thumb, don't touch anything that's aflame! Armor reduces damage from initial impacts against Lava or fireballs, but the burning damage itself is unmitigated, no matter what you're wearing.

If you're set ablaze, get into Water as quickly as possible to save yourself from heavy fire damage. If no lakes or rivers are nearby, dump a Bucket of Water over yourself. Carry one of these and have it on your hotbar at all times. It's especially important when you mine near Lava. Dousing yourself extinguishes the fire and turns Lava into Obsidian, so it's one of the only ways to make it out of a Lava pool alive.

Drowning

Armor does not reduce drowning damage.

A meter of air bubbles appears when you dive into Water. If this fully depletes, your character begins to take drowning damage. This does not bring immediate death, but you won't last too long. Find your way to the surface before this happens.

A neat trick here is to place certain items against a surface when you're desperate for air. Things like Torches create an air pocket for a very short time. The Water soon puts them out, but your character breathes comfortably for the moment before this happens. Ladders, Signs, Trapdoors, Doors, Fences, and Sugar Cane can create permanent air bubbles underwater. Use any of these items to save yourself from drowning.

Suffocation

Armor does not reduce suffocation damage.

Characters or monsters that are covered in Sand or Gravel start to take this type of damage because they cannot breathe. It even hurts tougher monsters, like Iron Golems, so that's interesting.

You can't do anything about this damage directly. The only escape is to free yourself. Use a Shovel to dig out of Sand and Gravel, or a Pickaxe if you've accidentally run into a harder block. Break free, and the damage stops.

Poison

Armor does not reduce poison damage.

Poison hits your character if you eat the wrong item, get bitten by a Cave Spider, or drink the wrong potion.

Poison inflicts damage over time, and you can't reduce it with armor. However, you can negate the poison by drinking Milk. Carry around a Bucket of Milk if you're worried about poison damage. A good time to do this is when you explore an abandoned mineshaft, because those places often host plenty of Cave Spiders.

The Wither Effect

Armor does not reduce Wither Effect damage.

Wither Skeletons place a minor poison-like effect on their targets. If a Wither Skeleton strikes you, expect to suffer additional damage over time. Armor doesn't help, so back off, keep your health and hunger bar as high as possible, and try not to take additional hits until you're back in good shape.

Lightning

Armor reduces lightning damage.

Lightning inflicts five damage points to your character if you're ever unlucky enough for it to strike you. This happens only outside, during thunderstorms. To stay safe, don't play outside during thunderstorms!

Falling Into the Abyss

Armor does not reduce damage from the void.

If you find a way to get below the Bedrock, your character falls into the void. This abyss of darkness has no salvation. Unless you can teleport back to safety with an Ender Pearl, your character will die.

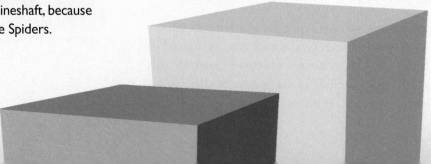

DEATH AND REBIRTH

Despite your best plans and intentions, you will get killed at some point in *Minecraft*. A lucky Creeper, a fall into Lava, or some other curse will befall you. When that happens, the game is not necessarily over. Let's see what happens.

Hardcore Mode

If you're playing *Minecraft* in Hardcore mode, well, then I guess the game *is* over. You get only one life in Hardcore mode, so death is the end of all things. You have to play very conservatively to survive on this setting. When your character does die, it's time to start over with a new game.

If you're really naughty, it's possible to create a copy of your save file and then restore that when your character dies. We don't mind telling you that this is possible, but we won't mention exactly how to do it. It's your responsibility if you choose to skirt the rules!

Death Penalties

THE COST OF DYING

- Huge loss of experience

- Potential loss of equipment and resources that you were carrying

- Time spent getting back to where you were

For any other mode, death is not the end. Your character drops everything that he or she is carrying when something reduces his or her health to zero. Unless you're on a tile that destroys objects, your inventory is still available to be retrieved for several minutes.

The clock has started! (Or not—we'll talk about this in a moment.)

Your character is reborn with full health and a full hunger bar at the last place you slept. Hurry toward your Chests of goodies and grab at least a full set of basic tools, a Sword, any armor that you still have, and a mix of food and Torches. Backtrack to the place where you died, keeping in mind the threat that took you down. If it's night outside and that's where you died, quickly sleep on your Bed to start the next day. This doesn't count against your timer; your loot is still out there.

If you make it back to your items in time, you get to keep them, along with *some* of the experience that your character had at the time of death. It isn't a great amount, but you won't have to start from scratch without any levels. Yay?

Lava deaths are the worst, because your items fall into the Lava and are burnt to cinders. There won't be anything left when you return, unless a few pieces flew up and out and then landed safely on a nearby shore. It's worth checking, but don't get your hopes too high. Lava is evil, and that's why you need a Bucket of Water wherever you go.

Explosive deaths can be nasty, too. Depending on the circumstances, some of your items might be destroyed by subsequent explosions or fires.

If you don't make it back to the place where you died within five minutes, everything goes away. Take a

deep breath, remember that you can always mine more treasure, and get back to doing what you like— that's *Minecraft*.

BUT WAIT! THERE'S STILL A CHANCE

There is a slight catch here, in your favor. You have to get close to the area where you died for the timer to really begin ticking down. Those five minutes don't start until you're in the same region (called "chunks") as your body.

Characters that die far away from home aren't always doomed. Get prepared before you enter the region that has your body, and then beeline toward your corpse. There's still some hope.

We still recommend trying to get to your body as soon as possible. It's easy to forget where you were, and the longer you wait, the more likely it is that you take a wrong turn and lose time trying to find the location.

TRAPS AND DEFENSES

There are many ways to rig traps around your home and mines. These work to kill monsters and possibly harm or kill other players that come into your territory without permission (on servers where PvP is allowed).

There are so many ideas for cool traps that we can't cover more than a sampling of them, but we want to get you started with a few general concepts.

Pressure Plates

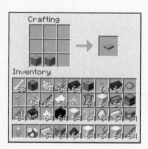

Pressure Plates are critical in many traps. These items activate a charge whenever anything steps on them. A block of TNT nearby turns this into an explosive mine. But that's pretty easy to spot. Almost anyone gets suspicious once they see TNT lying around. As an alternative, you can put the TNT below a Pressure Plate to add a layer of trickery. Consider making a Door into your house that you don't use. Put a Pressure Plate on the inside and have Gravel or Sand and TNT below that. Anyone who enters that way will have a bad experience. Just don't put anything valuable in that room, and make sure that it's easy to rebuild the area and the trap. This is better for a funny joke than for a serious defense.

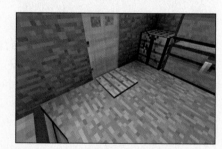

Pistons

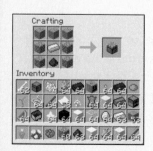

Pistons move blocks and make it possible to set up slightly more elaborate traps. Use Pistons for making mechanical doorways or to block passages. A Pressure Plate with Redstone channels and Pistons on the other side of a wall lets you open or close passages.

Combine this with secondary traps to make your dungeons even more deadly. Have someone step onto a Pressure Plate, use the Pistons to block the character into a small space, and then let another Piston push aside the stones holding back the Lava directly above him. Bye, bye!

Iron Doors

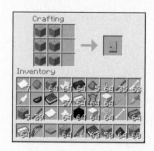

Iron Doors are excellent to pair with traps, because these items can't be opened manually. They must be activated with a Button, Pressure Plate, Lever, etc. Because of this, you should make it easy for other players to get into your target area; leave a Pressure Plate for them to walk over so that the door opens. Once they're in, the door closes automatically, and the trap has already been sprung. They can't turn around and leave without rushing to use their Pickaxe, and hopefully your TNT, Lava, or other deadly surprise is already on its way.

To make an Iron Door, use the standard Door recipe, but substitute Iron Ingots for Wooden Planks.

Pits

Most characters won't survive a fall 23 blocks down; they'll take full damage and die even if they have full health. Unless their armor has Feather Fall, it's Game Over.

Thus, many traps use long falls as a way to kill monsters and players. You can lure people onto blocks and tempt them to mine away, but this doesn't work very often. Few experienced players will mine directly downward, even if a sign says "FREE LOOT INSIDE!" So make things more interesting. Build a bridge that leads toward your base/safe area, and hide the drop with Pistons. Use a Pressure Plate to trigger a wall that pushes people into the deadly pit while they're crossing the bridge. This still isn't very subtle, but it sometimes works!

Many common pit traps have a top layer with a Pressure Plate, a piece of TNT underneath, and then a fall below that. This is too much work to use against monsters, but it's reliable against human intruders.

Trapped Chests

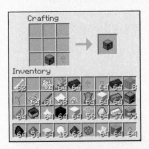

Trapped Chests have the normal function and use of standard Chests. Double them up for extra storage, and place what you want inside. However, these Chests have a red tinge around their lock and set off a Redstone signal when they're opened. Use this to activate TNT, Lava traps, pits, etc.

Water Suffocation Traps

Water is used to kill monsters and to funnel loot around your base. A waterway that flows down through a tunnel can be passed under a low ceiling, so the clearance is only a single block. This traps characters and other tall monsters so that they start to suffocate. This eventually kills the enemy in question and allows their loot to drop into the water. The current carries the loot to a place deeper inside your base, where you can safely collect it. Make multiple waterways converge in one area for maximum efficiency!

Monster Holding Areas

Build a large room near your main base. Leave it lit while you're constructing it, but destroy any Torches when you finish the entire task. Inside, create a long strip of water that flows down toward a single block. Make several of these strips converge at the same block for extra efficiency. For the final block, use a Sticky Piston and connect that to a Lever somewhere safe and convenient. Or use an open Trapdoor so that monsters wander onto it and then fall. Dig a pit that's 22 blocks deep under the Sticky Piston/Trapdoor.

Use this to capture monsters that get trapped by the water currents. Use the Lever to open the pit, or simply wait if you're using the Trapdoor method. Build a secondary tunnel inside your base leading to the monster holding area below. All of your foes are badly injured by the fall and die from a single hit from any decent weapon. You still get their loot and their experience.

If you don't care about the experience, make the pit a little deeper to inflict fatal injuries. This costs you certain types of loot as well, but it's safer if you aren't into fighting.

Soul Sand and Ice

You gather Soul Sand in the Nether, and it slows anything that tries to walk over it. Place Ice underneath Soul Sand for an even more potent slowing effect. This is a double whammy if you create a room with any other traps, because victims can't run away.

Monster Spawners

When you find Monster Spawners, don't just destroy them without thinking. These items are extremely useful for creating high-quality monster farms. You can use the techniques we've described in and around Monster Spawners to ensure that you gather and/or kill all of the creatures they summon.

The biggest downside of making a good monster farm with Monster Spawners is that you have to stay fairly close by to get the most out of them. Monsters don't spawn unless you're within range.

Thus, this works really well if you stay in a particular area to mine. Otherwise, go ahead and destroy the Monster Spawner, or wall it off for now and leave a Sign to remind yourself where it is.

MODERN CONVENIENCES

Some machines and items are quite useful for your character; they make your time in *Minecraft* easier to manage. Let's see what we can build!

Cobblestone Generator

Cobblestone isn't hard to get, but there's something nifty about making an infinite source of it. Having a Cobblestone generator in your base provides a limitless supply of the rock that you can harvest at will.

To create one of these generators, hollow out a decent room. Make a long trench surrounded by Stone; avoid placing anything that might catch on fire nearby. Bring two Buckets here, one with Water and one with Lava. Dump out each one at opposite ends of the trench, and watch the two fluids meet. Wherever they touch, Cobblestone forms. Break it, collect it, and repeat the process.

Water turns the actual Lava block into Obsidian if they ever touch, so avoid letting the water flow that far.

To make the generator more effective, use a Piston at the major point of contact between the two flows to push completed Cobblestone out of the way. This allows more Cobblestone to be created even when you're not there to mine everything. Use Clock Circuits to make sure the system triggers at a smooth, even pace.

Clock Circuits are very nice! These are made in a variety of ways. Clock Circuits are effectively a group of devices to ensure that your system toggles on and off on its own. You can have these set to different lengths of time, depending on the setup you install.

A common setup for a Clock Circuit is to use Repeaters. Place two Repeaters and connect them with a loop of Redstone dust. Add a Lever to control the initial energy of the circuit. Also add a Redstone Torch onto a powered block next to this circuit. The torch starts off generating power, but turns off around one-second later because it was placed onto a powered block. Your circuit now has power and is timed with a one-second pulse. Destroy the Powered Block and the Redstone Torch if you like (to use elsewhere) because the circuit is going to continue circulating its own power unless something damages it.

Garbage Pits

Several types of features make good garbage bins. Dig a small pit and fill it with Lava for dangerous but effective disposal of items that you're sick of keeping around. Take that, stacks of Dirt! Cacti accomplish the same task without the danger of burning down your house.

If you want something less effective but more aesthetically pleasing, a small fountain works well enough. Throw extra items in there and leave them for several minutes. They'll disappear on their own as long as you don't jump into the fountain to collect them.

Ender Chests

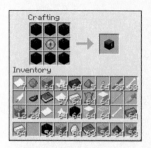

Once you kill enough Endermen, you start to get a supply of Ender Pearls. Craft these with Blaze Rods to make Eyes of Ender. Combine Eyes of Ender with Obsidian to make Ender Chests. These special

containers are linked, so any Ender Chest you make contains the items you placed in any of your other Ender Chests. If you have Ender Chests, you can effectively store items anywhere in the game and collect them anywhere else.

This is incredibly nice when you work in the Nether and The End. Place your treasure in the Ender Chest, and it'll be available back in your safe house even if you get killed!

Pressure Plate Doors

Tired of opening Doors for yourself like a sucker? Place a Pressure Plate in front of your Doors (on the inside of the house only). This lets you run out without stopping to mess with anything. Don't try this outside your home, because monsters can find their way in.

Maps and Compasses

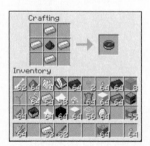

As we've mentioned before, you may face walls of Cobblestone at any time. Although all Cobblestones maintain the same orientation no matter how they're placed, it takes a moment of looking to figure this out. A better way to reference your orientation is to craft a Compass.

Compasses make it easier to navigate, so craft one as soon as you can, and pay attention to your movements. The more you do this, the more your sense of direction will improve.

If you still have trouble finding your way around, make Maps. Then expand on your Maps to make them cover more territory; do this by crafting the existing Map with even more Paper.

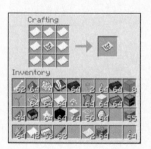

Carry your Map in your inventory so you can switch to it and figure out where you're going. This, combined with a Compass, makes exploration safer and easier.

Surface features like biome colors, Lava, Water, and elevation are all reflected in the Maps you make. Anything below the surface isn't shown, so you only get a position relative to your topside base when you're down in the tunnels.

THINKING OUTSIDE THE BLOCKS

This section is designed to give you some ideas for decorating your living space in your *Minecraft* world. Many recipes for functional items are already in the game, but what about fun, decorative items?

Like anything else in *Minecraft*, what you create is limited only by your imagination. Here, you'll find a few ideas to help you get started. With the right materials, you can make everything from a nice kitchen to a bathroom (complete with running water), or even a realistic forge.

Common Materials

Creating furniture doesn't require complicated materials. Mostly, you just need simple blocks (of anything) and the means to make Signs, Levers, Trapdoors, Tripwires, and Pistons. Some recipes call for something specific: a block of Wool in a certain color, or a chunk of Netherrack, or a Dispenser. The real challenge is using ordinary things in unusual ways. For example, Trapdoors can be used in more ways than just outside over pits; instead, try one on a wall next to a window as a shutter.

Ideas by Room

LIVING ROOM

Sofas

One of the simplest ways to make a sofa is to place two or more Slabs together to form the seat. Place two Signs on the far ends of the Slabs to create the sofa's arms. This type of sofa looks like a bench if you use wooden Slabs. If you like, you can use a wide Picture as the sofa's back.

You can make another common sofa using sets of Stairs. Put two Stair pieces beside each other and cap off the ends with Signs. Because Stairs can be made with Wood, Stone, Bricks, Nether Brick, Sandstone, and Quartz, you can choose from a wide range of sofa colors.

If you want a thicker sofa, create two Slabs as the seat and then surround the Slabs with blocks as the arms and back. You can make some very nice sofas this way using blocks of colored Wool.

Chairs

You can make a chair the same way as a sofa, except that the "seat" is only one square wide. So use one Slab or one Stair piece instead of two, as described for the sofas.

DINING ROOM
Tables

You can make a small table using a Fence Post and a Pressure Plate. All you have to do is place the Fence Post on the ground (it looks nice near a wall), and then put a Pressure Plate on top of the post as the table's surface.

You can make larger tables using Pistons, provided you don't completely dig out an underground basement for your house. Dig two blocks down and place a Redstone Torch at the bottom to power the Piston. Then put the Piston on top of the Torch, which causes the Piston to extend. Because you can put any number of Pistons next to each other with this method, you can make your table as wide or long as you like.

KITCHEN
Sink

You can construct a very easy sink using one Cauldron and one Tripwire Hook. The Cauldron forms most of the sink, and a Tripwire Hook against the wall above the cauldron makes a faucet. If you want your sink to be filled with Water, pour a Water-filled Bucket into the Cauldron.

Cabinets

To make cabinets, put any number of blocks against a wall. Iron blocks look very nice for this because they really stand out against Wood or Stone walls. Make cabinet doors by placing Trapdoors on the cabinets' front sides, facing you. If you use Bookshelves instead of blocks, it gives the illusion of having food or dinnerware within the cabinet.

BATHROOM
Toilets

Toilets are slightly more complicated than some other pieces of furniture. Most toilets are made in rooms with Slab floors, so they don't seem quite as large or unsightly. You need two spaces to make a nice toilet. The first space is filled by a Cauldron (you can fill it with Water by using a Bucket). Behind the Cauldron,

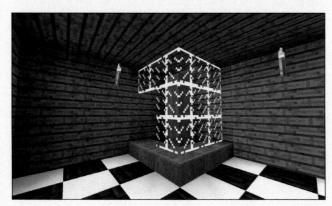

stack two large blocks. Put a button on one side of the upper block as a flusher. A Trapdoor over the Cauldron as a lid completes the toilet.

Showers and Bathtubs

Pick a corner and create the shower's base with Slabs. Then place a Piston in the ceiling or wall and a water source behind it. Fill in the space around the Slabs with Glass blocks or Glass Panes. A Lever linked with the Piston lets you turn the water on or off.

Dressers

Make a nice dresser by stacking two large Chests on top of each other. Another dresser uses four Stair pieces, two Trapdoors, and two Doors. Place two Stairs facing each other, so they form a "V." Stack two more Stairs directly on top of the first set, forming a hole in the center topped by another open "V." The Trapdoors then go on top of the dresser. Set the two Doors against the front of the Stairs, making a fully opening dresser.

Beds

Minecraft already has a recipe for a functional Bed, but you can do more with it to make it *yours*. To make a four-post bed, craft two Beds with the standard recipe. Make a headboard and footboard with a layer of blocks at the top and bottom. If you wish, you can use Wool blocks (dyed or natural) to complement the crafted Beds' red color; Glowstone blocks also create a nice effect. If you don't like the look of full blocks around the bed, try Slabs (but leave full blocks on the corners). By stacking Fences on top of the corner blocks, you can make the bedposts.

To create a canopy over a four-post bed, outline the area with either Fences or Gates to make a lattice. Using more Fences, connect the ceiling lattice to the bedframe. You can then fill in the rest of the area within the ceiling space with additional blocks of your choice.

OTHER
Fireplaces

Who doesn't love fire? Fireplaces are easy to build and are very dramatic. First, you need a place where you can dig down at least two squares. Put a block of Netherrack in the hole at the bottom. If you want a larger fire in your fireplace, make the "pit" larger.

Next, construct the fireplace's chimney with blocks of material, the most obvious being Stone or Brick. If you want your fireplace to narrow into a chimney, use Stairs to slim the larger section into a smaller column. Light the Netherrack using a Flint and Tinder, and the fire will burn continuously. For decoration, add a Glass Pane or Iron Bar front piece.

Note that fireplaces contain actual fire. If you don't surround your fireplace with a 3x3x9 area of nonflammable materials, adjacent objects run the risk of catching fire. You can accidentally set fire to your home or furniture if you don't make nearby walls, floors, and furniture out of Stone or Brick.

REDSTONE

You can mine Redstone deep underground in the Overworld. Once you start mining down there, Redstone collects quickly. Each vein yields a fair number of pieces, and it's hard to miss these veins even when you're running through a cavern, because they're bright red. Always keep an Iron Pickaxe handy. Lesser materials fail to break Redstone properly. Iron tools are required for quite a few of the special metals and ores, so an Iron Pickaxe isn't a special burden here.

You can craft blocks of Redstone to make pretty crimson decor around your house, but its real uses are much more impressive. Redstone is used to make Clocks, Compasses, Detector Rails, Dispensers, Droppers, Note Blocks, Powered Rails, Redstone Lamps, Redstone Repeaters, and Redstone Torches. That's a pretty big list!

This amazing material is also used in brewing to make potions last longer. But if that's not enough for you, you can also place Redstone on the ground as a red trail of dust. Redstone Dust lets you channel power from one area to another, allowing for the construction of complex machines.

Transmission of Redstone Power

Trails of Redstone Dust send power up to 15 blocks from their source. Power is generated by a number of objects. Pressure Plates, Redstone Torches, Levers, and Buttons are just a few examples of items that trigger some type of power. Placing Redstone Dust on a block next to these items lets their power transmit to somewhere else.

Create a trail of dust that goes where you need it to go, and make sure you don't shift the height of your trail more than one block at a time. Redstone Dust stops sending power if its elevation changes more abruptly than that. It also fails if you shift the trail up or down one block and don't leave either air or glass in between. Trying to send the trail up and under another heavy block doesn't work.

When power is continuous along a line of dust, the material turns bright red instead of dark red. This lets you see how well power is flowing along your lines. If the energy isn't going far enough, add additional sources of energy, such as a Redstone Torch.

VERSION CHANGE

```
Pocket versions of Minecraft still use Redstone in crafting but don't
let you use trails of Redstone Dust to trigger machines. You can't put
the material onto any blocks.
```

Redstone Machinery

Now things get a bit more complex. You know that Redstone can carry energy around, but what does that actually do? A good question! The energy from these signals lets you operate a range of mechanisms in the game, providing automation for farms, traps, transportation, and more. It's hard to get a handle on all of this when you first start *Minecraft*. In fact, this presents a steeper skill/learning curve than almost anything else in the game. Don't try to master this right away. Take your time, dabble in Redstone, and figure it out as you go.

When you're starting out, don't be afraid to look at other people's machines for inspiration. See how they did what they did. Most people need to see a few machines set up in the game before they start to understand Redstone's use and potential.

Now that we've said that, let's move forward. We'll try to keep this as simple as possible. Let's start by breaking down the major parts of a potential machine.

PIECES OF A MACHINE

■ **Power:** some device needs to provide power for your machine

■ **Transmission:** the power needs to be sent from its source to somewhere else of your choosing

■ **Mechanism:** the device that receives power and uses it to accomplish your goal

ITEMS THAT PRODUCE POWER

Power is produced by a wide range of items.

ITEM	HOW TO ACTIVATE IT	POWER PRODUCED
Button	Interact with it or use a Bow to shoot it.	Activate nearby dust/components for 1.5 seconds when touched, or 1 minute if shot by a Bow.
Daylight Sensor	Turns on during the day and off at night; the opposite is true if used below ground.	Adds more power as the day/night progresses.
Detector Rail	Adds power when a Minecart is detected nearby.	Powers itself and adjacent blocks.
Lever	Produces power when turned on.	Power remains on as long as the Lever is not turned off.
Pressure Plate	Provides power when touched; wooden Pressure Plates can be shot with Arrows to produce power.	Powers the block underneath it; any trails/components next to either the plate or the block below are activated.
Redstone Block	Always on.	Strong power for all nearby components.
Redstone Torch	Provides continuous power unless it receives power from another source—this turns it off.	Powers adjacent blocks but not the block to which it is attached.
Trapped Chest	Provides power when someone opens the Chest.	The Trapped Chest and the block underneath it power adjacent dust/mechanisms.
Tripwire Hook	Turns on if the wires are damaged or crossed.	The hook and the block that it's placed on produce power.
Weighted Pressure Plate	Adds increasing power based on how many objects are on top of it.	The plate and the block it's placed on produce power.

HOW TO TRANSMIT POWER

Power sources add energy to adjacent blocks, which is sometimes all you need. Add a mechanism next to a power source, and you're good to go. However, power transmission is wonderful if you need to make something happen several blocks (or more) away from the power source. The following three items let you send power this way.

Redstone Dust

This is the most basic way to send a Redstone signal along a short length of blocks. The power goes as far as the strength of the original signal. This means that a strong power source can send power 15 blocks away; a source with less power can transmit power only a portion of that distance. For example, a Daylight Sensor will send its signal farther as the day goes on and the sun rises higher in the sky.

Create a simple test to observe this. Make a Daylight Sensor with a trail of Redstone Dust that leads 15 blocks away from it. Watch the line of dust turn bright red across a greater distance as the day progresses—pretty neat!

Redstone Repeater

Sometimes, you may want to send a signal along a greater distance than 15 blocks. Redstone Repeaters let you strengthen a signal in a single direction. Place your line of Redstone Dust so that it leads up to the rear of the Redstone Repeater and then continues out its front side.

This strengthens your signal and allows it to reach greater distances. If you want, add more Repeaters so the signal continues toward any destination. There is a short delay in this process, but that's good too. Redstone Repeaters are often used as a way to slow down a signal so that it doesn't get to its final mechanism too quickly.

Redstone Comparator

Comparators are the most complex way of transmitting power. Like Repeaters, they have a front and a back, but they don't reinforce the signal. Instead, they have two modes: comparison mode and subtraction mode.

Comparators send their signals from back to front, and they output a signal that's equal in strength to the signal they receive. Thus, a trail of activated Redstone Dust that would normally travel five more blocks can enter the back of this device and exit the front to power five more blocks of dust. You might be thinking, "That doesn't seem to do anything important at all." Well, not yet.

The Comparator comes into play when there are signals coming into the back *and* the side of the device. This changes its output. In comparison mode, the signal is shut down if the value of the side signal is stronger than the one entering the rear. Thus, comparison mode gives you a way to shut down machines based on a separate circuit.

Subtraction mode *reduces* the signal strength of the main line by the strength of the signal entering the side of the comparator.

MECHANISMS

At the end of your signal, place a mechanism of some sort to use the power you're sending. Mechanisms can accomplish a wide range of tasks.

MECHANISM	EFFECT
Activator Rail	Triggers Minecarts that pass over them, detonating TNT, executing Command Blocks, or silencing Hoppers.
Command Block	Power causes the block to execute its command a single time.
Dispenser	Shoot one item from a random slot.
Door	Toggles between open and closed.
Dropper	Drops one item from a random slot in its inventory.
Fence Gate	Toggles between open and closed.
Hopper	Power stops Hoppers from pulling items into themselves.
Note Block	Creates sound.
Piston	Pushes the block in front of the Piston (and up to 12 total blocks beyond that).
Powered Rail	Speeds Minecarts.
Rail	Toggles junctions.
Redstone Lamp	Creates powerful light.
TNT	Begins the detonation sequence for the block of TNT.
Trapdoor	Toggles the position of the Trapdoor.

WHAT TO MAKE

Even though we just explained Redstone functionality, this barely scratches the surface. None of this information really means anything until you start to build your own devices.

Continue reading for some very simple ideas to get you started with Redstone.

Heavy Doors

Iron Doors keep out monsters on any difficulty, no matter how many of them there are. They don't even try to pound their way through. Use six Iron Ingots to craft a door, and use power to open and close it. On the inside of your house, a Pressure Plate in front of the Door works perfectly for easy escape. On the outside, you don't want that because monsters might walk right in.

Instead, use a Button outside your Door. Neither of these items leaves the power on continuously, so your Door closes as soon as you move away or wait too long.

Fast Minecarts

Place Powered Rails over long stretches so your Minecarts can travel across great distances. You can climb large inclines as well, making it easier to travel up and down from your mines without wasting time.

Easy Pits

Dig a pit near the front of your house and place a Trapdoor over it. On the inside of the house, place a Lever on a block that's adjacent to the Trapdoor. When you use the Lever as a power source, the block it's attached to gains power. This, in turn, transmits to the Trapdoor and activates it. You can now drop creatures into a pit from the safety of your home. If anyone you don't like comes up to your house, drop them into the pit. A deadly fall should do the trick nicely, but Lava and other fun toys work just as well.

Night Lights

Redstone Lamps, Redstone Torches, and Daylight Sensors let you craft lighting that turns on only when the light level falls to a certain point. Put the Redstone Lamps and the Redstone Torches next to each other, so they're turned on by default. Then, place a line of Redstone Dust that leads to the blocks underneath the Redstone Torches. Connect this to your Daylight Sensors. When there is enough light during the day, they'll provide power to the dust and turn off the Redstone Torches. As night falls, they'll lose power and the Redstone Torches will begin powering the Redstone Lamps again. This is an example of an inverter (i.e., using Redstone Torches to turn *off* a signal rather than turn it on).

The same technique lets you close Doors and Fence Gates in the evening, to prevent monsters from coming into your areas.

ENCHANTMENT AND USING EXPERIENCE

Minecraft isn't a run-of-the-mill RPG or any game where levels give you more health, damage, and other basic stats. You're a farmer, a miner, and a survivor. These stats aren't really going to change for you.

Instead, you use levels to enchant your weapons, armor, and tools, to make them better at doing various tasks. We'll now discuss gaining and using experience, and what you can get with the enchanting system.

Gaining Experience

Almost every activity in *Minecraft* gets you experience. This comes in the form of glowing orbs that appear when you do something important: kill monsters, breed animals, mine special items, smelt ores, etc. Collect these orbs by walking close to them; they'll try to reach you on their own if you go anywhere near them!

ACTIVITIES THAT GENERATE EXPERIENCE

- Animal breeding
- Bottles of Enchantment
- Cooking food and other various items in a Furnace
- Destroying Monster Spawners
- Fishing

- Killing monsters or having them die within several seconds of being damaged by your character
- Mining ore or smelting it
- Killing regular farm animals is worth experience too, but not much

LEVELS REQUIRE DIFFERENT AMOUNTS OF EXPERIENCE

Getting from level 1 to 2 takes much less experience than going from level 39 to 40. As you progress higher and higher in level, the amount of experience needed to go higher increases. You don't want to stockpile levels beyond whatever point you currently need. In general, level 30 (for Enchanting Table work) or level 39 (for Anvil work) is the highest that you ever need to go. Pushing for levels beyond this yields diminishing returns. You're much better off spending your levels to enchant something and then progressing in levels again.

EXPERIENCE REQUIRED TO GAIN A LEVEL

LEVEL(S)	EXPERIENCE REQUIRED	TOTAL EXPERIENCE REQUIRED	LEVEL(S)	EXPERIENCE REQUIRED	TOTAL EXPERIENCE REQUIRED
1	7	7	26	87	997
2	9	16	27	92	1089
3	11	27	28	97	1186
4	13	40	29	102	1288
5	15	55	30	107	1395
6	17	72	31	112	1507
7	19	91	32	121	1628
8	21	112	33	130	1758
9	23	135	34	139	1897
10	25	160	35	148	2045
11	27	187	36	157	2202
12	29	216	37	166	2368
13	31	247	38	175	2543
14	33	280	39	184	2727
15	35	315	40	193	2920
16	37	352	41	202	3122
17	42	394	42	211	3333
18	47	441	43	220	3552
19	52	493	44	229	3782
20	57	550	45	238	4020
21	62	612	46	247	4267
22	67	679	47	256	4523
23	72	751	48	265	4788
24	77	828	49	274	5062
25	82	910	50	283	5345

As you can see, the amount needed for a single level rises substantially over time. In earlier versions of the game there were specific levels where things got much harder, but that isn't as much the case now. Though the quantities needed to level up rise, they never go up by an alarming amount.

For many people, the ideal will be to get to level 33, enchant their favorite item, and level up to 33 again. This way, you always have access to the most powerful enchantments in case you need to enchant something else rather suddenly. However, it is slightly more efficient to ping pong between 27 and 30, if you're not worried about enchanting something at any given moment.

LOSING EXPERIENCE

Death causes your character to lose a huge amount of experience. *Some* of your experience falls to the ground, and you can retrieve it if you make it back to your corpse in time, but the rest is gone forever. Wear armor and stay away from deadly drops, Lava, and unwinnable fights to avoid death's experience penalty. Furthermore, spend your experience to invest in enchanted items and Books, so your experience isn't sitting around doing nothing.

Making an Enchanting Table

When you're ready to spend some experience levels, make an Enchanting Table. You need Diamonds, Obsidian, and a Book to do this. Make a Diamond Pick to mine the Obsidian, gather more Diamonds as needed, and use Leather and Paper to make your Book.

When you're done, you have an Enchanting Table ready to go, but it can't handle major enchantments. Basic Enchanting Tables only add low-cost enchantments to items. These are still nice, but the really incredible stuff requires more effort.

We Need More Power

To give your Enchanting Table more options, place Bookshelves around it. It takes 15 Bookshelves to fully power an Enchanting Table. Arrange these Bookshelves two blocks away from the table in either a U-shape around the table or wedged into a nearby corner.

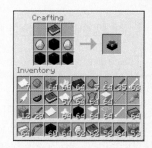

Bookshelves only count if they are two spaces away—they can't be adjacent to the Enchanting Table. Stack the shelves two high but not three high. Diagonal spaces count just fine. Given these double stacks, you can have 18 Bookshelves in your U, which is more than you need.

You need a huge amount of Leather and Paper to craft all of those Bookshelves. We suggest you create a large animal pen, lure at least two Cows there, and start breeding them as soon as possible. Visit the pen every five minutes to feed the Cows even more Wheat. Don't kill any of the Cows in your pen until you have roughly eight adults.

Once you hit that mark, perform some minor culling after each breeding session. After a major breeding session, slaughter two Cows and keep the count between six and eight adults every time you go out after that. The pen starts to fill really quickly, and you get quite a haul of Leather.

Grow Sugar Cane along local waterways and harvest it each time you go out. This stuff grows like a weed, so getting piles of it for Paper isn't a big deal. If it isn't going quickly enough, reinvest some of the harvested Sugar Cane into additional stalks to increase your yield.

The Finishing Touch

Now that you have 15 Bookshelves near your Enchanting Table, you can use high-level enchantments. Interact with the Enchanting Table to open the interface for enchanting items. Place a weapon, tool, or piece of armor in the slot on the left. You need to add Lapis Lazuli as well, but this material is easy to harvest while you're out looking for Diamonds and other precious underworld materials.

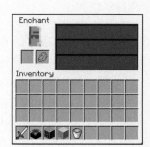

The strange lettering on the right is associated with the cost of your possible enchantments. The higher the cost (in levels), the better your potential enchantment will be. Items that are enchanted directly like this can end up with multiple effects, so you might get something really awesome out of this.

Items have three possible tiers of enchantments. Each tier costs one Lapis and one character level (so enchanting can cost you up to three levels per item). You are guaranteed at least one effect, which will be listed in the description of the item when you hover over it in the enchantment interface. You may also get other effects, but this is determined randomly after you decide what level of enchantment to give the item.

Also, there are minimum total character levels required for each tier. Even though a full enchantment only costs three character levels, you need to be character level 30 to unlock the ability to spend that much at once.

Select the cost that you're willing to pay, click on that bar, and enjoy your enchanted item. Anything you enchant gets a pretty glow to show that it's magical. This makes it easier to sort enchanted items in your inventory, so you don't lose them, put them in a Chest to be forgotten, or make some other mistake.

Other Means of Enchanting

There are several other ways to enchant your equipment. Let's go over those quickly.

PRIESTS

Villages often have Priests. These special Villagers can add specific enchantments to your items. They'll show the enchantment in the trading interface, so you don't have to guess what you'll get. Add the item you want enchanted, pay some Emeralds, and that's that. This is a somewhat costly process in terms of resources, but you don't need to spend a single level. That's neat!

ENCHANTED BOOKS

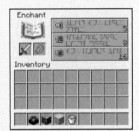

Craft Books and then enchant them at your Enchanting Table. You can stack multiple enchantments on a single Book and then transfer all of them onto another item when you have a combination that you like. You do this by working with an Anvil and using the Enchanted Book and the item that you're trying to enchant. This costs additional levels.

Book enchanting is a very costly process. You're likely to spend many more levels investing in the final item than you would by just going to the Enchanting Table with the same item. However, Enchanted Books are useful. They're the best way to infuse an item with a specific combination of powerful enchantments. Otherwise, you're playing a game of chance each time you spend your levels. You might end up with a fairly weak enchantment and produce a Diamond Sword that doesn't do anything you care about. That's a bummer.

ANVILS

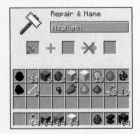

Anvils let you combine items, including their enchantments. The primary item is saved, and the secondary item is destroyed but all of its pertinent enchantments are transferred to the primary item. Enchantments that aren't allowed to affect a specific item are not transferred, so they're simply lost. Thus, you can't put armor enchantments on a Bow, even if you combine a Bow with an Enchanted Book that has multiple armor enchantments.

Anvils can also combine two regular items, as long as they're of the same type. Two Diamond Picks with the same enchantments could be used in the Anvil together. The second would be destroyed to repair the primary one.

Types of Enchantments

ENCHANTMENT TYPE	MAXIMUM RANKS	EQUIPMENT TYPE	DESCRIPTION
Aqua Affinity	I	Helm	Increases underwater mining rate dramatically
Bane of Arthropods	V	Sword	Increases damage to Spiders, Cave Spiders, Silverfish, and Endermites by 2.5 per rank
Blast Protection	IV	Any Armor	Reduces explosive damage and reduces knockback
Depth Strider	III	Boots	Reduces water's slowing effect by 1/3 per level
Efficiency	V	Tools	Increases mining/harvesting speed by 30% per rank
Feather Falling	IV	Boots	Reduces damage from falling and Ender Pearls
Fire Aspect	II	Sword	Adds 3 rounds of burn damage (or 7 at rank II)
Fire Protection	IV	Any Armor	Reduces fire damage and decreases burning duration
Flame	I	Bow	Sets your Arrows on fire, adding three rounds of burning to targets hit
Fortune	III	Tools	Multiplies the number of drops from Coal, Diamonds, Emeralds, Nether Quartz, and Lapis Lazuli
Infinity	I	Bow	You don't need more than one Arrow to fire your Bow forever
Knockback	II	Sword	Increases knockback against your targets
Looting	III	Sword	Slain monsters drop more regular loot and have a higher chance to drop their rare treasures
Luck of the Sea	III	Fishing Rod	Reduces the chance of getting poor results from fishing and raises the chance of getting higher quality items
Lure	III	Fishing Rod	Greatly improves the speed at which you fish
Power	V	Bow	Increases Arrow damage by 25% (+ 25% more per rank)
Projectile Protection	IV	Any Armor	Reduces incoming damage from Arrows, Blazes, and Ghasts
Protection	IV	Any Armor	Reduces many types of damage taken
Punch	II	Bow	Increases knockback by Arrows
Respiration	III	Helm	Lets you stay underwater for 15 seconds more per rank, improves vision underwater, and slows suffocation
Sharpness	V	Sword	Increases damage by 1.25 per rank
Silk Touch	I	Tools	Allows you to harvest resources directly to get Cobwebs, ore blocks, Ice, etc. (one of the most desirable enchantments)
Smite	V	Sword or Axe	Adds 2.5 damage per rank against undead monsters
Thorns	III	Any Armor	Adds a chance to wound attackers for 1-4 damage
Unbreaking	III	Anything	Increases durability of the item

BREWING

Brewing is a fun way to make potions. Potions help you endure tough fights, survive in dangerous areas, and even damage some of your enemies. You can't brew early in the game because you need a number of tricky ingredients to get anywhere with this art. We'll tell you what to do!

Collect Ingredients to Make a Brewing Stand

The first step is to gather the primary ingredients you need. Nether Wart and Blaze Rods are two of the toughest (and most important) things on the list, so let's focus on these.

Both materials are found in the Nether. Make a Nether Portal and bring ample supplies through to the other side. Search for a Nether Fortress until you find one, and then scour the place for Chests and for stairways with Soul Sand nearby. These are the only two places in the game where Nether Wart is available. Not all of the Chests have Nether Wart, and not all Nether Fortresses have the stair gardens. So it's luck of the draw for finding these items.

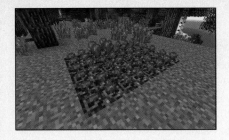

Blazes, on the other hand, are found frequently in Nether Fortresses. Fight them with ranged attacks, or retreat to draw them forward. Kill as many as you can to get Blaze Rods.

Once you have a few of these goodies, make a Nether Wart garden. You don't want to search Nether Fortresses every time you need more Nether Wart, so don't do any brewing just yet. Wait until you have an adequate Nether Wart garden.

Sadly, you can't use Bone Meal to speed up your garden; getting a large garden going is a fairly time-intensive process, but it's well worth your investment. Break all of your initial Nether Wart into Seeds, and plant all of them. Do the same thing with the yields from your initial planting, and continue to increase the garden from there, taking only one or two Nether Wart at first to play with, and then more as your garden reaches a substantial size.

Now craft a Brewing Stand, a Cauldron, and some Glass Bottles. Fill your Cauldron with Water. This is useful for filling Water Bottles, and they look cool in your brewing area anyway. Having an infinite Water source nearby isn't a bad thing, either.

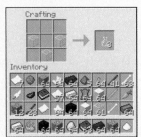
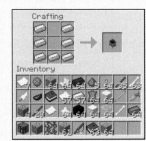

Place all of your crafted items in one room with a Chest or two, and grab your Nether Wart. With these and a number of other odds and ends, you're ready to start brewing.

Types of Potions

Potions come in two stages. You make the first stage by interacting with the Brewing Stand and adding a Water Bottle with some ingredients. After adding your ingredients, wait for the brewing to finish, and collect your finished potion.

There are five basic potions, as follows:

BASE POTIONS

POTION NAME	INGREDIENTS	EFFECT
Awkward Potion	Water Bottle + Nether Wart	Builds into much more powerful potions
Mundane Potion (Extended)	Water Bottle + Redstone	Used to make a Potion of Weakness (Extended)
Mundane Potion	Water Bottle + one of the following: Blaze Powder, Ghast Tear, Glistering Melon, Magma Cream, Spider Eye, Sugar	Used to make a Potion of Weakness
Potion of Weakness	Water Bottle + Fermented Spider Eye	Reduces melee attacks by .5 damage
Thick Potion	Water Bottle + Glowstone Dust	Used to make a Potion of Weakness

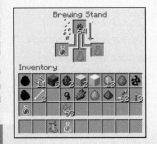

So far, it doesn't look like brewing is very useful. You can make a potion that reduces your own melee damage—yay? But trust us, this gets much better.

After you have a primary potion, use the Brewing Stand again. This time, you add one of the primary potions instead of a Water Bottle. Now you start having fun!

SECONDARY POTIONS

POTION NAME	INGREDIENTS	EFFECT
Potion of Fire Resistance	Awkward Potion + Magma Cream	3 minutes of fire immunity
Potion of Healing	Awkward Potion + Glistering Melon	Restores 4 damage
Potion of Leaping	Awkward Potion + Rabbit's Foot	Boosts jumping height and reduces falling damage for 3 minutes
Potion of Night Vision	Awkward Potion + Golden Carrot	Lets you see as if the area is perfectly lit for 3 minutes
Potion of Poison	Awkward Potion + Spider Eye	Poisons a target for one damage every 1.5 seconds (for 45 seconds)
Potion of Regeneration	Awkward Potion + Ghast Tear	Restores 2 damage every 2.4 seconds (for 45 seconds)
Potion of Strength	Awkward Potion + Blaze Powder	Adds 130% to your melee damage for 3 minutes
Potion of Swiftness	Awkward Potion + Sugar	Increases speed and jumping distance by 20% for 3 minutes
Potion of Water Breathing	Awkward Potion + Pufferfish	You don't need to breathe underwater for 3 minutes
Potion of Weakness (Extended)	Awkward Potion + Fermented Spider Eye	Reduces melee damage by .5 for 4 minutes

Now you start to see a lot of possibilities. Potions of Healing let you restore health instantly, unlike food. Fire Resistance is useful when you fight Blazes and Ghasts in the Nether. Regeneration is critical to your survival in boss fights, against Withers or the Ender Dragon.

Nether Wart and a few key ingredients allow you to make extremely useful potions, and you can brew even more powerful versions if you're willing to spend a bit more time and effort. Read on!

TERTIARY POTIONS

POTION NAME	INGREDIENTS	EFFECT
Potion of Fire Resistance (Extended)	Potion of Fire Resistance + Redstone	8 minutes of fire immunity
Potion of Healing II	Potion of Healing + Glowstone Dust	Restores 8 damage
Potion of Leaping II	Potion of Leaping + Glowstone Dust	You can jump even higher
Potion of Night Vision (Extended)	Potion of Night Vision + Redstone	Lets you see as if the area is perfectly lit for 8 minutes
Potion of Poison (Extended)	Potion of Poison + Redstone	Poisons a target for 1 damage every 2 seconds (for 2 minutes)
Potion of Poison II	Potion of Poison + Glowstone Dust	Poisons a target for 1 damage every second (for 22 seconds)
Potion of Regeneration (Extended)	Potion of Regeneration + Redstone	Restores 2 damage every 2.4 seconds (for 2 minutes)
Potion of Regeneration II	Potion of Regeneration + Glowstone Dust	Restores 2 damage every 1.2 seconds (for 16 seconds)
Potion of Strength (Extended)	Potion of Strength + Redstone	Adds 130% to your melee damage for 8 minutes
Potion of Strength II	Potion of Strength + Glowstone Dust	Adds 260% to your melee damage for 1.5 minutes
Potion of Swiftness (Extended)	Potion of Swiftness + Redstone	Increases speed and jumping distance by 20% for 8 minutes
Potion of Swiftness II	Potion of Swiftness + Glowstone Dust	Increases speed and jumping distance by 40% for 1.5 minutes
Potion of Water Breathing (Extended)	Potion of Water Breathing + Redstone	You don't need to breathe underwater for 8 minutes
Potion of Invisibility	Potion of Night Vision + Fermented Spider Eye	Turns you invisible (but not your weapon or armor) for 3 minutes
Potion of Invisibility (Extended)	Potion of Night Vision (Extended) + Fermented Spider Eye	Turns you invisible (but not your weapon or armor) for 8 minutes
Potion of Harming	Potion of Healing or Poison + Fermented Spider Eye	Inflicts 6 damage
Potion of Harming II	Potion of Healing II or Poison II + Fermented Spider Eye or Glowstone Dust	Inflicts 12 damage
Potion of Slowness	Potion of Fire Resistance or Swiftness + Fermented Spider Eye	Slows movement for 1.5 minutes
Potion of Slowness (Extended)	Potion of Fire Resistance (Extended) or Swiftness (Extended) +_ Redstone or Fermented Spider Eye	Slows movement for 3 minutes

There are a few simple ways to remember how the potion system works. Everything starts with Nether Wart. Your initial potion should almost always be made by adding Nether Wart to a Water Bottle. Done.

For tier-two potions, use your Awkward Potion from the first stage and add an ingredient to get whatever base effect you need. Look on the Secondary Potion table to figure out what you need/want.

To make potions last longer, add Redstone to a Secondary Potion.

To make potions stronger, add Glowstone Dust to a Secondary Potion.

To make potions work when thrown, use Gunpowder.

Gunpowder turns normal potions into Splash Potions. This makes Potions of Weakness and Potions of Poison useful against specific enemies. Potions of Poison II really add damage over time.

People often brew Splash Potions of Healing so they can heal themselves as quickly as possible. Tossing the potion onto the ground at your feet gives you health much faster than just about any other option. It's *way* faster than food and considerably faster than drinking a Potion of Healing in a normal way.

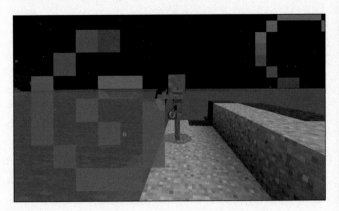

POISON DOESN'T ALWAYS WORK

Don't try to poison Spiders, Cave Spiders, or the Ender Dragon. They don't take any damage from poison.

Skeletons, Wither Skeletons, Withers, Zombies, and Zombie Pigmen are immune to poison and don't take damage from Potions of Harm, either. In fact, they heal from them instead! However, they take damage from Splash Potions of Healing.

Witches take reduced poison damage, so it's not worth your time.

TRAVELING THE WORLD

There are several ways to get around the world, and it's always nice to have options. Most of the methods we describe here either cost more in terms of crafted resources or food, but they're worthwhile when you can get where you're going faster and without any hassles.

Walking, Sprinting, and Jumping

Walking is the most basic travel method, but it's slow. Monsters easily catch up with you, and that means you end up fighting more often and taking damage.

Sprinting is faster by a fair margin—it's almost one third faster. Although you need to eat more often, it's useful to sprint once your character has a decent supply of food. Jumping and sprinting together makes your character move even faster, though the hunger increase is more substantial.

For the best possible walking and sprinting speed, use Potions of Speed.

Mounts

Horses are the best mounts for speedy travel. They vary in terms of maximum speed, but even the slow ones are pretty darn good. The best Horses are amazing and should be bred with other speedy Horses so you have a stable of racers. They're perfect for long-distance travel above ground.

Boats

Don't swim across large stretches of water. It's painfully slow. Construct a Boat and bring enough spare Wood to make more Boats in case your first one gets destroyed; this happens very easily if you bump into anything heavy. If you want to provide a nice impact cushion for your Boat, plunk down a piece of Soul Sand in front of it.

Boats are decently quick once they get going.

Railways

Railways are very fast. Put down a long stretch of regular Rails, and drop one Powered Rail with a Redstone Torch every 32 blocks. Your Minecarts rush across distance quite well in this manner, whether you're above ground or down in the depths.

Descending tracks have even less trouble maintaining speed, but flat railways are the easiest to create.

Ender Pearls

Throw Ender Pearls to teleport your character. This is a resource-intensive travel method, so it's best reserved for when you're in a tough spot and need to escape. Use these items to get away from battle, to cross ravines, or to reach really tricky spots in a cavern.

Be warned! Ender Pearls deal damage to your character when you teleport. They're not for the faint of heart. They also have a slight chance to spawn a monster when you throw them (the tiny but malicious Endermites).

The Nether Shortcut

The Nether and the Overworld are connected. A Portal placed in one of these worlds always corresponds to a sister portal in the other. The interesting thing about this is that the locations are related in relative direction—this requires an explanation.

If you make two Portals near your base, there will be two Nether Portals created in the Nether. If your portals in the Overworld are directly north/south of each other, then their Nether counterparts will also be directly north/south from each other!

However, the *number of blocks between* the Portals in each world is not the same. One block of distance in the Nether equals eight blocks in the Overworld. If you want to create bases far away from home in the Overworld, take a short trip inside the Nether and make a new portal somewhere else. You pop out fairly far away in the Overworld and can explore someplace completely new!

TRADING

In the "Special Areas" section, we talked about Villages where your character can meet people and trade with them by using Emeralds (or give them items that they request to earn their Emeralds).

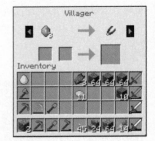

Though we've already covered the basics for how to do this, let's look at the items that are tradable from specific Villagers.

Blacksmith

WANTS

ITEM	VALUE
Coal	16-23/Emerald
Diamonds	4-5/Emerald
Gold Ingots	8-9/Emerald
Iron Ingots	8-9/Emerald

IS SELLING

ITEM	VALUE	ITEM	VALUE
Chainmail Boots	4-5 Emeralds	Diamond Shovel	7 Emeralds
Chainmail Chest	10-13 Emeralds	Diamond Sword	12-13 Emeralds
Chainmail Helm	4-5 Emeralds	Iron Axe	6-7 Emeralds
Chainmail Leggings	8-9 Emeralds	Iron Boots	4-5 Emeralds
Diamond Axe	9-11 Emeralds	Iron Chest	10-13 Emeralds
Diamond Boots	7 Emeralds	Iron Helm	4-5 Emeralds
Diamond Chest	16-18 Emeralds	Iron Hoe	4-5 Emeralds
Diamond Helm	7 Emeralds	Iron Leggings	8-9 Emeralds
Diamond Hoe	7 Emeralds	Iron Pickaxe	7-8 Emeralds
Diamond Leggings	11-13 Emeralds	Iron Shovel	4-5 Emeralds
Diamond Pickaxe	10-11 Emeralds	Iron Sword	7-10 Emeralds

Butcher

WANTS

ITEM	VALUE
Coal	16-23/Emerald
Gold	8-9/Emerald
Raw Beef	14-17/Emerald
Raw Pork	14-17/Emerald

IS SELLING

ITEM	VALUE
Leather Boots	2-3 Emeralds
Leather Chest	4 Emeralds
Leather Helm	2-3 Emeralds
Leather Leggings	2-3 Emeralds
Porkchop	6-7/Emerald
Saddle	6-7 Emeralds
Steak	6-7/Emerald

Librarian

WANTS

ITEM	VALUE
Books	11-12/Emerald
Gold	8-9/Emerald
Paper	24-35/Emerald
Written Book	1/Emerald

IS SELLING

ITEM	VALUE
Bookshelves	3 Emeralds
Clock	10-11 Emeralds
Compass	10-11 Emeralds
Glass	4-5/Emerald

Farmer

WANTS

ITEM	VALUE
Fish	9-12/Emerald
Gold Ingots	8-9/Emerald
Raw Chicken	14-17/Emerald
Wheat	18-21/Emerald
Wool	14-21/Emerald

IS SELLING

ITEM	VALUE
Apples	5-8/Emerald
Arrows	9-12/Emerald
Bread	3-4/Emerald
Cooked Chicken	7-8/Emerald
Cookies	8-10/Emerald
Flint and Steel	3 Emeralds
Melon Slices	5-8/Emerald
Shears	3 Emeralds

Priest

WANTS

ITEM	VALUE
Gold Ingots	8-9/Emerald

IS SELLING

ITEM	VALUE
Bottle of Enchanting	2-4/Emerald
Eye of Ender	7-10 Emeralds
Glowstone Blocks	2-3/Emerald
Redstone Ore	2-4/Emerald

THE NETHER

The Nether is a world of red stone, fire, and strange beasts. It's possible to enter this dimension after gathering several special materials from the Overworld. After you make a Nether Portal, it's possible to travel back and forth between these dimensions at will.

MONSTERS FROM THE NETHER

- Blazes
- Ghasts
- Magma Cubes
- Wither Skeletons
- Zombie Pigmen

RESOURCES IN THE NETHER

- Glowstone
- Nether Quartz
- Nether Wart
- Netherrack
- Soul Sand

Creating a Nether Portal

To access the Nether, you need to construct a Nether Portal. To do this, your character must have access to a source of fire (Flint and Steel), Diamonds (for a Diamond Pick), and Obsidian. Once you have access to all of these materials, mine 14 blocks of Obsidian and bring them to your base. Construct a Nether Portal by placing four blocks of Obsidian in a line on the ground. Build the two ends into pillars of Obsidian that are five blocks high, and then fill in the gap on top with two connecting blocks. Now use your Flint and Steel to light the inner hollow space of this Obsidian frame.

Now that the Nether Portal is active, you can jump into it and wait for the teleportation spell to zip you between worlds. Don't jump out from the portal on the other side until you make sure you won't fall into Lava or suffer any other ill effects.

What to Bring into the Nether

The Nether is one of the most dangerous places in *Minecraft*. Light is dim, Lava is plentiful and flows faster than usual, and monsters are deadlier than in the Overworld. It's very easy to die, so take only what you need to survive. Don't bring items that you can't afford to lose.

Diamond tools are not required in the Nether. You don't need to cut through any hard materials, so Iron Pickaxes are perfectly fine. Bring those, some Swords, a Bow, Arrows, Wood and Cobblestone (neither of which are found naturally in the Nether),

food, Torches, Flint and Steel, and anything else that might seem useful. The weapons are necessary to fight the Nether's monsters, and some items are standard equipment for any mining or exploration trip. You should bring Flint and Steel on any Nether trip; if your Nether Portal gets snuffed out over there (for example, by getting hit by a Ghast's fireball), you have to relight it.

When you arrive, make a central base as close to your portal as possible. Wall it off with Cobblestone from back home. Cobblestone doesn't burn; Netherrack, the natural stone of this area, does! Any long-term structure you build in the Nether should be made from heavier, non-flammable materials.

Your base needs to have a Crafting Table, Furnace, Chests, and preferably an Ender Chest once you can craft those. Put your best loot into the Chests each time you take a break to ensure you don't lose anything if your character falls or tunnels into Lava. In the Nether, this is not a rare occurrence.

New Rules

You can't use Water in the Nether. It boils away instantly, so that's pretty useless.

Beds aren't great to bring, either, unless you plan to use them as makeshift TNT. When you try to sleep in a Bed, the whole thing explodes. It's better to avoid the situation entirely unless you're interested in blowing things up with a piece of bedroom furniture.

What to Do in the Nether

Besides fun and exploration, you can accomplish several goals when you get to the Nether. Harvest Netherrack, Nether Quartz, Soul Sand, and Glowstone as soon as possible. These are fairly common materials, and you can't find them anywhere back home. Collect an ample supply of each.

Netherrack is the least useful. It burns forever, so you can make cool fire pits and fireplaces with it, but that's about it. The stone is way too ugly to be useful for nice bases or homes.

Nether Quartz is lovely. The blocks you make with it are really cool looking, though it takes a good while to farm enough Nether Quartz to make large buildings. We recommend making a wizard's tower out of Nether Quartz. So cool!

Glowstone is a bright material used to create blocks that are better than Torches; they work underwater and shine quite clearly even from long distance. Glowstone breaks into chunks when you mine it, so a Pickaxe with Silk Touch is useful, though not required.

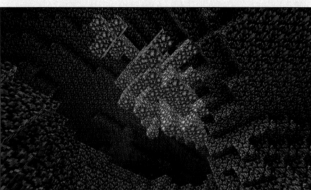

Soul Sand is hard to walk on. It's fun for making traps, slowing other players and monsters, or for a few specific tasks, like summoning the Wither. Look for Soul Sand when you travel, and get at least a partial stack of it.

LOCATING AND ASSAULTING NETHER FORTRESSES

Nether Fortresses contain even more valuable materials than the Nether itself. Blaze Rods and Nether Wart are both amazingly useful, and you won't find either of these without going to a Nether Fortress.

Search for Nether Fortresses by walking east or west from your starting point. Nether Fortresses are aligned north to south and are built along lines that go the entire length of the Nether. Once you bump into a Nether Fortress, you're set! Additional forts are located north *and* south from there, so exploration isn't as challenging.

Additionally, Nether Fortresses are large enough that you won't usually wander past them. They're made of compressed Netherrack, called Nether Brick. Their Fences, Stairs, and sundry monsters make them major landmarks.

Fight carefully through Nether Fortresses to snag Nether Wart from small growing areas near some of the stairs, and collect material from slain enemies. Wither Skeletons drop Wither Skeleton Skulls if you're especially lucky. You need three of them to summon a special boss monster, and it takes a long time to gather them.

Getting three skulls from Wither Skeletons takes more time than almost any other gathering task in *Minecraft*. It's tough, so do everything you can to improve your chances of finding these rare items.

Use enchanted Swords to deal maximum damage versus undead. It's even better if these weapons have Looting III on them. It doesn't quite double the rate of skull drops, but it's still a 60% improvement! Not bad.

If too few Wither Skeletons appear in your current Nether Fortress, don't be afraid to search for a new one. Thanks to differences in their layouts, some forts spawn more Wither Skeletons than others.

Ranged weapons are a must in these forts. Blazes have ranged attacks, and Wither Skeletons can too if they pick up a Bow. Also, some regular Skeletons spawn in Nether Fortresses, so be on the lookout for them.

You'll find Magma Cubes near the base of these areas, and they too drop useful items. Fight them at range to avoid damage, or go in for melee attacks if you're well armored and feeling lucky.

Not all Nether Fortresses have gardens of Nether Wart, but even the ones that don't often have Chests of loot. These can yield Diamonds, pieces of metal, Golden equipment, more Nether Wart (yay!), Saddles, and Horse Armor. Because of this, you can collect your first Nether Wart and start a garden of your own by searching carefully for Chests and growing areas along the steps.

Destroying a Wither

Once you hunt enough Wither Skeletons to get the three needed Wither Skeleton Skulls, bring them back to the Overworld with a supply of Soul Sand.

Choose a spot for battle in advance. Don't do this near your base, because the Wither's explosive attacks will wreck the whole area. Underground areas are a bit easier, because you won't have to navigate massive dirt chasms and such while racing back toward the Wither.

Use a Potion of Night Vision before the battle. Torches don't survive the Wither's explosions, and you won't want to fight in pitch darkness.

Also, bring the following useful items: a Diamond Sword (with Smite), Health Splash Potions, Strength Potions, an enchanted Bow (with Power), Diamond armor (Protection IV is almost a must), and an Enchanted Golden Apple.

To summon your Wither, build a small altar of Soul Sand—one block on the bottom, three horizontal blocks stacked above it. Then place the three skulls on top of the altar. This brings the Wither into being. Run! Immediately!

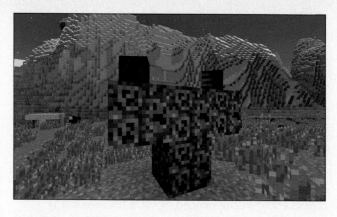

The Wither charges to full health and detonates the area around the altar when it reaches full power. You don't want to be around for this blast.

After you hear the strange explosion, return for battle. Use your Bow to reduce the Wither to half health. This isn't too hard, because the Wither's ranged attacks take a moment to reach you, so ranged combat provides an advantage. Dodge the explosive skulls that the Wither sends your way, and fire back as often as possible.

Drink potions to restore health if you get behind, and then use your Enchanted Golden Apple and Strength Potions when it's time to go for melee attacks. Withers become immune to ranged damage at half health, so you have to finish them with your blade.

Once you're buffed with the Enchanted Golden Apple's and Strength Potions' positive effects, charge toward the Wither and go for broke. Attack aggressively and kill it while the apple's regenerative effects are still working.

The Nether Star that drops is required to make Beacons, and these offer really neat bonuses for your character and any friends. Plus, you can get multiple achievements by going to the Nether, farming materials, summoning a Wither, and killing it. It's all worthwhile!

Light a Beacon

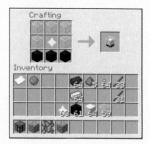

Once you have a Nether Star, return to your base and craft a huge pyramid of blocks. The largest effective pyramid has to contain 164 blocks of Iron, Gold, or Diamond. Each block costs nine ingots of the material in question, so it's quite a daunting amount of resources to gather.

You can always construct your pyramid in tiers. The first level only needs to have the Beacon on top

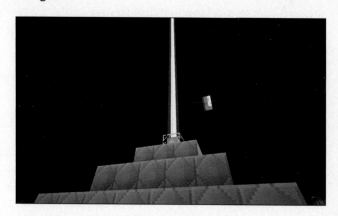

and then nine blocks in a square beneath it. That's only 81 ingots of material, so it isn't too bad. Once you have that, save up more resources until you can craft the second stage. Go on from there so you don't have to wait until you have the entire thing ready before getting the perks of having an active Beacon.

You can cluster multiple Beacons together by placing them on a large pyramid. In the end, this saves on space and materials by quite a large margin. A 2x2 top with four Beacons with a 4x4 tier beneath it is much more useful than creating a single large pyramid with one Beacon.

WHAT DO BEACONS DO?

Completed Beacons light the sky and look wonderful, but that's the least of their effects. Once constructed, you turn on Beacons by adding a single piece of Iron, Gold, Emerald, or Diamond. This activates a buff that influences your character and any friends that are within a certain range.

RANGE OF EACH PYRAMID

Tier I	20 Blocks
Tier II	30 Blocks
Tier III	40 Blocks
Tier IV	50 Blocks

A Beacon's range reaches horizontally by the number of blocks listed in the preceding table. However, the Beacon's powers reach upward (vertically) by 250 blocks. This is why many players construct Beacons near the bottom of the Overworld. Note that your Beacon has to have open access to the sky to work properly, so you have to dig a hole down toward the bedrock to let the Beacon shine free.

Normally, Beacons give you one power each. As you make larger pyramids, you get more choices for powers, but you don't get any secondary powers until tier IV. These maximum-sized pyramids let you make strong primary powers or get a free secondary regeneration effect.

Some of the primary effects are locked until you make a certain pyramid size. The initial choices are Speed and Haste. Resistance and Jump Boost require a tier-II pyramid. Strength requires a tier-III pyramid.

POSITIVE EFFECTS FROM EACH BEACON (CHOOSE ONE)

Haste	Faster mining
Jump Boost	Higher and longer jumps
Resistance	Improved armor rating
Speed	Faster walking and sprinting
Strength	Increased melee damage

For the best effect, craft four Beacons and use the wider pyramids to get almost all of these buffs. A tier-II pyramid built in this fashion needs to have "only" 52 blocks but gets you four primary powers. That's less than one-third of the cost of a single Beacon tier-IV pyramid.

If you ever get enough material together for a four-Beacon, tier-IV pyramid, life is great. The increased range really helps, and your total number of effects makes it a joy to mine, work, or farm near the Beacon.

Pocket Edition: The Nether Reactor

Pocket Edition players don't have access to the Nether, because it's not a world in that version of the game. Instead, they get to create a machine called the Nether Reactor, and it gives you a taste of the Nether while staying in your own happy world.

Start your quest by gathering Iron Ingots and Diamond. Use these to craft the Nether Reactor Core. Now that you have a core, find a place that is safely apart from your main base. This process creates a huge tower of Netherrack, and you don't want it to cut through territory that's already well landscaped.

The Reactor needs 4 Gold Blocks (36 Gold Ingots' worth of material), 14 Cobblestone, and the Nether Reactor Core. Build a small structure using the following pattern:

- **Tier One:** Gold Blocks at the corners of a 3x3 grid, Cobblestone in between

- **Tier Two:** Cobblestone at the corners, Nether Reactor Core in the center, empty spaces in between

- **Tier Three:** A "+" sign of Cobblestone with nothing at all in the corners

Hit the Nether Reactor Core when everything is in place, and watch the fireworks. Quite a few interesting items spawn from a somewhat random list. The most dangerous eventuality is that Zombie Pigmen appear, and they're aggressive in the Pocket Edition, so get ready for a fight when they come out.

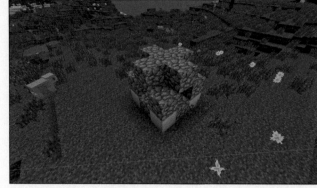

Keep a Diamond Pickaxe in your hand when you activate the Reactor. The expensive Gold Blocks in your design are about to turn into Obsidian. As soon as the Reactor starts to churn, hit those Gold Blocks and try to recover as many of them as possible before they change.

After the Reactor finishes spawning items, clean up the area and dig your way through the Obsidian to get the old Nether Reactor Core back. It can be used multiple times if you want a chance to get more cool loot.

THE END

The End is another special dimension in *Minecraft*. You cannot get there at first, but Endermen help you get there eventually.

Endermen and Eyes of Ender

Endermen are rare monsters, but you find them here and there throughout the Overworld. Large, dark areas that are at least three blocks high have a chance to spawn Endermen at any time.

Fight these enemies by attacking their feet. This prevents them from teleporting. Don't use ranged attacks, and don't look them in the eyes because that makes them aggressive before you're ready to fight.

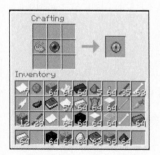

Kill enough Endermen, and you start to accrue Ender Pearls. These items are useful for instant teleportation. Throw them at your target—and bam!—you're there. This causes damage to your player, but it's still fun.

That said, you're best off saving most of your Ender Pearls; they are crafted into Eyes of Ender. These items help you find strongholds and then to activate portals that are located only within those strongholds.

Craft more than 12 Eyes of Ender when you want to reach The End. Use the Eyes to locate the nearest stronghold, attack that base, and look for the room with the End Portal. This is where Silverfish spawn. Track them back to that room, destroy their Monster Spawner, and then fill in the 12 slots around the End Portal with your Eyes of Ender. Doing so opens the way—you can now get to The End.

Note that you can't get back, so don't step through the portal until you stash your best items at home.

Going to The End and Killing the Ender Dragon

End Portals stay activated once you've found them and used your Eyes of Ender. That's good news, because your trip to The End won't always go well. We recommend against taking all of your good equipment for your first trip there. You should get your bearings, make sure your spawn location is "safe," and try to build a starting base with your first life there.

The game's final boss is here; it's called the Ender Dragon. This thing is so powerful that it breaks most blocks by flying through them. Obsidian and the End Stone that dominate this dimension are both exceptions. Bring enough Obsidian to quickly create a small room beside the portal where you spawn (not *on* it). Form this room and drop an Ender Chest there, if you have one. This lets you harvest End Stone and transport it back to the Overworld even before you're able to kill the Ender Dragon.

PREPARING FOR BATTLE

Once you're comfortable going to The End and getting your bearings, start to arm yourself for the final engagement. You want a Bow with the best Power enchantment you can get. A few stacks of Arrows won't hurt, though you likely won't need all of them unless things go very badly.

A good Sword helps, too. The Ender Dragon is too mobile to kill with a Sword, but Endermen also inhabit The End, and they are an additional threat. Swords should have either Fire Aspect or the highest possible damage output.

Diamond armor with Protection IV is your smartest bet for safety. Your helm can be either a Pumpkin or a Diamond Helm. The latter is better for survival. Pumpkins are better for avoiding extra fights with Endermen, because they don't attack when you look at them. This is a matter of personal preference.

Potions of Healing and Regeneration are both useful during the battle. Golden Apples or Enchanted Golden Apples are great, too.

Ender Pearls are helpful as well. They let players teleport from smaller islands over to the main island, possibly saving themselves if they're knocked over the edge during the boss fight.

SLAYING THE DRAGON

A series of End Crystals keeps the Ender Dragon alive and healthy. Each Crystal is placed on top of an Obsidian pillar, like the ones on which you arrive. Destroying these is a critical part of the boss fight. If you don't break the crystals, the Ender Dragon can stay at or near full health indefinitely, despite your best efforts.

Watch for the healing beams that emanate from the End Crystals. Their energy flows toward the dragon. Trace it back to figure out where the crystals are located, and use your Bow to shoot at them until they explode.

Once the crystals are no longer healing the Ender Dragon, turn the Bow on him! Head shots are the way to go if you want to win this fight anytime soon; they inflict quadruple damage. The best way to achieve these hits is to wait for the Ender Dragon to come after your character. Nail it in the head with a fully charged attack. Get another shot in immediately afterward, and then watch the dragon fly away. Chase it and wait for the boss to turn and come after you again. Repeat your attacks and wait for the kill!

THE AFTERMATH

The Ender Dragon drops so much experience that even a character with no experience will max out their levels almost immediately. It's better to bring a few friends to spread around the experience, or bring in materials for enchanting work so you can enchant multiple items and still max out your experience.

The Ender Dragon also drops a Dragon Egg. This doesn't have a use (yet). However, you can collect it. Clicking on the Dragon Egg causes it to teleport. Do this one time to get the egg away from the End Portal, which appears to take you home. You don't want the egg to fall into the End Portal and break.

After the Dragon Egg teleports, track it down. It sometimes appears below the ground. Tunnel until you find it, and then get two blocks beneath it. Destroy the End Stone there, place a Torch, and then destroy the block above to drop the Dragon Egg onto the Torch. This turns the egg into a resource and allows you to collect it.

And now, you have completed The End. Come back here to farm Endermen or End Stone, and use your new End Portal to return home at any time.

ACHIEVEMENTS

Achievements (and Trophies) are small rewards to let you know you're on the right track in *Minecraft*. These rewards are available in the PC and console versions of the game. You don't get any special items for unlocking these, but they're still fun goals to target, especially when you're a new player and don't know what to do first. By the time you figure out how to get most of these, you'll be an expert at *Minecraft*!

ACHIEVEMENT	REQUIREMENTS	DESCRIPTION	VERSIONS
Acquire Hardware	Complete "Hot Topic" and pick up an Iron Ingot	Smelt an Iron Ingot	PC, Console
Adventuring Time	Complete "The End?" and visit 38 specific biomes	Discover all biomes	PC only
Awarded All Trophies	Complete ALL trophies	All Trophies have been awarded	PS only
Bake Bread	Complete "Time to Farm" and pick up Bread	Turn Wheat into Bread	PC, Console
Beaconator	Complete "The Beginning." and place a Beacon with a four-tier pyramid	Create a full Beacon	PC only
Benchmarking	Complete "Getting Wood" and pick up a Crafting Table	Craft a Crafting Table with four blocks of Wood Planks	PC, Console
Cow Tipper	Complete "Time to Strike!" and pick up Leather	Harvest some Leather	PC, Console
Delicious Fish	Complete "Hot Topic" and remove any cooked Fish	Catch and cook a Fish	PC, Console
Diamonds to You	Complete "DIAMONDS!" and drop Diamonds for another target to pick up	Throw Diamonds at another player	PC only
DIAMONDS!	Complete "Acquire Hardware" and pick up a Diamond	Acquire Diamonds with your Iron tools	PC, PlayStation
Dispense With This	Complete "Acquire Hardware"	Construct a Dispenser	Console only
Enchanter	Complete "DIAMONDS!" and pick up an Enchanting Table	Use a Book, Obsidian, and Diamonds to construct an Enchanting Table	PC, PlayStation
Getting an Upgrade	Complete "Time to Mine" and pick up a non-Wooden Pickaxe	Construct a better Pickaxe	PC, Console
Getting Wood	Complete "Taking Inventory" and pick up a piece of Wood	Attack a tree until a piece of Wood pops out	PC, Console
Hot Topic	Complete "Time to Mine" and pick up a Furnace	Construct a Furnace out of eight Cobblestone blocks	PC, Console
Into Fire	Complete "We Need to Go Deeper" or "Into the Nether" and pick up a Blaze Rod	Relieve a Blaze of its Rod	PC, PlayStation
Into the Nether	Complete "Acquire Hardware" and enter a Nether Portal	Build a Portal to the Nether	Console only
Leader of the Pack	Complete "Monster Hunter"	Tame five Wolves	Console only
Librarian	Complete "Enchanter" and pick up a Bookshelf	Build some Bookshelves to improve your home	PC only
Local Brewery	Complete "Into Fire" and pick up a Potion	Brew a Potion	PC, PlayStation
MOAR Tools	Complete "Benchmarking"	Construct a Pickaxe, Shovel, Axe, and Hoe	Console only
Monster Hunter	Complete "Time to Strike!" and kill any monster	Attack and destroy a monster	PC, Console
On a Rail	Complete "Acquire Hardware" and travel by Minecart for 500 m (Console) or 1 km (PC)	Travel by Minecart for 500 m or 1 km	PC, Console
Overkill	Complete "Enchanter" and deal 18 damage to a target	Deal 8 hearts of damage in a single hit	PC only
Overpowered	Complete "Getting An Upgrade" and Craft an Enchanted Golden Apple	Use 8 Blocks of Gold and an Apple to craft an Enchanted Golden Apple	PC, Console
Repopulation	Complete "Cow Tipper"	Breed two Cows with Wheat	PC only
Return to Sender	Complete "We Need to Go Deeper" or "Into the Nether" and kill a Ghast using a Ghast's Fireball	Destroy a Ghast with a Fireball	PC, PlayStation
Sniper Duel	Complete "Monster Hunter" and kill a Skeleton with a Bow from long range	Kill a Skeleton with an Arrow from 50 m or more	PC, PlayStation

ACHIEVEMENT	REQUIREMENTS	DESCRIPTION	VERSIONS
Taking Inventory	Open your inventory	Press the default Inventory key to open your inventory	PC, Console
The Beginning.	Complete "The Beginning?"	Kill the Wither	PC only
The Beginning?	Complete "The End."	Spawn the Wither	PC only
The End.	Complete "The End?" and use a Portal to exit The End	Defeat the Ender Dragon	PC, PlayStation
The End?	Complete "Into Fire" and enter an End Portal	Locate The End	PC, PlayStation
The Lie	Complete "Time to Farm" and pick up a Cake	Use Wheat, Sugar, Milk, and Eggs to make a Cake	PC, Console
Time to Farm	Complete "Benchmarking" and pick up a Hoe	Use Wood Planks and Sticks to make a Hoe	PC, Console
Time to Mine!	Complete "Benchmarking" and pick up a Pickaxe from the Crafting Table	Use Wood Planks and Sticks to make a Pickaxe	PC, Console
Time to Strike!	Complete "Benchmarking" and pick up a Sword	Use Wood Planks and Sticks to make a Sword	PC, Console
We Need to Go Deeper	Complete "DIAMONDS" and enter a Nether Portal	Build a portal to the Nether	PC only
When Pigs Fly	Complete "Cow Tipper," use a Saddle on a Pig, and cause the Pig two hearts of falling damage	Fly a Pig off a cliff	PC, Console

How to Earn Specific Achievements

ACQUIRE HARDWARE

REQUIREMENTS	DESCRIPTION	VERSIONS
Complete "Hot Topic" and pick up an Iron Ingot	Smelt an Iron Ingot	PC, Console

Here's an easy one. Construct a Furnace, interact with the Furnace, and put one piece of Iron Ore into the top slot. Put any type of fuel in the lower slot (Coal is always good). After a short time, the Iron Ore burns away and leaves an Iron Ingot. Pick it up!

ADVENTURING TIME

REQUIREMENTS	DESCRIPTION	VERSIONS
Complete "The End?" and visit 38 specific biomes	Discover all biomes	PC only

Visit the Nether and The End, and then travel the Overworld as well to find as many biomes as possible. This is one of the hardest and most time-consuming achievements in the game. If you look up a world with an existing seed, people can give you coordinates for the biomes you still need to find. This can really help, but it's still a labor of love.

AWARDED ALL TROPHIES

REQUIREMENTS	DESCRIPTION	VERSIONS
Complete ALL trophies	All Trophies have been awarded	PS only

The PlayStation version of *Minecraft* gives you this trophy if you finish all the other available Trophies. Read through this section to find out how to get all of them.

BAKE BREAD

REQUIREMENTS	DESCRIPTION	VERSIONS
Complete "Time to Farm" and pick up Bread	Turn Wheat into Bread	PC, Console

Put three pieces of Wheat onto your Crafting Table, side by side. This gets you a piece of Bread! Pick it up, and enjoy your easy achievement.

BEACONATOR

REQUIREMENTS	DESCRIPTION	VERSIONS
Complete "The Beginning." and place a Beacon with a four-tier pyramid	Create a full Beacon	PC only

Kill a Wither to collect a Nether Star. Use this to craft a Beacon (which requires five Glass Blocks, the Nether Star, and three Obsidian on the bottom). Build your Beacon and then bring it to a wide open space. Create a pyramid there, using blocks of Iron, Gold, or Diamond. You need a four-tier pyramid for this achievement; this means you need 164 blocks of whatever mineral you plan on using.

BASE	9X9 (81 BLOCKS)
Tier 2	7x7 (49 Blocks)
Tier 3	5x5 (25 Blocks)
Tier 4	3x3 (9 Blocks)
Top	Beacon on top

BENCHMARKING

REQUIREMENTS	DESCRIPTION	VERSIONS
Complete "Getting Wood" and pick up a Crafting Table	Craft a Crafting Table with four blocks of Wood Planks	PC, Console

After you chop down a block or two of Wood from a local tree, put the blocks of Wood into your crafting window. Fill all four spaces with Wood and make a Crafting Table. Grab it, set it up, and keep on crafting.

COW TIPPER

REQUIREMENTS	DESCRIPTION	VERSIONS
Complete "Time to Strike!" and pick up Leather	Harvest some Leather	PC, Console

Find Cows and attack them with a Sword (or whatever you feel like using). Kill the animals and grab any Leather that drops. That's all you need to do.

DELICIOUS FISH

REQUIREMENTS	DESCRIPTION	VERSIONS
Complete "Hot Topic" and remove any cooked Fish	Catch and cook a Fish	PC, Console

Craft a Fishing Rod and go to your nearest body of Water. Equip your rod and use it to toss the lure out into the Water. Watch carefully for any ripples, and don't pull the Rod up until you see the lure dip into the Water. That's when you use the Rod to grab your Fish.

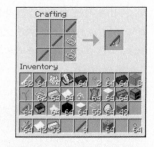

Once you have something to cook, go back to a Furnace, put the Fish into the upper slot, and wait for it to cook. Grab the cooked Fish when it's done, and you're finished.

DIAMONDS TO YOU

REQUIREMENTS	DESCRIPTION	VERSIONS
Complete "DIAMONDS!" and drop Diamonds for another target to pick up	Throw Diamonds at another player	PC only

Drop Diamonds in front of a Zombie or, better yet, a player that you trust. If the target picks up your Diamond, you get this achievement. Kill any Zombies involved to get your Diamonds back, or ask nicely to get them back from your friend.

DIAMONDS!

REQUIREMENTS	DESCRIPTION	VERSIONS
Complete "Acquire Hardware" and pick up a Diamond	Acquire Diamonds with your Iron tools	PC, PlayStation

Make an Iron Pickaxe and dig down toward the Overworld's bedrock (a "Y" value of 15 or lower). Dig through tunnels in all directions until you see a clear, bluish stone embedded in the rock. Cut it out using your Iron Pickaxe and grab the Diamonds. Never use a Wood or Stone Pickaxe for this task; it destroys your precious loot.

DISPENSE WITH THIS

REQUIREMENTS	DESCRIPTION	VERSIONS
Complete "Acquire Hardware"	Construct a Dispenser	Console only

Get a Bow, Cobblestone, and some Redstone, and craft these items into a Dispenser. That's all that's needed for this achievement.

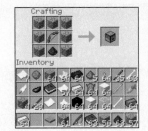

ENCHANTER

REQUIREMENTS	DESCRIPTION	VERSIONS
Complete "DIAMONDS!" and pick up an Enchanting Table	Use a Book, Obsidian, and Diamonds to construct an Enchanting Table	PC, PlayStation

Make Paper (from Sugar Cane) and gather Leather from Cows or Horses. Use these to craft a Book.

Then go deep into the mines and gather two Diamonds and four blocks of Obsidian. You need a Diamond Pickaxe to mine the Obsidian, so it'll take five total Diamonds to complete this if you haven't already made a Diamond Pickaxe.

Once you have all of these items, craft an Enchanting Table and start saving experience for some cool item enhancements!

GETTING AN UPGRADE

REQUIREMENTS	DESCRIPTION	VERSIONS
Complete "Time to Mine" and pick up a non-Wooden Pickaxe	Construct a better Pickaxe	PC, Console

After you've made a Wood Pickaxe, start mining Stone. If you don't see any nearby, dig into the ground and head downward until you find a pocket of Stone. Get three or more pieces of that, and return to your Crafting Table. Use two Sticks and three Cobblestone to make a Stone Pickaxe. Boom! Done.

GETTING WOOD

REQUIREMENTS	DESCRIPTION	VERSIONS
Complete "Taking Inventory" and pick up a piece of Wood	Attack a tree until a piece of Wood pops out	PC, Console

Upon starting your game, charge the first tree you see. Hit it with your fists without releasing the Attack button. Before long, the Wood breaks and falls to the ground. Pick it up by walking over it.

HOT TOPIC

REQUIREMENTS	DESCRIPTION	VERSIONS
Complete "Time to Mine" and pick up a Furnace	Construct a Furnace out of eight Cobblestone blocks	PC, Console

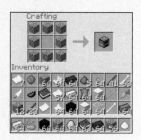

Mine eight pieces of Cobblestone and take them to your Crafting Table. Add them as ingredients and make your Furnace. It's as simple as that.

INTO FIRE

REQUIREMENTS	DESCRIPTION	VERSIONS
Complete "We Need to Go Deeper" or "Into the Nether" and pick up a Blaze Rod	Relieve a Blaze of its Rod	PC, PlayStation

Go into the Nether and search for a Nether Fortress. They're extremely large structures, so you won't have any doubt when you see one. Climb up the Nether Brick staircases and hunt for the fiery Blazes that fly around each fort's upper reaches. Kill them with ranged attacks or back around corners to lure them into melee range.

Loot the ground after Blazes die and search for their Blaze Rods. Quite useful items!

INTO THE NETHER

REQUIREMENTS	DESCRIPTION	VERSIONS
Complete "Acquire Hardware" and enter a Nether Portal	Build a Portal to the Nether	Console only

Make a Diamond Pickaxe, fill a Bucket with Water, and search for a pool of Lava (on the surface or down near the bottom of the Overworld). When you find Lava, use the Bucket to pour Water over the Lava. The Water cools the magma and turns it into Obsidian. Make a large, safe place to mine, light it well with Torches, and collect many pieces of Obsidian by using your Diamond Pickaxe (nothing else works).

You can make a Portal to the Nether with 10 pieces of Obsidian. For your first Portal, we'd suggest 14 pieces just because it's easier and looks nice.

When you have everything you need, find a safe place for your Portal. Make a line of Obsidian four stones long. Stack more Obsidian on the stones at each end until there are two pillars five stones high. Then complete the top of the Portal. It should look like a large zero or a frame with an empty center. Use a fire source, such as Flint and Steel, to light the Portal's empty center. Now you can jump back and forth between the Overworld and the Nether. The corners are optional, which is why only 10 pieces of Obsidian are required, but the Portal works either way. Consider blocking Portal rooms with a doorway, in case anything decides to wander in from the Nether.

LEADER OF THE PACK

REQUIREMENTS	DESCRIPTION	VERSIONS
Complete "Monster Hunter"	Tame five Wolves	Console only

If you're out in a taiga biome, bring a large supply of Bones with your character. Use these Bones to try to tame any Wolves you meet. Keep doing this to get a large pack and complete your achievement. It's easier to breed Wolves than to tame them, so feed the Wolves meat to bolster their numbers once you get the achievement out of the way.

LIBRARIAN

REQUIREMENTS	DESCRIPTION	VERSIONS
Complete "Enchanter" and pick up a Bookshelf	Build some Bookshelves to improve your home	PC only

Six Wooden Planks and three Books combine to make a Bookshelf. You need these to improve your Enchanting Table's power, so quite a bit of Paper, Leather, and Wood are required to max out your Enchanting Table.

For maximum power, your Enchanting Table needs to have 15 Bookshelves positioned two blocks away from it. For this to happen, you need 45 Books and 90 Wood Planks. In terms of total resources, you need 45 Leather, 135 Sugar Cane, and 90 Wood Planks.

LOCAL BREWERY

REQUIREMENTS	DESCRIPTION	VERSIONS
Complete "Into Fire" and pick up a Potion	Brew a Potion	PC, PlayStation

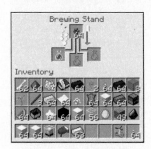

Fight Blazes in the Nether until you get a Blaze Rod. Bring it home and use it with three pieces of Cobblestone to craft a Brewing Stand. Next employ three Glass Blocks to make Glass Bottles, and use those in the Brewing Stand to begin playing with potions.

Powerful potions are based on rare ingredients, like Nether Wart. Try that and a Water Bottle to make your first interesting potion. Things get much more involved from there, but you've already done enough to get credit for Local Brewery!

MOAR TOOLS

REQUIREMENTS	DESCRIPTION	VERSIONS
Complete "Benchmarking"	Construct a Pickaxe, Shovel, Axe, and Hoe	Console only

Use basic recipes to craft each of the four common tools. These take eight Sticks and a modest supply of Wood or Cobblestone. It's easy to gather all of these, and we explain them in the "Let's Begin with the Basics" chapter.

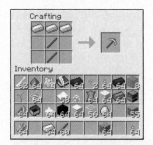 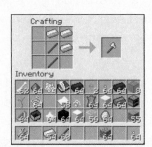 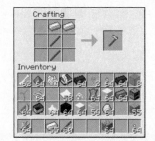 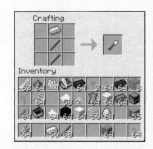

MONSTER HUNTER

REQUIREMENTS	DESCRIPTION	VERSIONS
Complete "Time to Strike!" and kill any monster	Attack and destroy a monster	PC, Console

Craft an Axe or Sword and use it to kill a monster the next time night falls.

ON A RAIL

REQUIREMENTS	DESCRIPTION	VERSIONS
Complete "Acquire Hardware" and travel by Minecart for 500 m (Console) or 1 km (PC)	Travel by Minecart for 500 m or 1 km	PC, Console

This achievement takes a long time to complete. You need to make a railway that stretches 500 blocks (console versions) or 1,000 blocks (on the PC). That's a major time commitment.

We recommend you work as a team to get On a Rail. Everyone can get credit from the same project, because the railway doesn't get torn up while each person travels along it. This means you can send off one worker, then another, then another, until everyone who participated in the project ends up with the achievement. The more people who participate, the more fun this is!

The good news is that this isn't very difficult apart from the labor. You need to harvest a massive quantity of Iron. You need smaller amounts of Redstone, Wood, and Gold as well, because Powered Rails are better for this.

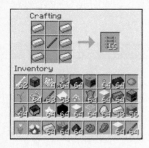 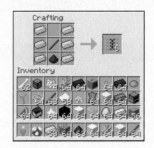 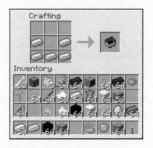 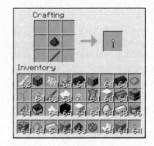

Don't try to go up or down or deal with curves. Make a straight rail that burrows through any mountains that you encounter. Put down 31 regular Rails for every Powered Rail. Drop a Redstone Torch next to the Powered Rails to give them juice.

To be really clever, have one of the participants put a sign down every four Powered Rails. Note the number of tracks that have been deployed so far: 128, 256, etc. This way, you know how much farther you need to go without having to guess.

OVERKILL

REQUIREMENTS	DESCRIPTION	VERSIONS
Complete "Enchanter" and deal 18 damage to a target	Deal eight hearts of damage in a single hit	PC only

Make a Diamond Sword, an Enchanting Table, and get the best enchantment you can for dealing damage (Bane of Arthropods or Smite). Focus on the correct target for the enchantment you use, so Spiders for Bane or undead for Smite.

When you fight these monsters, jump and swing to try to score critical hits; these blows enhance damage. Bane or Smite at level 3 with a jumping critical and Diamond Sword should be enough for an Overkill!

OVERPOWERED

REQUIREMENTS	DESCRIPTION	VERSIONS
Complete "Getting An Upgrade" and craft an Enchanted Golden Apple	Use eight Gold Blocks and an Apple to craft an Enchanted Golden Apple	PC, Console

The process for this is very simple; it's just a basic crafting recipe. The only trouble is harvesting that much Gold. Don't do this until you're very late in the game and can spare such a huge sink for your spare Gold. When you're ready, turn the Gold Ingots into Gold Blocks (at a cost of nine Gold Ingots per block). Use eight blocks to make your Enchanted Golden Apple.

YOU CAN DO ANYTHING WITH A LITTLE PRACTICE

REPOPULATION

REQUIREMENTS	DESCRIPTION	VERSIONS
Complete "Cow Tipper"	Breed two Cows with Wheat	PC only

Find two Cows that are fairly close together and feed both of them Wheat. Happy hearts will appear over their heads to indicate they're in breeding mode. They'll sing sweet songs to each other and have a baby Cow. That's all you need to do.

RETURN TO SENDER

REQUIREMENTS	DESCRIPTION	VERSIONS
Complete "We Need to Go Deeper" or "Into the Nether" and kill a Ghast using a Ghast's Fireball	Destroy a Ghast with a Fireball	PC, PlayStation

Go to the Nether and take out any melee object, such as a Sword. Find a Ghast and wait for it to notice your character. Stand still so you're an easy target, and watch as the Ghast shoots a fireball at you. Swing at the last

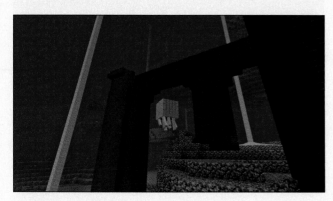

minute before the fireball hits, and try to aim your cursor at the Ghast while you do this. A successful strike sends the fireball back into the Ghast. Score a killing blow to win the fight and get the achievement.

When you try to do this, come to the field with full health, stay away from Zombie Pigmen, and don't start if you have a bunch of experience saved up. It's best to do this when you're low level. That way, it isn't as big a deal if you die. Also, stay close to your Overworld Portal. Otherwise, you might not get your gear back.

SNIPER DUEL

REQUIREMENTS	DESCRIPTION	VERSIONS
Complete "Monster Hunter" and kill a Skeleton with a Bow from long range	Kill a Skeleton with an Arrow from 50 m or more	PC, PlayStation

Look for Skeletons in the Overworld at night. Hit them with your current weapon to find out how many blows it takes to kill one of them. Once you do this, heal back to full health and find a new Skeleton. Slap it enough times with your weapon to *almost* kill it, and then back off. Go to very long range and draw your Bow. This usually takes a number of Arrows, so be sure to have a decent supply on hand in case you have trouble hitting the Skeleton. Fire from extremely long range until you get your kill.

To make the battle easier, there is a more involved way to do this. Craft several Fence pieces ahead of time. When you find your Skeleton victim, rush forward and fence it in. Place Torches nearby. Wound the Skeleton, as usual, and then back off over 50 blocks. You now have a stationary target, making the sniping duel easier to win.

TAKING INVENTORY

REQUIREMENTS	DESCRIPTION	VERSIONS
Open your inventory	Press the default Inventory key to open your inventory	PC, Console

When you enter the game, use the key/button that's bound to your inventory. Simple.

THE BEGINNING.

REQUIREMENTS	DESCRIPTION	VERSIONS
Complete "The Beginning?"	Kill the Wither	PC only

To beat the Wither, use high-end, enchanted Diamond weapons and armor. Prepare yourself with a Potion of Night Vision, and construct Snow Golems in advance. Use all of these to your advantage and kill the Wither. This is quite doable even when you're alone, but bringing allies for the fight makes the encounter even more epic.

THE BEGINNING?

REQUIREMENTS	DESCRIPTION	VERSIONS
Complete "The End."	Spawn the Wither	PC only

This is a fairly late-game achievement. You need to spend a huge amount of time hunting Wither Skeletons in the Nether, until you collect three Wither Skeleton Skulls. They're a rare drop, so you have to fight in Nether Fortresses for a good while. Grab some Soul Sand on the way out of the Nether, and then find a safe tunnel deep inside the Overworld. Build a T-shaped stand of Soul Sand (a block on the bottom with three blocks of Soul Sand stacked horizontally above). Place the Wither Skeleton Skulls on top of the Soul Sand, and spawn the Wither!

THE END.

REQUIREMENTS	DESCRIPTION	VERSIONS
Complete "The End?" and use a portal to exit The End	Defeat the Ender Dragon	PC, PlayStation

Once you get access to The End, build an assortment of end-game equipment: Diamond Armor, a Diamond Sword with high-end enchantments, plenty of potions, a great Bow, and as many Arrows as you want to carry. Go to The End, break the Ender Crystals, and shoot the Ender Dragon again and again until it dies. Strategies for this are discussed earlier in this chapter.

THE END?

REQUIREMENTS	DESCRIPTION	VERSIONS
Complete "Into Fire" and enter an End Portal	Locate The End	PC, PlayStation

Kill as many Blazes and Endermen as possible to collect Blaze Rods and Ender Pearls. Craft a large collection of Eyes of Ender, and use them to find a stronghold in the Overworld. Siege the stronghold and find the End Portal that is dormant within the compound. Use your Eyes of Ender to activate the End Portal. Go through the Portal, into The End when you're done.

THE LIE

REQUIREMENTS	DESCRIPTION	VERSIONS
Complete "Time to Farm" and pick up a Cake	Use Wheat, Sugar, Milk, and Eggs to make a Cake	PC, Console

Make three Buckets and gather Milk in them. Use Sugar Cane to make two units of Sugar, find Chickens to steal an Egg, and harvest three Wheat. Combine all of these at a Crafting Table to make your first Cake.

YOU CAN DO ANYTHING WITH A LITTLE PRACTICE

TIME TO FARM

REQUIREMENTS	DESCRIPTION	VERSIONS
Complete "Benchmarking" and pick up a Hoe	Use Planks and Sticks to make a Hoe	PC, Console

Use two Sticks and two Wooden Planks to craft your first Hoe. Now you can till Dirt or Grass into fertile land for growing crops.

TIME TO MINE!

REQUIREMENTS	DESCRIPTION	VERSIONS
Complete "Benchmarking" and pick up a Pickaxe from the Crafting Table	Use Wood Planks and Sticks to make a Pickaxe	PC, Console

Use two Sticks and three Wooden Planks to craft your first Pickaxe.

TIME TO STRIKE!

REQUIREMENTS	DESCRIPTION	VERSIONS
Complete "Benchmarking" and pick up a Sword	Use Wood Planks and Sticks to make a Sword	PC, Console

While you're making other simple items, stay at the Crafting Table and use one Stick and two Wood Planks to make a Sword. It's not a very good sword, but Stone upgrades aren't far in your future.

WE NEED TO GO DEEPER

REQUIREMENTS	DESCRIPTION	VERSIONS
Complete "DIAMONDS" and enter a Nether Portal	Build a Portal to the Nether	PC only

Make a Diamond Pick and use Water on Lava to create dark Obsidian blocks. Harvest these with the Diamond Pickaxe (carefully), and then return to your base when you have a large pile of them. Use 10-14 Obsidian to create a large O-shaped portal four blocks wide and five blocks tall. Don't fill in any of the portal's interior; leave that space entirely empty. Then use Flint and Steel to light the portal area (i.e., the empty space in the center). It can now take you between the Overworld and the Nether.

WHEN PIGS FLY

REQUIREMENTS	DESCRIPTION	VERSIONS
Complete "Cow Tipper," use a Saddle on a Pig, and cause the Pig to lose two hearts from falling damage	Fly a Pig off a cliff	PC, Console

Zombies occasionally drop Carrots. Once you get a Carrot, make a garden for it and use Bone Meal to quickly develop a small pile of Carrots. Use these Carrots to lure a Pig back to your base. Gather a

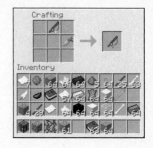

Saddle from a Chest in a dungeon or similar area (or trade for it). Then craft a Carrot on a Stick as the finishing touch.

Put the Saddle on your Pig, climb onto it, and use the Carrot on a Stick to guide the Pig toward a medium-sized drop. Don't get your cute piggy killed, but make sure it falls far enough to take decent damage. Once you run the Pig over the edge, it lands and gives you credit for the achievement.

PLAYING WITH FRIENDS

Minecraft is great even when you're alone, but it's even better if you find a place to play with your friends. There are many ways to do this, if you're interested. There are servers online at all hours of the day, and you can join them without any trouble. You can also play locally with friends who are on the same network as your computer. For an even larger group of people to game with, you can set up a server for yourself and anyone who wants to join over the internet!

Let's explain how to do all of this, and then we'll discuss *Minecraft* etiquette, so you know a few of the common dos and don'ts of playing the game with other people.

JOINING SERVERS

The simplest way to play with other people is to join an existing multiplayer server. Launch *Minecraft*. Next, make sure you have the information for the server on which you'd like to play. If you have no idea where to go, then let's take a moment to find out!

Searching for a Multiplayer Server

Use your favorite internet browser, type in something like "Minecraft Servers," and then search. Your search results should provide a decent list of sites that spread information about *Minecraft* servers.

The sites that share this information usually have blurbs about the type of community to which its server caters. Are they PvP servers? Playing to build? Survival? Look for an indicator that these people are interested in the type of gameplay you seek. Also, check to see how many people are logged into the server. If it's too empty or too full, then maybe it's not a great choice for you. Personal taste takes priority here, so look for whatever you like. Maybe a small server is more your style. Or maybe you enjoy having tons of people to interact with.

What Do the Terms Mean?

It's tough to figure out where to go when you have no idea what people are talking about. Let's break down the types of *Minecraft* servers, so you have an idea of what you're getting into. Some servers use their own terms or have unique styles of play, but the following list should give you a fair idea of what to expect.

Survival	Mostly non-PvP focused, standard rules
Freebuild/Anarchy	Unrestricted
Creative	Building servers, no combat, no risk
Roleplay	For creating a character, a story, and playing your role
PvP	Player versus player; combat between players, but there may be rules
Hardcore PvP	Player versus player; anything goes, at any time
Faction	PvP in teams
Hunger Games	Competitive PvP
Prison	Work your way up and out
Challenge/Mini Games	Specific goals are set forth
Economy	Build, trade, and expand
City	More rigid about where you can build; often involves heavy trade

Once You Choose Where You Want to Go

Look up the IP address of the server that interests you. The sites that discuss these servers almost always provide this information. Highlight the address itself, and then copy it. Go back to *Minecraft*, select Multiplayer, and then Add Server. Paste the address you copied into the Server Address bar and proceed. You can now get to that server whenever it's online.

Make sure your login information is accurate. If you type in your user name incorrectly, the game won't let you join multiplayer servers. You must have a valid Mojang account to do this.

LOCAL PLAY

You don't always need to hang out with 300 people to enjoy *Minecraft*. Maybe you're just in the mood to host some of your friends visiting your home. Local Play is easy to do in *Minecraft*. Have one person in your house start a regular, single-player game. Once they're in, hit Escape and then select "Open to LAN" to make the game multiplayer. Other people on your network will soon see the game pop up in their multiplayer menus, and they can join.

Console editions of the game let people join in for split-screen local play. That's pretty neat too, as long as you have a good TV to play it on.

CREATING YOUR OWN SERVER

For the best of a few worlds, you can create your own server and have friends and strangers come through to enjoy *Minecraft*. Note that this is very involved stuff compared with playing on someone else's server. Hosting is quite a commitment, so don't get into this unless you're extremely excited about messing around with the ups and downs of server management.

We don't go into this in depth, because some of the routing challenges, security issues, and other complexities go far beyond the scope of this book.

INTERACTING WITH OTHER PEOPLE

Now that you're ready to go online and have fun, take one more minute to stop and read. Following are a number of tips that help to avoid trouble with other people. Let's talk about etiquette, so you can be one of the cool folks that everyone likes to have around!

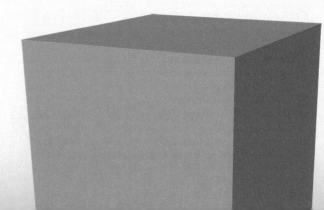

Griefing Is Bad!

There is a time and place for trouble. If you want to wreck people's houses, attack their characters, slaughter their animals, and ruin everything you see, go to a Hardcore PvP or an Anarchy server—a place where this behavior is tolerated. This is perfectly fine. Just make sure you end up playing with other people who want the same thing! Combat rocks. It's nice to compete and hunt people down, if they're cool with that.

Don't go into regular Survival servers or other cooperative modes and try to ruin things for everyone else. This is incredibly lame. It'll get you kicked off of the server sooner rather than later, and there's just no point. Treat people the way you want to be treated, and everything will go just fine most of the time.

What Counts as Griefing?

- Attacking other players unless the server is PvP focused, or the other player says they're interested in fighting

- Stealing from other players' chests or taking things from their homes

- Damaging other players' property with Lava or TNT, removal of light sources, destruction of walls, leading monsters to them, and so forth

- Inappropriate speech or text

GET AWAY FROM GRIEFERS

If it seems like a server has a ton of people griefing and causing trouble, find a new server. Keep searching until you discover a place that has cool people. Why bother playing online if you don't like the players that you bump into, right?

Have a Thick Skin, But Not Too Thick

Try not to overreact if people are a little bit rude from time to time. It's the internet. It happens. Ignore the person who is being a pain, and focus on the players that you like spending time with.

That said, report people to the server's administrator or moderators if you start seeing really nasty stuff. Anything really hurtful, cruel, or upsetting should not be tolerated. It's totally fine to stick up for yourself and others!

What You Can Say and Type

If you're worried about saying anything wrong around other people, go by a simple rule: pretend that your parents and your younger siblings are in the same room. Don't do anything online that you wouldn't do when they are listening. Following this guideline avoids quite a few "Oops, I didn't mean to upset you" moments.

SAMPLE MULTIPLAYER CHALLENGE

We thought it would be exciting to show off the type of challenges that we give to each other when trying out multiplayer *Minecraft*. This one is a perfect weekend game that we sometimes do while waiting for everyone to arrive. The people who are available ahead of time try the "One Hour Challenge." That's when we set a timer and try to create the coolest thing that we can with only one hour after the world is created. To make things extra tricky, we do this in Survival Mode so resources are highly limited. You have to work with what you're given, and that makes the game very intense.

RULES: You have one hour to build the coolest structure you can and to equip yourself as well as possible.

PLAYERS: Kathleen Pleet, Chris Burton, Michael Lummis

Kathleen Pleet

When I first started, I had high hopes. Lots of ideas. I was going to make a beautiful little house in a woodland, filled with flowers and joy. But an hour isn't much time, and I figured I'd have to cut a few corners. Just a few, though.

It all went horribly wrong.

The first thing that happened was I found myself in a sparse island swamp. There weren't all that many trees around, but there were plenty of Pigs. Ah well. If you can't find Wood, there's always Stone!

Scratch the pretty wooden farmhouse: we're going underground. I gathered enough Wood to make a few pieces of equipment and looked for a place to start my dungeon.

This was easier said than done, though. I had to find a spot that wouldn't fill with Water as soon as I began to dig. I went through a lot of Dirt. And then Gravel. Where was the Stone?

Well, there wasn't much Stone, but at least I found a good vein of Iron. That's something.

Unfortunately, I made my way out of my early tunnel only to find that it was getting dark outside. I had only a primitive mineshaft and no shelter. I started a mad scramble to construct walls around the mine, and I used anything and everything in my inventory to do so.

It was completely dark as I constructed my crude perimeter. I used most of my stuff on the walls, so I had to dig out Cobblestone to make a Furnace. But I also used all my Wood, and that meant that I had nothing with which to make light. Or a Door.

Going outside proved extremely dangerous. In addition to Zombies, there was also a Slime. Before I started this mineshaft, I should have killed some of those Pigs for meat. Oops.

I was quick enough to grab a few logs of Wood, but the Zombies came at me and I had to rush back to my hideaway. I managed to make a Door, but I couldn't place it. Suddenly, there was a swipe from the shadows, and I became stuck on the ledges of my mineshaft as a Zombie attacked me. I couldn't see to attack the Zombie back.

How did I survive? I didn't.

It was now fully night outside. I respawned with nothing; it was some distance to my house, and in between me and my paltry abode were a multitude of enemies.

There were still Zombies *everywhere*! I made my way back to the house and only managed to get a little turned around (that's an achievement for me; I'm not known for my sense of direction, especially in the dark).

I ran in and grabbed all my stuff as quickly as I could. Not surprisingly, the Zombie that got me was still there, and it attacked me. I used the first weapon I could get to—an Axe—and hit the Zombie. When it was pushed back, it fell into the ledges leading down to my mine tunnel, and it was so dark that it was hard to tell where it was and when it was making its approach. After one good strike, I ran up my staircase and placed the Door, so nothing else could find its way to me. Finally, I dispatched the Zombie. I thought that I was safe.

I had a brief enough moment to start to make some Charcoal. I hadn't found any Coal, so that was the only way to get light and make a Torch. It was then that I realized that I still wasn't alone. There was a second Zombie in there! With that one dispatched, I could finally rest.

The Wood in the Furnace yielded a precious piece of Charcoal, and I made a few Torches. I put them around the top of my home. Thankfully, dawn was approaching.

In preparation for my next foray, I worked on the house to finish any straggling walls and then gave

my place a ceiling. The last thing I needed was for it to rain Zombies the next night.

I also killed a few Pigs for their meat. I figured that I'd need it, even if I did feel a bit guilty about it.

I started cooking the Pork and then made my way back down my mine, hoping to accomplish something productive.

The mine proved to be a bottomless pit of empty shaft and endless Cobblestone. Apart from the small vein of Iron, I found nothing else useful. It soon became clear that if I wanted any type of light, I would have to get it from forestry. The swamp trees were my only source of energy, so I spent some time chopping down a few.

I figured, at this point, at least I could make sure that my house wasn't a total wreck. I'd been caught out the first evening and used too many materials to make my walls. This evening, I replaced everything with Cobblestone, which made it look marginally better. I had no shortage of Cobblestone.

I also had enough Iron to make a Bucket, which served me well. I made two Iron Pickaxes (sadly, they proved useless in the end because I never found anything but Stone in the mine).

Finally, I did a small scout of the nearby area. Although it could be very dangerous, filled with Slimes, Creepers, and nightly Zombies, there were abundant natural resources above ground. I found Sugar Cane as well as Cows and Chickens. I didn't have to hunt for Water, and there were more than a few patches of pretty blue flowers.

As the challenge moved toward its conclusion, I decided it was time to create something attractive on the property, as best I could. I'm usually compulsive: I like the tunnels that I create to be regular and smooth, and if I have enough patience, I sometimes even make the walls out of smooth stone (or anything other than Cobblestone) after I've harvested a vein of something. I obviously didn't have time for that, but I also never found anything that would mess up my mining tunnels either.

I expanded my entry room and made a few Chests in which to store things. There wasn't much space in the entry area, so I chose the bottom of the mine as my area of beautification.

I used my Bucket to grab Water, went downstairs, and hollowed out a room. I removed the Granite blocks in the room, because they were somewhat unattractive. A small outline of Diorite blocks provided

contrast, and I made a fountain, with a waterfall tucked into the back wall. Finally, flowers made it look a little brighter down there.

I left the mine and went upstairs to find that it was dark once again. Well, if you only have a brief amount of time, best live it up! I wandered outside and planted a Carrot (dropped by one of the many Zombies in the region). You never know when a carrot will be useful!

Sadly, despite all the wildlife, I never found Sheep. So I couldn't make a bed. I spent the remaining time trying to make the house look a bit nicer by adding a couple more flowers in front.

I have to say that although it wasn't the paradise that I first envisioned, this place did have real potential. It was a fixer-upper, but one that held a lot of promise.

FINAL LEVEL: 5

EQUIPMENT: Nothing of Note. But at least I had a Bucket!

TYPE OF BUILDING: Survival Cottage

Chris Burton

The random world that I was put in had good access to basic resources, with handy trees and a nice mountain range for Stone and (hopefully) Coal and Iron. A quick runaround knocking down trees got me the basic tools needed for further expansion. The grassy plains supported numerous herds of cattle, which provided lots of food for the rest of the build. Fifty-one Steaks will take you a long way in *Minecraft*!

My initial dig yielded Coal within the first layer, and quickly broke through into a small tunnel system. Going left took me to a small Sandstone deposit and underground pond, but the right path was far more extensive.

The moans of Zombies prompted me to seal the right tunnel off quickly with Dirt. No need to take any risks!

Without a Bed (or Sheep), I was going to have to make a choice. I could push on, hoping to find Sheep quickly, or I could risk it all and go without sleeping.

Despite the risk of respawning far away from familiar surroundings, I decided to proceed without a safety net. I'd just have to stay cautious, keep everything well lit, and watch my steps.

The first night cycle came all too fast. I sealed off my tunnel to the surface and concentrated on mining the Sandstone cave and converting what little Iron I found into useable ingots. I had a couple of minor mishaps. A Creeper somehow got behind me, but my panicked punching caused it to fall off the ledge and into the underground pond, where it exploded without killing me. I also found a random block of Silverfish but managed to kill the obnoxious little thing before it caused any trouble.

Daylight let me come out of the cave and explore a bit. I had noticed a few cacti over the hill and wanted to see if there was a more extensive desert. I kind of wanted to do something with the Sandstone, so I was very

happy when I crested the hill and found a Mesa biome. In addition to a very good view, it had lots of Sand, a large lake that I could use as a water source, and some Cacti and Sugar Cane that I could use as decorations.

I decided I wanted to make a floating oasis. I would make a new home base of Sand and Sandstone, floating in the sky, accessible by waterfall. I had nearly everything I needed. I quickly shoveled a couple of stacks of Sand and used my precious Iron to make Buckets and an Iron Pick.

With nightfall approaching, I wanted to get the basics in place. I made a pillar of Dirt in the middle of the lake, and then built the foundation of my new floating home around the top of the Dirt pillar. There were no apparent monsters (and I was on a floating Sandstone platform), so I wasn't too worried about working through the night. I had three Buckets of Water, so when I ran out of Sandstone, I lit the place with Torches and used the water to make a waterfall. I'd have an easy way back up, and getting down was as simple as jumping off the edge into the lake!

The remainder of the night was spent mining Sandstone, refilling Buckets, and waiting for the sun to come back up.

I had one more day/night cycle (20 minutes) left in the challenge, so it was full speed ahead. I had all the materials, so the first order of business was finishing the foundation. Once that was done, I put Sand on top and around the edges. Filling the pool in the middle of the oasis was as simple as using Bucket after Bucket of water from the lake below, with the waterfall providing a handy way back to my new home. Once the structure was completed, I removed the initial Dirt pillar. Night fell during the final construction, so I was coming to the end.

With night well underway, I put Torches around the edge to light everything. A Crafting Table let me build Chests for storing the remaining items, and a Forge served to cook a nice celebratory Steak dinner. Some Sugar Cane and Cacti added a touch of color to the oasis. There was only one thing missing: a Bed.

With five minutes left, I ran around the plains near my initial dig site looking for Sheep. As the clock ticked down, I saw them in the distance: there was a small herd of the fluffy white creatures! With no time for subtlety, I "sheared" them with my Shovel and ran with the Wool back to my base. With just a minute remaining, I finished my new home with a lovely new Bed to sleep in. As the challenge ended, I thought that it might be interesting to create a system of sky islands going higher and higher, with waterfalls pouring into one another.

But that would have to wait for another time! The last second of the clocked ticked, and the challenge was over.

FINAL LEVEL: 9

EQUIPMENT: No armor. Stone Sword and Iron Pickaxe.

TYPE OF BUILDING: Hanging Garden

Michael Lummis

The world popped to life, and I saw Pigs, Grasslands, a few Trees, and no immediate dangers. This was a nice area, but I still decided to immediately grab some Wood and begin digging deep. My hope was to get plenty of Stone, Iron, Coal, and maybe some rare materials so my structures at the end of the period wouldn't be simple Cobblestone. I wanted to do better than that!

The initial dig down was dangerous. I dug directly under my feet (usually a no-no), but I had few materials to lose and was willing to take the risk. Only 10 blocks in, I broke through an open cavern and had a minor fall. It didn't do any serious damage to my character, but I saw several monsters moving around in the shadows. That wasn't good. I kept digging as quickly as possible.

A Zombie fell onto my head after a few seconds, but luckily I'd crafted an Axe and was able to switch to it, kill the darn thing, and continue digging. Nothing else fell on top of me, though I was half expecting a bad case of Creeper head. Phew. In a 1x1 space, any Creeper would have obliterated me.

I soon reached a Y Value of 12; that's my favorite spot for digging because it lets you see plenty of possible locations for Diamonds. There was Redstone all over the place, but I didn't find Coal immediately. Without Torches, life was difficult for a short time. But I grabbed Stone, made a Furnace, and then used a small amount of Wood to burn my old wooden tools. I turned them into Charcoal to get a few Torches made. With that, I had light!

From there, I started on some tunnels. Coal and Iron were almost immediate finds, so I switched to Iron tools. There was no reason to hold on for the future, because we only had an hour to work with. Why waste even seconds just to save on Iron?

With a decent supply of Redstone coming in, I began to wonder what I could build. I'd need to make a passage to the surface if I wanted to make a building up there. But maybe I could create something nifty down here in the deep instead. That would save the minutes it would take to make it back up. Hmmmmm. A lava cave would be perfect, and that was what I wanted to break into the most. Every time I heard bubbling, I dug around in several directions to try and find where it was coming from.

I continued to tunnel and search until almost 25 minutes had gone by. I found an eight-stone Diamond vein! I also got more than enough Iron to do whatever I needed. But I'd been foolish and hurried down here before gathering enough Wood or food. This was a major mistake, because I was suddenly low on Sticks for additional tools and Torches. And my character was going to begin starving soon.

In addition to that, I hadn't found a lava cavern. An underground lava fort would have rocked. But needs must be met, and dying there in the deep wouldn't help me very much. I tunneled to the surface, stocked up on a little Wood, and killed nearby Rabbits and Pigs with my Diamond Sword. Totally necessary.

With only half of my time left, I might have to create a surface building instead of an underground one. That was fine. It would still be very interesting to see what I could do. And I had enough interesting materials to spice up the building.

The next 15-minute burst was frantic. I had some decent things to work with, but time was running short. Now on the surface, I ate, searched quickly for a scenic spot, and found a lake nearby. That was what I decided to focus on. I could make a beachfront building maybe.

Or I could be a little more ambitious. Instead of heading down to the beach, I used a local hill to build out and over the lake. Crouching for safety, I laid the blocks under my feet and created a foundation in the middle of the air. Initially, I threw down Cobblestone just to get an idea what I was doing, but then I trashed the floor and started to replace it with Glass blocks (there was ample Sand below, and that was quick to harvest and cook). Having a Glass floor was nifty because it made the place look kind of scary.

There is never enough time in these challenges, so the last 15 minutes put me under a lot of pressure. There was so much more that I'd been planning to do, but that's why this event is so hard. I tried to decorate quickly.

Using Diorite and Granite, I gave the ceiling a bit more style, and I finished the Glass floor. Then I destroyed the land bridge that I'd made to start the place, and added supports underneath the four corners of the building. This made the place look more natural and enjoyable. The next day dawned, and that was that. I then went to see what everyone else made!

FINAL LEVEL: 13

EQUIPMENT: Iron Tools, Diamond Sword, almost a full suit of Iron Armor.

TYPE OF BUILDING: Fort Overlooking a Lake

MORE FUN WITH FRIENDS

You can obviously expand challenges like this to encompass more people, longer durations, or have specific goals in mind. Largest buildings, the highest level, etc. As with most of *Minecraft*, you can really go anywhere and do anything you want with these games.

Playing like this on a LAN is one of the best ways to bring your friends together to enjoy the game, but it's still fun to have people join the same server even if they're coming from all over the world. Consider setting up a voice server of some sort to make the game even more fun. There are many ways to do this, even if you don't want to spend any money.

TOOLS, RESOURCES, AND CONSUMABLES

This chapter shows you all of the items in *Minecraft*. The following index has everything in one place. After the index, we break all of the information into more detailed entries.

INDEX

NAME	CATEGORY	PAGE
Dragon Egg	Blocks and Resources	143
Dropper	Crafting	174
Dyed Wool	Crafting	175
Egg	Food and Food Ingredients	203
Emerald Ore	Blocks and Resources	143
Empty Map	Tools	216
Enchanted Book	Crafting	175
Enchanted Golden Apple	Food and Food Ingredients	204
Enchantment Table	Crafting	175
End Portal Block	Blocks and Resources	144
End Stone	Blocks and Resources	144
Ender Chest	Crafting	176
Ender Pearl	Common Items	159
Eye of Ender	Crafting	176
Farmland	Blocks and Resources	144
Feather	Common Items	160
Fence	Crafting	177
Fence Gate	Crafting	177
Fermented Spider Eye	Crafting	177
Fire	Blocks and Resources	144
Fire Charge	Tools	217
Fireworks	Common Items	160
Fishing Rod	Tools	217
Flint	Common Items	160
Flint and Steel	Tools	217
Flower Pot	Crafting	178
Furnace	Crafting	178
Ghast Tear	Common Items	160
Glass Bottle	Crafting	178
Glass Pane	Crafting	179
Glistering Melon	Crafting	179
Glowstone	Crafting	179
Glowstone Dust	Common Items	161
Gold Block	Food and Food Ingredients	204
Gold Ingot	Crafting	180
Gold Nugget	Crafting	180
Gold Ore	Blocks and Resources	145
Golden Apple	Food and Food Ingredients	204
Golden Carrot	Food and Food Ingredients	205
Granite	Crafting	180
Grass	Blocks and Resources	145
Gravel	Blocks and Resources	145
Gray Dye	Crafting	181
Gunpowder	Common Items	161
Hardened Clay	Blocks and Resources	145
Hay Bale	Crafting	181
Helmet	Weapons and Armor	220
Hoe	Tools	218
Hopper	Crafting	181

TOOLS, RESOURCES, AND CONSUMABLES

BLOCKS AND RESOURCES

This section covers the objects that make up most of the world in *Minecraft*. Most of the blocks here are for either ground cover, such as Dirt, Stone, Bedrock, and Netherrack, or for structures that appear on top of those blocks (including various flowers and decorations).

Air

LOCATION	GATHERED WITH	USES
Empty space throughout all worlds	N/A	N/A

You cannot mine or collect air. It is all around, making up the *Minecraft* world's empty space, but it has a major use for your character.

When you remove an object from an area, air is left behind. This is true even when surrounded by Water or Lava, though these substances quickly flow into the empty space unless there is something to stop them.

Allium

LOCATION	GATHERED WITH	USES
Flower Forest	Anything	Magenta Dye Recipe

Allium is a pink flower found in Flower Forest areas. You can harvest it with your bare hands and use it to create Magenta Dye. One piece of Allium creates two pieces of Magenta Dye.

Azure Bluet

LOCATION	GATHERED WITH	USES
Plains, Sunflower Plains, and Flower Forests	Anything	Light Gray Dye

Azure Bluet is a light-colored flower found in multiple biomes. Each piece harvested can be replanted for decoration or used to make Light Gray Dye in a 1:1 ratio.

Banner

LOCATION	GATHERED WITH	USES
Crafted	Anything	Awesome decorations

Banners are crafted to decorate regions with many different styles. You can place Banners on the ground, onto walls, put them in Item Frames, and arrange them in different orientations. Creatures can move through Banners as if they weren't there, so don't count on these as barriers against enemy movement.

The initial Wool color determines the base color of the Banner you're making. Once completed, you can then decorate the Banner by crafting it with a huge array of materials. This can be a costly process, if the ingredients are hard to come by. To compensate for that, it's possible to copy Banner patterns. This way you can make multiple awesome-looking Banners and only need to spend the Wool and Sticks for each new Banner while retaining your symbol. Do this by crafting using your completed Banner and a plain Banner of the same color.

RECIPE

INGREDIENTS	CRAFTING RECIPE	RESULT
Wool (6), Stick	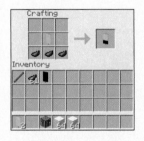	Banner

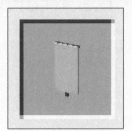

RECIPE

INGREDIENTS	CRAFTING RECIPE	RESULT
Banner (2)	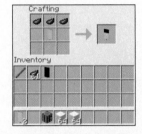	Both Banners must have the same base color, and one Banner must be free of patterns; it will receive the final pattern of the other Banner

Stripe Patterns

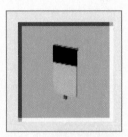

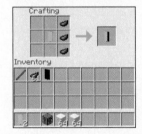

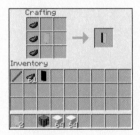

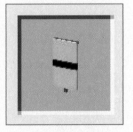
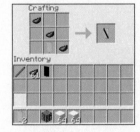

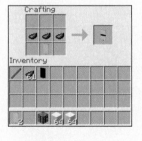

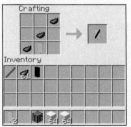

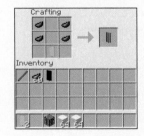

Stripe Patterns (continued)

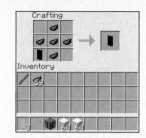

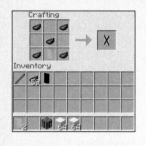

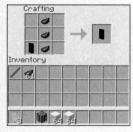

Halftone Patterns

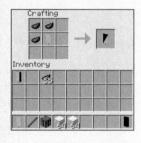

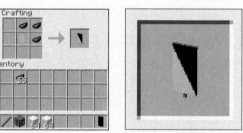

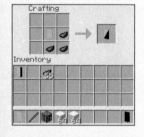

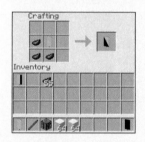

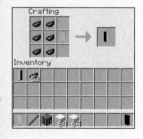

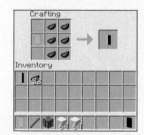

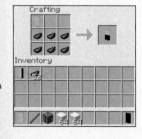

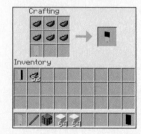

Shapes

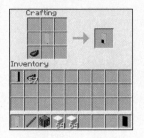 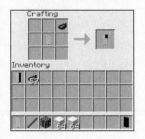 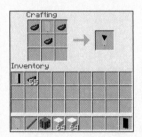  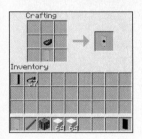

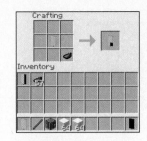 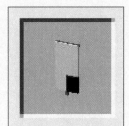 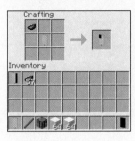 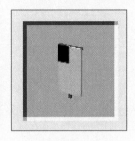  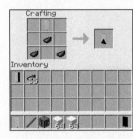 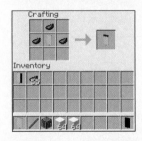   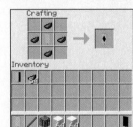

    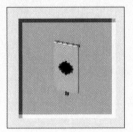

Borders

  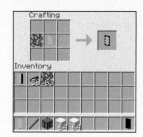 

Backgrounds

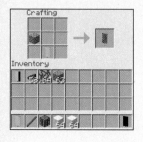 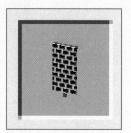 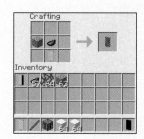 

Gradients

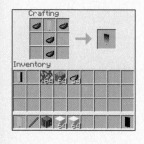 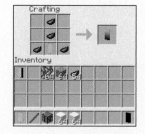 

Symbols

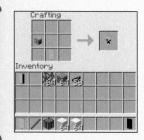 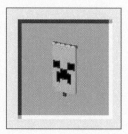 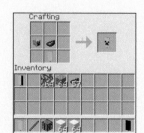 

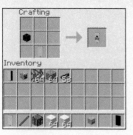
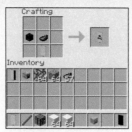
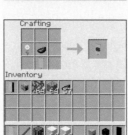

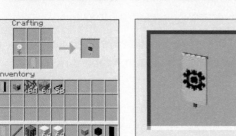
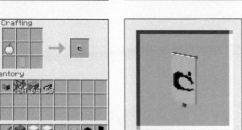
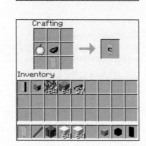

Bedrock

LOCATION	GATHERED WITH	USES
Bottom of all worlds and at the top of the Nether	N/A	N/A

Bedrock normally prevents players from getting outside the borders of the world. You find it commonly near the bottom of the Overworld (until eventually it covers everything). It's also at the bottom and top of the Nether. Normal mining and explosions do not damage Bedrock. Only special cheat codes or specific circumstances can be used to damage even a single piece of the rock.

When you see Bedrock, that's your hint that it's time to mine outward instead of downward!

Blue Orchid

LOCATION	GATHERED WITH	USES
Swamps	Anything	Light Blue Dyes

Blue Orchids are found in Swamp biomes and make Light Blue Dye in a 1:1 ratio. They're quite pretty, so it's nice to gather them for Flower Pots if you like their color.

Cactus

LOCATION	GATHERED WITH	USES
Deserts, Mesas	Axe	Refined into Cactus Green (a dye), trash pits

Cacti are spiky plants that you usually find in the desert. They hurt any player or monster that tries to bump into them, so be careful when you walk near a patch of these things. Use an axe to chop a few down if you'd like to harvest them. If you dig out the block beneath a cactus, that also causes the plant to drop.

A very fun trick is to make a garbage pit with Cacti inside. These plants destroy almost anything that comes into contact with them. You can dig out a modest pit with room for Cacti on each side, and then throw anything you're done with into the pit.

Note that Cacti grow on sand, so harvest some while you're in the area. Bring the plants home and create your own patch as decoration or to injure monsters that come close to your home.

Coal Ore

LOCATION	GATHERED WITH	USES
In areas of Stone blocks	Pickaxes	Burning in a furnace

Coal Ore is a fairly common sight in large, stony areas. Dig through the Stone until you see flecks of dark material in the walls, and focus on harvesting those as often as possible. This nets a fair amount of experience for your character, and it gives you free fuel for your furnaces! Coal is a long-lasting material for burning, so you can smelt ore, cook food, and keep your home looking nice and cozy for days on end.

Cobblestone

LOCATION	GATHERED WITH	USES
Seen in special areas (such as Strongholds and Dungeons)	Pickaxes	Construction material, used for making stone tools, Furnaces, Dispensers, and many other items

Cobblestone is one of the most common crafting ingredients in the game. You get it by cutting into Stone with a Pickaxe; simply beating on Stone with your bare hands will not work. Make a Wooden Pickaxe, break a few Stones, and then go back to make a Stone Pickaxe for yourself. Now you're ready to harvest Cobblestone in large quantities.

You can make buildings, tools, and decorative items all with the same Cobblestone. It's great stuff, and you can always get more without investing much time. Dig down into the soil, and there's likely to be more Stone waiting to be found.

Because Cobblestone always orients itself the same direction after you place it, these blocks offer a way to see which direction you're heading. Look very closely at the top of a Cobblestone block. In the block's upper-left, when you're facing north, there is a small "L" on the stones. Use this as a way to tell where you're going if you can't see the sun or moon and don't have a map or compass.

Cobweb

LOCATION	GATHERED WITH	USES
Mine Shafts	Shears that have Silk Touch	Slows movement (when walking or falling)

Cobwebs are naturally found in abandoned mine shafts. They slow down anything that tries to move through them, so put them in areas with your traps to make them even more effective.

You cannot harvest Cobwebs with normal equipment because they're fragile. You need a set of Shears enchanted with Silk Touch to gather Cobwebs without breaking them. Afterward, you're free to hang these Halloween decorations wherever you like. Place them near a Tripwire with a nasty trap or two.

Cocoa

LOCATION	GATHERED WITH	USES
Grow on Jungle Trees	Anything	Making Cookies and Brown Dye

Cocoa grows on Jungle Trees, so it's exclusive to specific biomes. Once you find the trees, harvest some Cocoa Beans to bring home and plant on the trunk of a Jungle Tree to start your own Cocoa farm. You need only a single block of a Jungle Tree to work with, so grow such a tree and cut it down except for its trunk.

Then plant your Cocoa Beans and wait for their third growth stage to harvest them. Break them open, collect the Beans, and you're ready to replant and repeat the process. You can use Cocoa Beans to make Cookies (a low quality food item) or a dark brown Dye.

Command Block

LOCATION	GATHERED WITH	USES
Special	N/A	Use specific commands when activated by a Redstone current

You can put Command Blocks into custom maps by using the following text entry:

```
command /give <player name> minecraft: command_block
<desired quantity>
```

Command Blocks are complex items that most players don't mess around with. However, if you're making a world for Adventure mode, these handy tools let you create teleporters, traps, and even control the game world directly.

Dandelion

LOCATION	GATHERED WITH	USES
Common grassy flower	Anything	Makes Dandelion Yellow Dye, or is used as decoration

Dandelions are easy to find because they grow in many biomes: Plains, Forest, and others as well. You won't have trouble getting your hands on these. A single flower can be turned into Dye whenever you like, or you can plant them on your own in grass, tilled dirt, or regular dirt.

And that's about all there is to Dandelions. They're pretty much weeds.

Dead Bush

LOCATION	GATHERED WITH	USES
Hot/Arid areas of the Overworld	Shears	Decoration only

Dead Bushes are available in warmer areas and cannot be gathered without using Shears. They're drab in color and aren't used in any crafting recipes. If you want to make a place look inhospitable, they're somewhat useful for that.

Diamond Ore

LOCATION	GATHERED WITH	USES
Deep inside the Overworld	Iron or Diamond Pickaxes	High-quality tools

Diamond blocks are found in the Overworld's lowest levels. If you press F3 to look at your character's position, you can see your "Y" value. This tells you how close you are to the bottom of the world. Diamond is found only between 0-15 in the "Y" values. This means you have to dig far down into the earth to collect any of them, and it's rare even at those depths.

Also, bring at least an Iron Pickaxe when you hunt for diamonds. It's impossible to mine these blocks when you have inferior equipment. If you find Iron Ore on the way down, you can always make a Workbench, a Furnace, refine the Iron, and craft an Iron Pickaxe right there.

The tools you make with Diamonds are the best in the game. Always focus your best enchantments on them, because these items last for a very long time. They're amazing!

Dirt

LOCATION	GATHERED WITH	USES
The Overworld	Shovels	Construction and farming

Dirt is one of the easiest things to gather in *Minecraft*. Use it to make sod buildings, obstacles, or to lay the foundation for some farmland (many crops grow on Dirt). Grass blocks become Dirt when you dig them up, and Dirt that you place in direct sunlight often shifts to a Grass block eventually.

Shovels let you dig into Dirt very effectively, but any object can be used to harvest Dirt, including your bare hands. To turn regular Dirt into tilled Farmland, use a Hoe.

Dragon Egg

LOCATION	GATHERED WITH	USES
The End	Special Technique	None yet

Dragon Eggs fall when you slay the Ender Dragon. You cannot walk up and harvest a Dragon Egg normally; it'll teleport away from your character and could even end up being irretrievable. Instead, you need to dig underneath the Dragon Egg two blocks down. Place a Torch there, and then break the block between the Dragon Egg and the Torch. Collect the egg after it "breaks" on the Torch. Use this same technique to quickly harvest Gravel or Sand by dropping their blocks onto a Torch. It's a neat trick.

Emerald Ore

LOCATION	GATHERED WITH	USES
Extreme Hills biomes, well below the surface	Iron or Diamond Pickaxes	Trading with villagers

Emerald Ore is brutal to find. Don't even look for it outside of Extreme Hills; you must locate one of those biomes and then create a mine that leads below a "Y" value of 30. Emeralds are down there, but not very many of them. They're spread out and don't occur in veins, so finding them requires patience.

If at all possible, bring a Pickaxe with Fortune any time you hunt for Emeralds. These enchantments make your time so much more productive because you get many extra Emeralds (2x - 4x, depending on how good your enchantment is and how lucky you are).

End Portal Block

LOCATION	GATHERED WITH	USES
Strongholds	N/A	Create a Portal into The End

Each Overworld has several Strongholds hidden within a certain area, not too far from where the first player begins his or her journey. End Portal Blocks (also called End Portal Frames in some versions of the game) are inside these Strongholds.

Insert Eyes of Ender into these blocks to complete a Portal. Every End Portal Block must be charged by Eyes of Ender before the Portal begins to function. When it does, you can travel into The End and face the threat of the Ender Dragon!

End Stone

LOCATION	GATHERED WITH	USES
The End	Pickaxe	Construction material

End Stone is a block type that dominates The End. It's resistant to damage and explosions, so it's a decent building material if you manage to harvest enough of it. The only problem is you can't easily pop back and forth to The End until you slay the Ender Dragon. That said, there is a way to gather this stone even if you haven't killed the dragon yet. To do this, place an Ender Chest in The End, harvest the stones, and put your loot in the chest. This way, when you die in The End and respawn in the Overworld, your stones will be waiting in any Ender Chests you place there!

At this time, there aren't any crafting recipes that use End Stone.

Farmland

LOCATION	GATHERED WITH	USES
Villages	Shovels	Growing crops

Farmland is created when you use a Hoe on Dirt or Grass blocks. This nice, tilled soil lets you grow a variety of items, with Wheat being the most common. Plant seeds in your Farmland and give them time to grow to create a renewable source of food.

Proper growth requires light (from any source), a Water block that is at most four tiles away, and time. We discuss farming in detail at several points in this book, because it's a great way to keep your characters fed!

Fire

LOCATION	GATHERED WITH	USES
The Nether	N/A	Destruction or decoration

You can find Fire on its own in the Nether, but it can be triggered in other areas with the use of Lava, Flint and Steel, lightning strikes, and from various enemy attacks. Whenever fire touches vulnerable wooden objects, it spreads, igniting them as well. This can destroy wooded areas and buildings and put characters at risk.

To fight fires, either attack the flames directly by hitting the object that's on fire, put blocks on top of the fire, or douse the area with Water. Whatever you do, work quickly! A small fire can quickly become one that's too large to handle.

Gold Ore

LOCATION	GATHERED WITH	USES
Deep inside the Overworld	Iron or Diamond Pickaxes	Create Gold Ingots that are used for golden tools, clocks, armor, and a few special items

You can find Gold between the Bedrock and "Y" values up to 30 in the Overworld. It's a bright yellow ore that is very easy to spot once you uncover it. Make sure you use an Iron or Diamond Pickaxe, and then harvest it like you would any other type of ore.

Once refined into Gold Ingots, you can do many things with this metal. Golden tools, weapons, and armor are pretty but not terribly effective. It's best to save most of your gold for Clocks, Golden Apples, and Redstone construction (because certain powered items require Gold).

Grass

LOCATION	GATHERED WITH	USES
Dirt areas that are exposed to decent levels of light	Shovels	Same as Dirt

Grass blocks are found wherever Dirt is given good light and time to grow. Grass itself grows on top of Grass blocks; flowers and shrubs can also grow this way. Dig into Grass blocks to collect Dirt, or cut through the Grass above with any object to grab Seeds. The best way to get material for a Wheat farm is to rip up huge swaths of Grass until you have enough Seeds to start your farm. If the Grass is thick enough, you can get dozens of Seeds in just a minute or two of running around. That's enough to kick start a farming project.

Gravel

LOCATION	GATHERED WITH	USES
The Overworld	Shovels	Gathering Flint

Gravel appears in areas with Dirt and Stone. It has a more rugged surface, so you can tell what is Stone and what is Gravel with just a glance. When tiles underneath Gravel are destroyed, the Gravel blocks above fall into place as if affected by gravity. This is true for Sand as well. Make sure to avoid standing underneath Gravel when you mine, because your character takes damage if you're struck by falling Gravel.

A quick way to harvest this material is to dig down two blocks under the stack of Gravel. Put a Torch underneath the Gravel stack before destroying the block of Stone or Dirt that holds the Gravel in place. This causes the entire stack of Gravel to fall onto the Torch, destroying the blocks and turning them into a resource that's easy to gather. Quick mining without even damaging your tools. That's pretty nifty, eh?

Hardened Clay

LOCATION	GATHERED WITH	USES
Mesas, Deserts, and River areas	Pickaxe	Construction material

Clay is a natural block in the Overworld. You can find heavy concentrations of it in certain biomes, such as Rivers and Mesas. Collect these blocks as if you're mining Stone. Bring them back to your house to use as a construction material with even more decorative options.

You can make Hardened Clay by cooking Clay in your Furnace. Hardened Clay can then be stained with any dyeing agent to give it a more desirable color.

Huge Mushroom

LOCATION	GATHERED WITH	USES
Mushroom Islands and Roofed Forests	Axe	Gathering Mushrooms, Shade Farming

Mushrooms grow in low or no-light areas. Huge Mushrooms are really cool-looking and grow naturally in somewhat uncommon biomes. If you want to reproduce these interesting features, use Bone Meal to grow regular Mushrooms into their giant cousins.

Because Mushrooms prefer areas with low light, they're great for making underground farms.

Ice

LOCATION	GATHERED WITH	USES
Cold areas	Any tool with Silk Touch	Decoration, Transportation

Ice forms in cold regions of the Overworld. One often sees it on the surface of Water, but it can also be on open ground. You can smash Ice with a Pickaxe (or any other object if you're willing to spend more time).

Movement on Ice is fast and slippery. This makes it possible to cross distances quickly and jump a bit farther as well.

Placing smaller blocks on top of Ice is interesting. For example, a Stone Slab on top of Ice retains the slippery characteristic that is common on Ice. If you run Water over Ice, this property works as well, so Water transportation over Ice is faster than it otherwise should be. Some players use this as a way to rapidly funnel objects that fall into Water to a central area.

Iron Ore

LOCATION	GATHERED WITH	USES
Underground, in the Overworld	Pickaxe	Powerful tools

Iron Ore is a modestly common mineral that appears throughout the world. It can appear at practically any elevation, as long as there are Stone and Dirt blocks present. Look for a brownish, rusty tinge to a Stone block. That's what Iron Ore looks like.

After mining Iron Ore, you must smelt it in a Furnace before it turns into Iron Ingots; these are what you need for your recipes. Toss all of your Iron Ore into the Furnace and wait for it to cook completely. Remove the Iron Ingots and try making a variety of tools with it, including improved basic tools (Pickaxes being the best choice), Shears, Buckets, and more.

Smelted metals give you experience after you remove them from a Furnace. It's not a huge bonus, but it's still nice to get.

Lapis Lazuli Ore

LOCATION	GATHERED WITH	USES
Deep under the Overworld	Pickaxe	Decorative elements

Lapis Lazuli is a blue mineral found in very deep tunnels under the ground. Your "Y" location value should be near 15 to find Lapis Lazuli. It's easy to mine with any decent Pickaxe, and it doesn't take long to gather. Veins of this mineral often yield a large amount of the blocks, so you come back with a good haul if you find even one or two veins.

Large Fern

LOCATION	GATHERED WITH	USES
Grass blocks	Shears or any tools	Decoration

Ferns grow in Jungles, Taigas, and Mega Taigas. They appear on grass blocks, much like regular Grass, Dead Bushes, and Tall Grass. You can find smaller and larger Ferns, but the main difference between them is that you get two Ferns if you cut them down with Shears.

Ferns can be broken with any tool to get Seeds, or cut down with Shears to harvest for decoration. If you want to make an area look nice with Ferns, build Flower Pots and plant Ferns in them around your property.

Ferns are usually spaced out a bit, so they're not necessarily a great source of Seeds. Thick areas of Grass are superior, because you can harvest it much faster.

Lava

LOCATION	GATHERED WITH	USES
The Overworld or the Nether	Bucket	Light, Furnace fuel, garbage disposal

One frequently finds Lava in the deep recesses of the Overworld, and it's even more common in the Nether, where it is practically the world's lifeblood. You can sometimes even find Lava near or on the Overworld's surface if you're lucky. Or unlucky, as the case may be.

Lava is quite dangerous. It sets flammable things on fire if they come into contact with it or stay too long beside it. Anything that catches fire takes damage over time—armor can't save you from this. If you're on fire, jump into Water or pour out Water from a Bucket to save yourself. It's possible to survive Lava without Water, but you must have a great deal of health before you're set aflame.

Lava makes a telltale bubbling noise when you're nearby. Always use caution when you hear this noise so you don't wander over an edge and fall in. It's difficult to swim out of Lava once you're in it.

Pour Water over Lava to create Obsidian blocks, a type of dark, hard rock that can be used for special construction. If Lava is poured over Water instead, you end up with Cobblestone.

Leaves

LOCATION	GATHERED WITH	USES
On Trees	Shears	Decoration

Trees automatically spawn Leaves around themselves. These blocks prevent easy movement, so they're sometimes quite annoying. Destroy them with any tool that you have, or use your bare hands if you like. Shears gather Leaves instead of destroying them, but at least they're very quick about finishing the task.

Breaking Leaves provides a chance to drop items, including Saplings of the Tree that spawned the Leaves. You might also get an Apple here and there, but this isn't a reliable way to get much food.

If you destroy every Wood block on a Tree, the Leaves nearby begin to disappear, dropping Saplings or Apples as if they were destroyed by hand. If you want to clear Leaves and have some time, simply kill the Tree and walk away. The Leaves go away on their own, and you don't have to bother with anything.

Lilac

LOCATION	GATHERED WITH	USES
Forest and Flower Forest biomes	Anything	Magenta Dye

Lilacs are harvested from certain forests, and you can easily turn them into Magenta Dye. If you cut them with Shears, you can plant them as decoration around your house. They have a pleasing color, so you might as well grab a few if you find a place where they grow.

Lily Pad

LOCATION	GATHERED WITH	USES
Grows on Water blocks in swampy areas	Anything	Decoration, bridges

Lily Pads grow on top of the Water in swamps, and you also occasionally find them when you fish. These items are decorative, but they have minor functionality as well. It's possible to walk on top of Lily Pads, so they're sometimes used as bridges when people don't feel like bringing blocks of heavier material all the way out to a waterway.

Monster Egg

LOCATION	GATHERED WITH	USES
Deep in the Overworld	Anything	Spawns Silverfish

Stone isn't always what it appears to be. Certain blocks of Cobblestone, regular Stone, and Stone Bricks are actually Monster Eggs. They break to reveal Silverfish, nasty little beasts that try to call their friends to swarm you.

One most often finds Silverfish in strongholds and underneath Extreme Hills biomes. It takes a bit more time to break a Monster Egg compared to a normal block of the same type, so it's possible to realize that you're dealing with one before you unleash the beast. When this happens, it's best to back off and mine elsewhere.

Monster Spawner

LOCATION	GATHERED WITH	USES
Special areas	Pickaxe	Creates monsters!

Monster Spawners are found in rare areas: dungeons, abandoned mineshafts, Strongholds, and Nether fortresses. These blocks create a specific type of monster; you can tell which by looking inside the Spawner's cage.

Conditions must be right for a Monster Spawner to create one of its creatures. If you illuminate an area around a Monster Spawner, then it cannot generate any creature that wouldn't normally appear in bright areas. This provides a way to deactivate Monster Spawners without breaking them. Make the conditions poor for the monsters, and then you have the option of setting up a kill room. Monster Spawners with deadly traps are a great way to generate free experience for your character!

TOOLS, RESOURCES, AND CONSUMABLES

Moss Stone

LOCATION	GATHERED WITH	USES
Dungeons, jungle temples, and Mega Taiga biomes	Pickaxe	Decoration and construction

Moss Stones are blocks of Stone that have vines growing on top of them. They're pretty cool-looking and let you spice up your home base. Gather these with any normal Pickaxe, or make your own by crafting Cobblestone and Vines together.

RECIPE

INGREDIENTS	CRAFTING RECIPE		RESULT
Cobblestone, Vines		→	Moss Stone

Mycelium

LOCATION	GATHERED WITH	USES
Mushroom Islands	Shovel	Mushroom farming

Mycelium is a special type of Dirt block. You find it all around Mushroom Islands, and it allows Mushrooms to grow well even in direct light. If you want to spread Mycelium, cut Grass off of the Dirt blocks around Mycelium to give it space to grow!

Nether Brick

LOCATION	GATHERED WITH	USES
Nether Fortresses	Pickaxe	Construction

Nether Bricks are the general foundation of Nether Fortresses, a special set of areas in the Nether. These dangerous locations have powerful monsters but the potential for a few rare prizes as well.

Smelt Netherrack to make smaller Nether Bricks. These are crafted in quantities of four to make blocks of Nether Brick. It's non-flammable, but otherwise has no special properties. If you're building a defensive area in the Nether and don't have Cobblestone to use, this is a fair alternative.

RECIPE

INGREDIENTS	CRAFTING RECIPE		RESULT
Nether Brick (4)		→	Nether Brick Block

Nether Quartz Ore

LOCATION	GATHERED WITH	USES
The Nether	Pickaxe	Special tools

Nether Quartz Ore is found commonly in the Nether; it's a pale vein of minerals seen inside of the Netherrack. It looks alarmingly like marbled flesh. Mine Nether Quartz Ore and then smelt it to get Nether Quartz. That material is used for several decorative elements, as well as for Redstone Comparators and Daylight Sensors. Neat stuff!

Nether Wart

LOCATION	GATHERED WITH	USES
The Nether, in Nether Fortresses	Anything	Brewing

Nether Wart is an herb that appears naturally only in the Nether. It grows on top of Soul Sand, so you must have both Nether Wart and Soul Sand anywhere you want to have a Nether Wart garden.

You can't do any substantial brewing work without Nether Wart. It's a core ingredient that leads to almost all good things. So brewing isn't particularly fun or viable until you gather these herbs.

To get them, go into the Nether and search for Nether fortresses. They contain gardens of Nether Wart along certain staircases, and you sometimes find Nether Wart inside Chests in these forts as well.

Netherrack

LOCATION	GATHERED WITH	USES
The Nether	Pickaxe	Construction and decorative fireplaces

This type of stone is found in the Nether, and it's that area's most common resource. It's easy to mine Netherrack, but it doesn't have many uses. It isn't a pretty stone to work with, and it can be a hazard because any fire that gets onto Netherrack burns *forever*.

However, this does point to one neat use of Netherrack. A fireplace is great if you put a piece of Netherrack underneath its viewing area. Light the Netherrack with Flint and Steel, and encase the fire in some type of nicer stone fireplace, so your house doesn't burn down. That's pretty cool.

If you wish, you can also turn Netherrack into Nether Bricks by smelting it. Nether Bricks aren't flammable, so they're more useful and look a little nicer.

Obsidian

LOCATION	GATHERED WITH	USES
Anywhere	Diamond Pickaxe	Construction, Enchanting Tables, Portal to the Nether, specialty items

Obsidian is formed when Lava and Water crash together. This can occur naturally (especially in impressive underground caves) or encouraged by dumping a Water-filled Bucket on top of a Lava pool. The end result is a dense black stone impervious to everything but a Diamond Pickaxe, and even that takes a bit to penetrate the material.

Obsidian has a number of specialty uses in addition to being an impressive construction material. First, you need it to construct Enchanting Tables (which, in turn, can provide enchantments to help you mine Obsidian). It's also required in constructing Nether Portals, the only means to travel to the Nether. It can be used to make Ender Chests, which allow you to access anything stored in them, across any location. Finally, Obsidian is used to make Beacon Blocks, which create skyward light beams and provide status effects to nearby players.

Oxeye Daisy

LOCATION	GATHERED WITH	USES
The Overworld	Anything	Decoration, makes Light Gray Dye

Oxeye Daisies are white flowers with yellow centers. They grow on Grass or Dirt areas in plains and flower forests. They can be used to make Light Gray Dye, but mostly they are simply pretty to look at and add some color to your garden or environment.

Packed Ice

LOCATION	GATHERED WITH	USES
Ice Plains Spikes biome in the Overworld	Pickaxe (with Silk Touch enchantment)	Decoration and construction

Packed Ice is only found in the rare Ice Plains Spikes biome, and it can be harvested only by using the Silk Touch enchantment. Packed Ice blocks are darker, not transparent, and can't melt. If you (or a monster) walk on them, you can slide, which makes Packed Ice walkways slightly faster. Most often, Packed Ice is used to create decorative ice spikes, similar to the area where it's naturally found.

Peony

LOCATION	GATHERED WITH	USES
The Overworld	Anything	Decoration, makes Pink Dye

Peonies are pink flowers that grow on Grass or Dirt in forests or flower forests. They're very pretty plants and can spruce up your home garden, or they can be used to make Pink Dye.

Poppy

LOCATION	GATHERED WITH	USES
The Overworld	Anything	Decoration, makes Rose Red Dye

Bright red poppies are among the most common flowers in the Overworld, found pretty much everywhere except swamps. They make any location more festive and add drama to any dense forest. You can pick Poppies and plant them all around your house and grounds. They can also be crushed down and used in Rose Red Dye.

Prismarine

LOCATION	GATHERED WITH	USES
Crafting Item	Crafted	Decoration

Blocks of Prismarine are used to decorate people's homes and tunnels. Their various forms are made with Prismarine Shards and Ink Sacs (in the case of Dark Prismarine).

Prismarine is a rare type of stone that you won't find except around ocean temples. Make sure to harvest this if you ever see it, because the stones are very useful for colored accents and have their own animation changes over time. Seriously awesome stuff.

RECIPE

INGREDIENTS	CRAFTING RECIPE	RESULT
Prismarine Shard (4)		Prismarine Block
Prismarine Shard (9)		Prismarine Brick
Prismarine Shard (8), Ink Sac		Dark Prismarine

Redstone Ore

LOCATION	GATHERED WITH	USES
Underground, deep in the Overworld	Iron Pickaxe or better	Redstone circuits, Blocks of Redstone, brewing, creating bright lights, Clocks, Compasses, specialty items

You can find Redstone Ore in the bottom 16 levels of the Overworld. You have to dig deep, but once you get there, it isn't too tough to find. Make sure you have at least an Iron Pickaxe with you, because nothing else will release the glowing red ore.

The glow of Redstone is linked to its most wonderful property: it can transmit and conduct energy. Redstone Ore itself produces light and bright red particles when anything nearby touches it, making it useful as a monster alert system.

You can use the Redstone gained when you split Redstone Ore apart even more creatively. Redstone Torches form a power source, and Redstone Dust (also called Redstone Wire) can be sprinkled along a path to transmit that power. Thus, you can use Redstone to make any number of electromechanical creations that can move or shift whenever you want. This includes working Dispensers, Repeaters, Pistons, Droppers, and much more. Any working mine needs a long Minecart rail system marked with Redstone torches and strengthened by Redstone-linked Powered Rails.

You can also use Redstone to make your daily *Minecraft* life a bit more regular; it's a necessary ingredient in both Clocks and Compasses. Clocks help you to plan out your day, and a Compass is a vital piece of equipment for any explorer—it can be a life saver.

Finally, Redstone is a component employed in brewing. It's used to make Mundane Potions (the base for many other potions), and it can be used to strengthen other potions or revert them back to a lower tier.

Redstone Dust (Redstone Wire)

LOCATION	GATHERED WITH	USES
Anywhere	Anything	Redstone circuits

The moment you plunk down a piece of Redstone in the world, it crumbles into Redstone Dust. The pieces of dust make a line capable of transmitting Redstone power from one location to another, which leads to another name for this material: Redstone Wire. Any energy flowing through the line makes it glow bright red.

The essence of Redstone Dust is that it allows you to create working, moving, and shiftable mechanical creations. It's a vital component of Redstone-based circuits. The Redstone Dust links a power source, such as a Redstone Torch, a Lever, or Button, to a transmitter component, such as a Door, a Repeater, a Piston, or an Activator Rail to start a Minecart. This allows you to transmit energy to create a desired effect. For example, you can make a door on the far side of your house open by pressing a button. Or you could climb into a Minecart and ride down into the underground depths. Any types of things are possible with Redstone-powered materials, and you're limited only by your quantity of Redstone Dust and your imagination.

For more information on Redstone, check out the Redstone section in the "You Can Do Anything with a Little Practice" chapter.

Rose Bush

LOCATION	GATHERED WITH	USES
The Overworld	Anything	Decoration, makes Rose Red Dye

These are shy plants, found only in forests and flower forests. However, if you stumble upon them, Rose Bushes are renowned for their beauty. They make a gorgeous addition to any garden, and they can be used to make Rose Red Dye.

Sand

LOCATION	GATHERED WITH	USES
The Overworld, along coasts and in deserts and some mesas (as Red Sand)	Shovel	Construction, Sandstone Blocks, Glass, TNT, farming

Some people may discount Sand as an unimpressive material, but they'd be wrong! While Sand may not seem exciting, it definitely has its uses. Sand can be stacked on its own, as in a seawall against the ocean, or compressed into Sandstone and used to construct anything else. It's also a necessary ingredient for Glass; all you have to do is melt it in a Furnace.

Sand is a wonderful base on which to grow Cacti and Sugar Cane, so it's a nice addition to your farm. Most areas have at least some Sand nearby, so it usually isn't difficult to acquire.

Finally, add some Sand to your Gunpowder to make an explosive creation! TNT can be used to blow up mountains, expand your mines, and generally stir up some fun. You owe it to yourself to at least try to blow something up.

Slime Block

LOCATION	GATHERED WITH	USES
Crafted item	Anything	Transportation

Slime Blocks look almost like living Slime monsters, which makes sense; they're made from Slimeballs. Slime Blocks have a few unique properties. They can make anything bounce that lands on them—including you! If you want a trampoline, you can make a pretty fun one with Slime Blocks. Additionally, they can slow down things that move over them, which makes them useful for traps. Finally, if Water flows over a Slime Block, it speeds up anything moving over it. Build a Slime Block pathway with guard rails just under a river, and you have a perfect transport device. Have your character use it as a quick slide, or shift materials down the river like an old-fashioned logging operation.

Soul Sand

LOCATION	GATHERED WITH	USES
The Nether	Shovel	Traps, transportation, farming, making a Wither

The Nether holds a number of dangers, and wandering into a stretch of Soul Sand doesn't help. This gray-brown substance, often found near large Lava fields, slows down anything walking through it. It's also slightly smaller than most other blocks, adding a slight challenge to getting out of it.

However, Soul Sand's slowing property makes it perfect for traps! A track of Soul Sand around your property can slow down and corral large numbers of monsters, which you can then mow down en masse. This also works against players in PvP multiplayer situations.

Soul Sand is the only material on which to grow Nether Wart, the primary component of all potions. If you're interested in brewing, make sure you have an ample supply of Soul Sand!

Finally, Soul Sand can also be used to summon a horrible monster, a Wither. But you should really know what you're facing before you do this; you don't want to mess with Withers unless you're prepared in advance.

Sponge

LOCATION	GATHERED WITH	USES
The Overworld (Underwater)	Anything	Decoration or absorbing water

Sponges, when dry, absorb up to 65 blocks of Water from the area that they're placed in. Once full, they become Wet Sponges and won't absorb any more Water until they've been dried out in a Furnace.

Sponges are sometimes found when you kill Elder Guardians near an ocean temple. There are also rooms inside some of these temples that have Wet Sponges already inside of them. Break them to steal these rare items and take them home as loot!

Stone

LOCATION	GATHERED WITH	USES
The Overworld	Pickaxe	Construction, some specialty components

Stone is something you seek out in your early days of *Minecraft*. It's one of the most common materials in the Overworld, but sometimes you have to dig before you get to it, depending on your circumstances. From that point on, though, you face no shortage of Stone and Cobblestone (the material produced when you break Stone).

If you want to form your Cobblestone back into Stone, all you have to do is smelt it in a Furnace, turning it back into Stone blocks. You can use these to make Stone Slabs or Stone Bricks. You can also make a few specialty components: Redstone Comparators and Redstone Repeaters.

The most common use of Stone is as a general construction material. It's pretty durable and fairly nice looking, and it has a very realistic appearance. Try using Stone to make a truly impressive castle or bridge!

Stone Brick

LOCATION	GATHERED WITH	USES
Crafted item	Pickaxe, Furnace	Construction, decoration

Stone Brick is a decorative material made from Stone, and it provides a different look than other building materials. Stone Bricks are very similar to Clay Bricks, except they require slightly less material and time to make.

Strongholds and temples use Stone Bricks in their construction, so you can get an idea of what they look like when you visit these locations. Additionally, Stone Bricks can be chiseled (Chiseled Stone Bricks) or covered in moss (Mossy Stone Bricks) for even more decor choices.

Sugar Cane

LOCATION	GATHERED WITH	USES
The Overworld, near Water	Anything	Farming, making Paper and Sugar

You can find Sugar Cane growing as a series of three long, thin, green tubes anywhere near Water. Farming your own supply is pretty simple; knock down the top two pieces and plant it along the Water's edge. It grows as a stack, and you can harvest the top pieces as they become available. Of course, you can always make more impressive Sugar Cane farms. All you need is the Sugar Cane itself, Water, something nice for it to grow on (Dirt and Sand), and your imagination.

It's a good idea to have a fair supply of Sugar Cane as your game progresses. You need Sugar Cane to make Paper, and without Paper, you can't make Bookcases. And without Bookcases, you can't have a fully powered Enchanting Table. Any excess Sugar Cane can be processed into Sugar, which is useful for making Cakes and some potions.

Sugar Cane itself creates air pockets in Water. You can intersperse Sugar Cane within Water to make small airlocks. It can also block the flow of Lava, which is a pretty neat trick for a simple plant.

Sunflower

LOCATION	GATHERED WITH	USES
The Overworld, in Sunflower Plains	Anything	Decoration, Dandelion Yellow Dye

These lovely yellow flowers are found only in special Sunflower Plains, where they add a bright counterpoint to the smooth green landscape. You can pick Sunflowers at your leisure, and they make a nice addition to your living space. If you want, you can crush them to make a nice yellow dye, the same dye made with Dandelions.

Tripwire

LOCATION	GATHERED WITH	USES
Anywhere	Anything	Traps

No trap would be complete without a Tripwire! Made when you place a piece of String, the small gray Tripwire connects signals from Redstone-powered circuits to Tripwire Hooks on opposite ends. When something collides with the Tripwire, a pulse is sent to the Tripwire Hooks, triggering the trap.

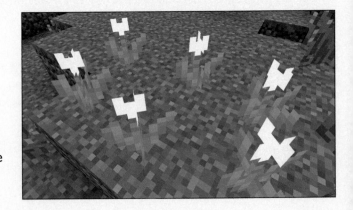

It's very difficult to see a Tripwire unless you really look for it. If you do see one, though, you can cut it with Shears, which disarms the trap.

Traps are much more common in multiplayer games, but they do occur in jungle temples in single-player. If you ever explore a jungle temple, it's best to keep your eyes open and your Shears ready for Tripwires! This can spare you from a painful arrow to the knee or a falling rock pile.

Tulip

LOCATION	GATHERED WITH	USES
The Overworld	Anything	Decoration, making Dyes

What flower grows between your nose and your chin? Easy! Tulips—get it? Two lips! Okay, well, maybe not… Instead, you can find Tulips on the plains, including sunflower plains, and in flower forests. They come in a wider variety than most other flowers; you can find white, pink, orange, and red Tulips.

Like other flowers, Tulips can be put around your house as decoration. You can also make dyes, depending on the color of your Tulips: Light Gray Dye from white Tulips, Orange Dye from orange Tulips, Pink Dye from pink Tulips, and Rose Red Dye from red Tulips.

TOOLS, RESOURCES, AND CONSUMABLES

Vines

LOCATION	GATHERED WITH	USES
The Overworld, in swamps and jungles	Shears	Transportation, decoration

Jungles and swamps are covered in dense vegetation, and the trees are surrounded by quickly growing Vines. However, these Vines provide some real benefits: they can be climbed, just like Ladders, and they can hide you or anything you build from sight.

To climb a Vine, simply move onto it from any solid block. "Sneaking" on a Vine causes you to stop; you can use this to hover in place. Falling onto a Vine greatly reduces falling damage, so they make a good safety system.

If you want to grow your own set of Vine "ladders," you must harvest the Vines with Shears. Vines grow only on solid blocks, and they grow down into any empty space below them. They don't need light to grow, either. Vines are perfectly happy to take over any territory beneath them, under any condition. Vines block line of sight, so monsters (even Endermen) and other players won't see things behind them. You can make secret passageways and hidden nooks using hanging Vines. They can even be placed over Chests, making them perfect for creating your own jungle temple.

Wood

LOCATION	GATHERED WITH	USES
The Overworld	Axe	Construction, making Wooden Tools, making crafting materials, fuel

Wood: it's what you gather your first day, every time. Most biomes have at least a reasonable supply of trees, and if you don't find any, it's worth running and searching for them. Wood comes from any type of tree (Oak, Spruce, Birch, Jungle, Acacia, and Dark Oak), and you need Wood (as Wooden Planks) to make your Crafting Table. From there, you use Wood to make your first set of Wooden Tools, especially a Wooden Axe to get more Wood, and then to create other useful items, like Chests and Torches. Other useful items you make from Wood include Fences, Ladders, and Doors. And if you can't find any Coal early on, Wood is your first means of making your own light; burning it in your Furnace helps stave off the darkness and creates Charcoal in the process.

As you become more comfortable with the game and gain access to additional materials, Wood becomes less valuable, but you never want to be completely without it. Even if you deforest the area around you, it's worth starting a sapling farm. Without Wood, you can't make any tools at all, and that is a true problem.

COMMON ITEMS

Bone

LOCATION	GATHERED WITH	USES
The Overworld and The Nether	Weapons; Fishing Rod	Taming Wolves, fertilizer, making Bone Meal (white) Dye

You can tell that Skeletons and Wither Skeletons have a Bone to pick with you—they leave it behind when they die! But what can you do with this grisly trophy?

Bones can be turned into Bone Meal, and that's the best way to grow a huge number of plants and trees quickly. You can also use Bone Meal to dye Wool white, but this is a waste of its potential; there are much easier ways to get white Wool. Additionally, you can use Bones to tame Wolves. A tame Wolf will defend you from harm and makes a loyal companion, so if you want your own dog, be sure to keep some Bones around.

If you don't like the idea of hunting the Overworld for Skeletons or the Nether for Wither Skeletons, you can always make a Fishing Rod. You have a chance to hook a Bone instead of a Fish during your fishing trip.

Bottle of Enchanting

LOCATION	GATHERED WITH	USES
The Overworld, in Villages	Trade from a Priest Villager	Gaining experience

The Bottle of Enchanting is also called an Experience Potion, because breaking it releases experience orbs (between 3 and 10 points). Unlike other potions, you can't brew Bottles of Enchanting; they require a bit of diplomacy and some trading expertise. Bottles of Enchanting are made only in Villages, and only by specific Villagers at that. Priests offer two to four Bottles of Enchanting for one Emerald. Of course, Emeralds are pretty rare, and the best way to get them is to trade with other Villagers, who sometimes give Emeralds if you offer them something they want—Librarians that need Paper, for example. All of this necessitates, of course, that you've discovered a nearby Village, you have Villagers with the right mix of tradable items, and you have those items to trade.

However, if you don't have that nice combination, Bottles of Enchanting are a good way to farm experience. They are an easy source of renewable experience that doesn't demand many risks.

Cactus Green

LOCATION	GATHERED WITH	USES
Crafted item	Furnace	Decoration, used for dyes and in fireworks

Burning a piece of Cactus in your Furnace creates Cactus Green. You can use this material to color a number of products green, including leather armor, Wool, and Glass (for Stained Glass). Other dyes use Cactus Green as an ingredient; Cyan Dye is made with Lapis Lazuli and Lime Dye with Bone Meal.

If fireworks are your thing, add Cactus Green to Gunpowder to make a Fireworks Star. Like any other dye, Cactus Green can be added to fireworks to create a "fade to color" effect.

TOOLS, RESOURCES, AND CONSUMABLES

Charcoal

LOCATION	GATHERED WITH	USES
Created by burning Wood	N/A	Burned in Furnaces, used to craft Torches

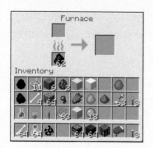

Charcoal has the same general purpose as Coal. It's primarily used as a fuel for Torches and Furnaces in the early game, when you have better access to Wood but might not have much time to mine Coal out of the rocks below.

To make Charcoal, burn blocks of Wood inside your Furnace. Use Sticks or wooden tools to light your first fire. Burn a block of Wood to make a single piece of Charcoal, and then put that into your fuel slot. Now use that piece to burn even more blocks of Wood, and you're good to go from there.

Coal

LOCATION	GATHERED WITH	USES
Underground in the Overworld	Pickaxe	Fuel for Furnaces

Coal is a somewhat common sight in the Overworld's underground areas. You see chunks of this dark ore in the rocks, and they're easily mined with any Pickaxe. Mining Coal is a good way to get experience, because each block gets you a small chunk of XP.

Bring Coal back to your base to use in your Furnaces; it's a very efficient fuel. Coal is also a major ingredient in Torches and Fire Charges.

Diamond

LOCATION	GATHERED WITH	USES
Deep underground in the Overworld	Iron or Diamond Pickaxes	High quality tools and equipment

Diamond is one of the rarest materials in *Minecraft*. It's found only near Bedrock, at the bottom of the Overworld. Make sure you're below 15 on the "Y" scale. Or dig down to the Bedrock and go up only about a dozen blocks from the bottom.

Search for this light ore and mine it with Iron or Diamond Pickaxes. Nothing else is strong enough to cut through the Diamond. Bring the ore home to use in tools, weapons, armor, and special crafting recipes: Enchantment Tables, Firework Stars, Jukeboxes, and Nether Reactor Cores (Pocket Edition only).

Ender Pearl

LOCATION	GATHERED WITH	USES
Carried by Endermen	Kill Endermen	Teleportation and crafting Eyes of Ender

Ender Pearls are dropped when you kill Endermen. These are very important items for reaching the late game because you can't find Strongholds without crafting Eyes of Ender, and those require Ender Pearls.

Used on their own, Ender Pearls are short-range teleportation devices. Use them to cross ravines or to save yourself if you're knocked off a high edge and react quickly. Even if you don't fall, Ender Pearls cause falling damage to your character when you use them, so be careful.

Feather

LOCATION	GATHERED WITH	USES
Dropped by Chickens	Kill Chickens	Crafting

Feathers are a key ingredient in Arrows, a Book and Quill, and Firework Stars. Of these, Arrows are easily the most common item that you craft. It takes many Arrows to get through the game, and most targets are safer to kill with Bows than with Swords.

To ensure you have a huge supply of Feathers, create a pen or barn for any Chickens found in the wilderness. Don't kill them! Use Seeds to lure them home and keep them safe in your pen. Breed them, using Seeds, and only kill excess Chickens. This gets you plenty of Feathers over time.

Fireworks

LOCATION	GATHERED WITH	USES
Crafted item	Crafting	Fun

Firework Rockets require a special, complex crafting recipe. They have variable ingredients so you can vary the effect of the rocket when it's fired.

Firework Rockets need Paper and Gunpowder to work. Extra units of Gunpowder make the rockets go higher when they're fired. If you want an attractive explosive effect, add Firework Stars to the recipe as well. You're allowed to add as many Stars as you have room in the crafting box.

RECIPE

INGREDIENTS	CRAFTING RECIPE	RESULT
Paper, Gunpowder (1-3), Firework Star (0-7)		Firework Rocket

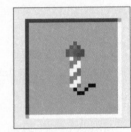

Flint

LOCATION	GATHERED WITH	USES
Found in Gravel	Shovels	Crafting

You sometimes find Flint when digging through Gravel. It's a useful material, so bring a Shovel when mining and don't avoid Gravel deposits. Slowly dig them out, don't get trapped when they fall, and collect all the Flint you find.

Flint is used to make Arrows, as well as Flint and Steel. Both of these are quite useful, so save all your Flint until it's needed!

Ghast Tear

LOCATION	GATHERED WITH	USES
In the eyes of sad Ghasts	Kill Ghasts	Brewing

Ghast Tears drop fairly often when you kill Ghasts. They are used to make Mundane Potions and Potions of Regeneration. The latter are quite useful in dangerous battles that take a long time to win.

TOOLS, RESOURCES, AND CONSUMABLES

Glowstone Dust

LOCATION	GATHERED WITH	USES
The Nether, often up high	Anything	Firework Stars and brewing

You gather Glowstone Dust by breaking Glowstone blocks in the Nether. You sometimes get it from killing Witches, but that's a hard way to get a decent amount. Instead, go to the Nether and look along the ceilings for large deposits of Glowstone. Each piece of Glowstone breaks into several Glowstone Dust.

Console players can farm Glowstone Dust by killing Blazes. Blazes drop small amounts of Glowstone for those players. Pocket Edition players do the same thing by creating and using Nether Reactors.

Use Glowstone Dust to make Firework Stars, Thick Potions, or to increase the power of other potions: Harming, Healing, Poison, Regeneration, Strength, Swiftness.

Gunpowder

LOCATION	GATHERED WITH	USES
Carried by Creepers	Killing Creepers	Crafting

Kill Creepers (without detonating them) to get Gunpowder. Ghasts and Witches also carry it, though both of these are harder to find and farm compared to Creepers.

Gunpowder itself is used to make Fire Charges, Fireworks, and TNT—boom! It's also useful in brewing to turn normal potions into Splash Potions; these activate when thrown. They're great for fast-acting Healing Potions or as a way to attack targets with Potions of Harming, Weakness, or Poison.

Horse Armor

LOCATION	GATHERED WITH	USES
Special treasure Chests	Open the Chest	Protect your beloved Horse

Horse Armor cannot be crafted. You have to explore the world and find this barding. One usually finds it in dungeon or temple Chests. Sometimes Village Blacksmiths have it as well, or you bump into it in Nether fortresses.

Once you have Horse Armor, interact with your Horse and equip the armor as you would your own. This makes it much harder for monsters to kill your mount. Horse Armor comes in Iron, Gold, and Diamond varieties. Interestingly, Gold Horse Armor is superior to Iron and doesn't have any durability to worry about!

Ink Sac

LOCATION	GATHERED WITH	USES
Carried by Squids	Kill the Squids	Making dark dye

One normally acquires Ink Sacs by killing Squids in deep Water, but you sometimes find them while fishing, too. As a crafting item, Ink Sacs are useful for making Gray Dye, Light Gray Dye, Black Wool, Black Stained Glass, Black Stained Clay, a Book and Quill, and Black Firework Stars.

In the Pocket Edition, they're also used to create Cocoa Beans when combined with Orange Dye.

Iron Ingot

LOCATION	GATHERED WITH	USES
Cooked Item	Cook Iron Ore in a Furnace	Crafting

Iron Ingots are created when you smelt Iron Ore inside a Furnace. Iron Ore is brought up from the Overworld's underground areas, and it's brownish in color.

Use Iron Ingots to create Iron weapons, armor, and tools. It's one of the most common items in the game for crafting purposes, so you need to mine a ton of it!

Leather

LOCATION	GATHERED WITH	USES
Carried by Cows and Horses	Kill Cows and Horses to harvest their Leather	Armor, Books, and Item Frames

Leather is a required ingredient for Books, so it's a vital resource for enchanting. For people who are light on Iron, Leather is also a good resource for armor. You need a fair amount of material to create a full suit of Leather Armor, but it's doable.

To harvest Leather, search for Cows or Horses. Breed these animals heavily until you have a large, working population of the beasts. Then slaughter a number of adults each time they successfully breed. Keep your Leather, and continue culling the population each time there are too many adults in your barn/pen.

Music Disc

LOCATION	GATHERED WITH	USES
Dungeon Chests, carried by Creepers	Search dungeons or kill Creepers (*)	Play Music Discs in Juke Boxes to change the game's music

Music Discs are either hard to find or tricky to get. You find them in dungeon treasure Chests when you're lucky. Bring them home and craft a Juke Box. Then put your discs in a Chest next to the Juke Box and play music whenever you like. Neat!

For a more reliable way to gather these discs, go outside at night. Get away from your base to avoid damaging it during monster attacks, and look for Creepers and Skeletons. Lure the two into the same area, and wound the Creepers. Get them close to death and then stop attacking them. Sprint to get a Creeper between your character and a Skeleton. Keep backing up and wait for the Skeleton to accidentally Snipe your Creeper buddy. This forces them to drop Music Discs. Huzzah!

Name Tag

LOCATION	GATHERED WITH	USES
Dungeon Chests, rare fishing treasure	Open the Chests or use a Fishing Rod on Water	Names creatures

Search through dungeons or fish extensively to find Name Tags; they're rare loot, so you won't get too many of them. Use them in your Anvil to put a name on them. Then find a monster and use the Name Tag to assign that name to the creature. This uses up your Name Tag, but causes anyone who targets the creature to see the name you've given it.

Try naming something Dinnerbone or Grumm to see what happens. Naming a Sheep jeb_ is rather interesting, too.

Redstone

LOCATION	GATHERED WITH	USES
Deep underground in the Overworld	Iron or Diamond Pickaxe	Brewing, Crafting, Machines

Redstone is the most complex material in the game. It's mined in the Overworld's darker tunnels, and then used to extend the length of potions, to construct rare tools, or to activate machines. Redstone Dust transmits power, while Redstone Blocks are used for power or decoration. There is an entire section dedicated to Redstone in the "You Can Do Anything with a Little Practice" chapter.

Saddle

LOCATION	GATHERED WITH	USES
Chests or Villages	Open the Chests	Ride Horses

Saddles cannot be crafted. They're found inside treasure Chests. Save any that you find, and use them after taming Horses. Saddled Horses are easily ridden and let you get around quickly. Make sure to breed your toughest and fastest Horses, so you have a good selection of animals to saddle. Pigs can also be saddled, but they're not quite as fast!

Slimeball

LOCATION	GATHERED WITH	USES
Carried by Slimes	Kill Slimes to get them	Crafting

Slimeballs are dropped when you kill Slimes. They're often found in swamps, but specific underground areas can also spawn them. If you find a place that has Slimes, mark it with Signs so you know where to find it again later. Slimeballs frequently spawn there and you can harvest the area more than once.

With these items, you can craft blocks made of Slime, Leads to control animals, Magma Cream, and Sticky Pistons. These are pretty useful crafting recipes, so find a steady source of Slimes whenever you can.

String

LOCATION	GATHERED WITH	USES
Cobwebs and Spiders	Shears, or by killing Spiders	Crafting

Spiders and Cave Spiders drop String when slain, so they're very good sources of this material. Dark caves that are just a single block high are perfect for spawning Spiders, because they're one of the only creatures small enough to get through the space. Cutting down Cobwebs in abandoned mineshafts also produces String.

Craft String into Bows, Fishing Rods, and Leads. It also makes White Wool, but this is a major waste of your String. It's better to use the default Wool acquired from most Sheep. It's already light in color and doesn't require you to use four String per piece!

String also forms a Tripwire when attached to Tripwire Hooks. This is a great way to set traps in your base or in tunnels where people have to follow a certain passage.

CRAFTING

Activator Rail

LOCATION	GATHERED WITH	USES
Crafted item	Crafting	Triggers Minecarts that are carrying Command Blocks, Hoppers, or TNT

Activator Rails are used to set off explosions, turn off Hoppers, or to use commands that are coded into Command Blocks. Any monster or person riding in a Minecart that hits an Activator Rail is thrown out of the cart as it passes over the rail. So Activator Rails are also used to set traps for invaders who try to use your rail system to get into your base.

RECIPE

INGREDIENTS	CRAFTING RECIPE		RESULT
Iron Ingot (6), Stick (2), Redstone Torch		→	Activator Rail

Andesite

LOCATION	GATHERED WITH	USES
Underground in the Overworld	Pickaxe	Decoration

This newer type of rock is found in the Overworld, in any location where Stone blocks appear. Use it to decorate areas where you want more variety than Stone or Cobblestone blocks can offer.

RECIPE

INGREDIENTS	CRAFTING RECIPE		RESULT
Diorite, Cobblestone		→	Andesite
Andesite (4)		→	Polished Andesite

Anvil

LOCATION	GATHERED WITH	USES
Crafted item	Crafting	Naming, Repairing, and Combining Items

Anvils require a huge amount of Iron to craft. Investing over 30 Iron into anything is a big deal, especially in the early game. Don't craft one of these until you have a steady supply of Iron tools and armor.

When you craft an Anvil, a block is produced. Put it somewhere safe in your base, and don't drop it on anyone you like; Anvils cause major damage if dropped on something.

Interact with the Anvil to name or repair items. It's possible to combine items of the same name/type. Like enchanting, it costs your character levels to use Anvils, but they offer the potential to make your powerful items last for a very long time.

RECIPE

INGREDIENTS	CRAFTING RECIPE		RESULT	
Iron Ingot (4), Block of Iron (3)		→		Anvil

Armor Stand

LOCATION	GATHERED WITH	USES
Crafted item	Crafting	Holds and displays wearable items

Armor Stands are crafted with simple materials and then can be placed around your home to make it more visually exciting. Once placed, these structures hold armor or monster heads. You already know how to get armor, but heads are found when many types of enemies are killed by a charged Creeper explosion. In the case of Wither Skeletons, you can also simply farm their heads (but it's a slow process).

RECIPE

INGREDIENTS	CRAFTING RECIPE		RESULT	
Stick (6), Stone Slab		→		Armor Stand

Beacon

LOCATION	GATHERED WITH	USES
Crafted Iron	Crafting	Beneficial effects

Beacons are crafted with special materials. The Glass and Obsidian aren't too hard to get, but Nether Stars certainly are. You get these from killing Withers, a type of boss monster that cannot be summoned or killed easily. The "You Can Do Anything with a Little Practice" chapter has a section explaining how to create one of these monsters, and a section on using Beacons as well.

After you craft a Beacon, it provides special powers to nearby characters, as long as it's activated and placed on top of a pyramid of Iron, Emerald, Diamond, etc. Building a functional Beacon is a huge investment in time and resources, but it's awesome once you make it work.

RECIPE

INGREDIENTS	CRAFTING RECIPE		RESULT	
Glass (5), Obsidian (3), Nether Star		→		Beacon

Bed

LOCATION	GATHERED WITH	USES
Crafted item	Crafting	Advances night to day

Beds are pieces of furniture that you can use only at night or during thunderstorms. Sleeping in a Bed lets you advance until the night/storm is over, and it also saves your location. Should your character be killed, you reappear in the last place that your character slept.

Beds cannot be used in the Nether or The End; they turn into massive explosives.

RECIPE

INGREDIENTS	CRAFTING RECIPE	RESULT
Wool (3), Wood Planks (3)	→	Bed

Blaze Powder

LOCATION	GATHERED WITH	USES
Crafted item	Crafting	Brewing, Special Recipes

It's easy to create Blaze Powder by breaking a Blaze Rod in your inventory or at a Crafting Table. This gets you two pieces of Blaze Powder. They can then be used to craft Eyes of Ender, Fire Charges, or Magma Cream.

Blaze Powder is also a direct ingredient in brewing. It's used to make Mundane Potions (meh) and Potions of Strength, which are amazingly useful!

RECIPE

INGREDIENTS	CRAFTING RECIPE	RESULT
Blaze Rod	→	Blaze Powder (2)

Block of Quartz

LOCATION	GATHERED WITH	USES
Crafted item	Crafting	Decoration

Blocks of Quartz are crafted from several pieces of Nether Quartz, as found in the Nether. These blocks make lovely decoration for any building you're working on; the stone has a light color that is really attractive.

Use a Stonecutter to make blocks of Quartz if you're playing with the Pocket Edition. Otherwise, you can craft them even if you aren't at a Crafting Table.

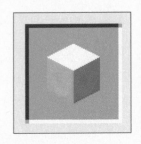

RECIPE

INGREDIENTS	CRAFTING RECIPE	RESULT
Nether Quartz (4)	→	Block of Quartz

Boat

LOCATION	GATHERED WITH	USES
Crafted item	Crafting	Sailing the seven seas

Boats are wooden objects to place in the Water and ride inside—no surprise there. They're crafted with five Wood Planks, so they don't require a big investment. Make a Boat any time you need to cross a large body of water. Try not to run into anything; Boats shatter if they run aground or bump into anything substantial.

Interact with Boats to start riding in them, and use the Sneak command to get out of the Boat.

RECIPE

INGREDIENTS	CRAFTING RECIPE	RESULT
Wood Plank (5)		Boat

Bone Meal

LOCATION	GATHERED WITH	USES
Crafted item	Crafting	Fertilize crops

Break a single Bone into a few pieces of Bone Meal, and use those to make crops or other vegetation grow very quickly. It sometimes takes a few Bone Meal applications to get something to mature, but the process is still extremely efficient.

Save your Bone Meal for new crops that you don't already have in abundance. That way, you can kick-start a major farming effort without spending a few hours getting up to speed.

Try Bone Meal on trees for an impressive effect. Making an orchard has never been so easy.

RECIPE

INGREDIENTS	CRAFTING RECIPE	RESULT
Bone		Bone Meal (3)

Book

LOCATION	GATHERED WITH	USES
Crafted item	Crafting	Enchanting

Books let you make an Enchanting Table, and they're the backbone of Bookshelves, which you also need for high-tier enchanting. You have to craft quite a few Books if you plan on becoming a great enchanter.

Pocket Edition users don't need Leather to craft Books. They only need the Paper. That's very easy, because a large garden of Sugar Cane yields all the necessary Paper.

RECIPE

INGREDIENTS	CRAFTING RECIPE	RESULT
Paper (3), Leather		Enchanting

Book and Quill

LOCATION	GATHERED WITH	USES
Crafted item	Crafting	Entertainment or trading

Use a Book and Quill to make a Written Book. These let you write lore for the world you're creating (to show to other people), or they're traded to villagers at a very nice rate.

Equip a Book and Quill in your hotbar, use it to open the Book, and start writing.

RECIPE

INGREDIENTS	CRAFTING RECIPE		RESULT
Book, Ink Sac, Feather		→	Book and Quill

Bookshelf

LOCATION	GATHERED WITH	USES
Crafted item	Crafting	Enchanting

Bookshelves make your Enchanting Table even stronger; your table can put higher-level enchantments onto items if it's two blocks away from your Bookshelves. Craft 15 Bookshelves and place them close to your Enchanting Table to give it maximum power.

Bookshelves are fairly expensive. The investment of Wood isn't too big a deal, but making three Books per Bookshelf is painful. Get a large ranch of Cows or Horses before starting this, and breed them well. You need tons of Leather to make all of those Books.

RECIPE

INGREDIENTS	CRAFTING RECIPE		RESULT
Book (3), Wood Plank (6)		→	Bookshelf

Brewing Stand

LOCATION	GATHERED WITH	USES
Crafted item	Crafting	Brewing

Brewing Stands are required for making potions. You must find Nether fortresses before making these because Blaze Rods are required to make a Brewing Stand. Also, Nether Wart is the primary ingredient for all useful potions, and Nether Wart is also located in Nether fortresses.

Once you have a Brewing Stand, find a safe place for it inside your base. Keep a Chest there for special ingredients, and a Cauldron for decoration and filling up Water Bottles.

RECIPE

INGREDIENTS	CRAFTING RECIPE		RESULT
Cobblestone (3), Blaze Rod		→	Brewing Stand

TOOLS, RESOURCES, AND CONSUMABLES

Brick and Blocks of Bricks

LOCATION	GATHERED WITH	USES
Cooked Item	Put Clay in a Furnace	Decoration

Cook Clay to turn it into a single Brick. Turn your Bricks into a block of Bricks by crafting four of them together, or make them into Flower Pots with only three Bricks.

RECIPE

INGREDIENTS	CRAFTING RECIPE	RESULT
Brick (4)		Bricks

Button

LOCATION	GATHERED WITH	USES
Crafted item	Crafting	Burst of power

Buttons trigger power for a short period, making them useful for opening Doors, triggering traps, and other sudden activities. It's possible to make Buttons out of Stone or Wood, so you can have them stand out against the wall to which they're attached. Or they can blend in if you're trying to be subtle.

After placing a Button on a surface, interact with it to trigger the Button and anything that's attached to it—nearby mechanisms or Redstone Dust.

RECIPE

INGREDIENTS	CRAFTING RECIPE	RESULT
Stone or Wood Plank		Button

Carpet

LOCATION	GATHERED WITH	USES
Crafted item	Crafting	Decoration

Use any two pieces of Wool to make three sections of Carpet. Lay them on top of blocks to add a neat decoration to your room. Dyed Wool lets you spruce up your base with a variety of colors.

RECIPE

INGREDIENTS	CRAFTING RECIPE	RESULT
Wool (2)		Carpet

Carrot on a Stick

LOCATION	GATHERED WITH	USES
Crafted item	Crafting	Leading Pigs

Use a Saddle to get onto a Pig, and then equip a Carrot on a Stick to lead the Pig wherever you like. You end up with a slow mount that isn't terribly effective, but it's pretty darn funny.

If you use the Carrot on a Stick actively, its durability decreases by a fair amount but gets your Pig moving much faster for 40 seconds or so.

RECIPE

INGREDIENTS	CRAFTING RECIPE	RESULT
Fishing Rod, Carrot		Carrot on a Stick

Cauldron

LOCATION	GATHERED WITH	USES
Crafted item	Crafting	Hold Water

Cauldrons are a nice, decorative way to hold Water. They're great to keep near Brewing Stands to give your setup an air of authenticity. However, Cauldrons aren't required for this. Any source of Water is good for brewers. Using a Cauldron is more a matter of taste than necessity.

RECIPE

INGREDIENTS	CRAFTING RECIPE	RESULT
Iron Ingot (7)		Cauldron

Chest

LOCATION	GATHERED WITH	USES
Crafted item	Crafting	Holds items

Chests are storage devices that help you sort items and keep your inventory organized. Drop off valuable or unneeded goods in your Chests by interacting with them, and then you don't have to worry about losing anything if your character dies.

For added Storage, place two Chests next to each other. They merge, giving your player even more storage in one shared super Chest!

RECIPE

INGREDIENTS	CRAFTING RECIPE	RESULT
Wood Planks (8)		Chest

TOOLS, RESOURCES, AND CONSUMABLES

Chiseled Quartz Block

LOCATION	GATHERED WITH	USES
Crafted item	Crafting	Decoration

Chiseled Quartz Blocks are attractive stone blocks that require some crafting work to prepare. Use Nether Quartz to make several Nether Quartz Blocks. Turn those into Slabs, and then use two of those Slabs to produce Chiseled Quartz Blocks. Functionally, they aren't much different from other Quartz blocks, but they have a more intricate texture.

RECIPE

INGREDIENTS	CRAFTING RECIPE	RESULT
Quartz Slab (2)		Chiseled Quartz Block

Chiseled Sandstone

LOCATION	GATHERED WITH	USES
Crafted item	Crafting	Decoration

Use two Sandstone Slabs to craft these neat-looking blocks. They're perfect for pyramids and other desert-inspired buildings.

RECIPE

INGREDIENTS	CRAFTING RECIPE	RESULT
Sandstone Slab (2)		Chiseled Sandstone

Clay Block

LOCATION	GATHERED WITH	USES
Crafted item	Crafting	Decoration

Clay Blocks are soft and easily dug out or damaged. However, they look nice and are useful as interior blocks for your base. Decorate rooms with them for fun. Or cook Clay Blocks to harden them, and then use dyes to turn the Hardened Clay into Stained Clay for even more visual options.

RECIPE

INGREDIENTS	CRAFTING RECIPE	RESULT
Clay (4)		Clay Block

Crafting Table

LOCATION	GATHERED WITH	USES
Crafted item	Crafting	Make more elaborate items

Use the default space for crafting in your inventory to make a Crafting Table by using four Wood Planks. Set up your table somewhere accessible, and interact with it to open far more crafting options.

RECIPE

INGREDIENTS	CRAFTING RECIPE	RESULT
Wood Plank (4)		Crafting Table

Cyan Dye

LOCATION	GATHERED WITH	USES
Crafted item	Crafting	Light-blue staining

This pleasing light-blue dye is used to change the color of Wool, Sheep, Stained Clay, etc.

RECIPE

INGREDIENTS	CRAFTING RECIPE	RESULT
Lapis Lazuli, Cactus Green		Cyan Dye

Dandelion Yellow

LOCATION	GATHERED WITH	USES
Crafted item	Crafting	Yellow staining

Turn a single Dandelion or Sunflower into this yellow dye. It's used for changing the color of Wool, Sheep, Stained Clay, armor, etc.

RECIPE

INGREDIENTS	CRAFTING RECIPE	RESULT
Dandelion or Sunflower		Dandelion Yellow

Daylight Sensor

LOCATION	GATHERED WITH	USES
Crafted item	Crafting	Outputting power based on the time of day/night

Daylight Sensors that are exposed to the sky put out a Redstone signal based on the time of day. It gets stronger as the day progresses, and shuts down at night. Used with a Redstone Torch, the Daylight Sensor can be inverted, making it into a Nighttime Sensor instead.

These are used to automate machines around your base depending on the time of day. People often use them to close Fences and Doors or to turn on lights when the sky starts to darken.

RECIPE

INGREDIENTS	CRAFTING RECIPE	RESULT
Glass (3), Wood Slab (3), Nether Quartz (3)		Daylight Sensor

Detector Rail

LOCATION	GATHERED WITH	USES
Crafted item	Crafting	Create a signal if a Minecart passes over it

Detector Rails allow you to trigger machines based on the approach of a Minecart. Use them to set off traps, alert people (with Note Blocks, Door opening/closing, etc.), or to make sure carts speed through in only one direction.

RECIPE

INGREDIENTS	CRAFTING RECIPE	RESULT
Iron Ingot (6), Redstone, Stone Pressure Plate		Detector Rail (6)

Diorite

LOCATION	GATHERED WITH	USES
Crafting Item	Crafted	Decoration

Blocks of Diorite are used to decorate people's homes and tunnels. They're made with Cobblestone and Nether Quartz, so they're much more costly than basic Stone-based blocks.

Put four blocks of Diorite together to check out Polished Diorite for even more visual options.

RECIPE

INGREDIENTS	CRAFTING RECIPE	RESULT
Cobblestone (2), Nether Quartz (2)		Diorite (2)
Diorite (4)		Polished Diorite (4)

Dispenser

LOCATION	GATHERED WITH	USES
Crafted item	Crafting	Shooting Items

Dispensers hold items, such as a Chest, but shoot them back out if they receive power from any source. Use Redstone to trigger Dispensers so they fire Arrows, Fire Charges, potions, or anything else you want to send at friends or enemies. You can even set up armor Dispensers to quickly armor yourself by walking over a series of Pressure Plates.

Use only new Bows to craft Dispensers. The recipe won't work if you try to craft one using a Bow that's taken any durability damage, even from a single firing.

RECIPE

INGREDIENTS	CRAFTING RECIPE	RESULT
Cobblestone (7), Redstone, Bow		Dispenser

Door

LOCATION	GATHERED WITH	USES
Crafted item	Crafting	Limiting accessibility

Doors allow you to block off areas without totally sealing them. Wooden Doors are easy to open and close; interact with them to toggle between these two settings and walk through the opening whenever you want. Wooden Doors keep out enemies fairly well, but concerted attacks can break through them.

Iron Doors require Redstone power to open and close, so they're a bigger hassle to build. However, they keep out almost any type of attacker, except for other players. Use Pressure Plates or Buttons to operate Iron Doors and have them shut automatically.

Note that the type of wood used to create a standard Door determines the visual appearance of that Door. Try this to see which styles of Door you enjoy the most. This controls the color and the texture of the door, including changes in the windows and style of the entire item.

RECIPE

INGREDIENTS	CRAFTING RECIPE	RESULT
Iron Ingot or Wood Plank (6)		Door

Dropper

LOCATION	GATHERED WITH	USES
Crafted item	Crafting	Moving items

Droppers drop items from their inventory whenever they are powered by a Redstone signal. Because they have inventories and the ability to push items into another block, Droppers can be chained together.

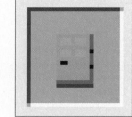

RECIPE

INGREDIENTS	CRAFTING RECIPE	RESULT
Cobblestone (7), Redstone		Dropper

Dyed Wool

LOCATION	GATHERED WITH	USES
Crafted item	Crafting	Decorative Wool

Use a dye to change Wool to another color and make Wool items in whatever color you like. Another way to do this is to dye Sheep before shearing them. The Wool received is colored the same as the dye used. This is more efficient than dyeing Wool directly because you get multiple colored pieces per dye.

RECIPE

INGREDIENTS	CRAFTING RECIPE	RESULT
Wool + Dye	→	Dyed Wool

Enchanted Book

LOCATION	GATHERED WITH	USES
Crafted item	Crafting	Putting specific effects onto your tools or equipment

Regular Books can be enchanted just like your armor, tools, and weapons. Use an Enchantment Table to put special effects onto your Books to turn them into Enchanted Books. This process can be done multiple times, adding more abilities onto the Enchanted Book each time.

When an Enchanted Book is taken to an Anvil, its powers are added to another item, and the Enchanted Book is destroyed. Any powers allowed to go onto the item type will transfer, but powers that are not allowed on the item are lost and wasted. This is a costly but useful process when you want to create extremely powerful items.

Enchantment Table

LOCATION	GATHERED WITH	USES
Crafted item	Crafting	Improving tools, weapons, and armor

Craft an Enchantment Table once you have access to Diamonds and Obsidian. Place the table in your base, and bring items to it once your character is higher in level. You're allowed to spend your levels to add special abilities to your items and equipment. Place the desired item into the Enchantment Table interface, and use the table on the right when deciding how many levels to invest in the object.

Surround your Enchantment Table with 15 Bookshelves to give it even more enchanting power. This lets you place much stronger enchantments on your equipment.

RECIPE

INGREDIENTS	CRAFTING RECIPE	RESULT
Book, Diamond (2), Obsidian (4)	→	Enchantment Table

Ender Chest

LOCATION	GATHERED WITH	USES
Crafted item	Crafting	Storing items in multiple places

Ender Chests are more expensive than regular Chests because they require Obsidian and Eyes of Ender. However, they have a powerful special ability; all Ender Chests are connected. Anything you put inside one Ender Chest is available in every Ender Chest you own.

Place these by your remote mining operations or in the Nether and The End as a way to safely keep items whether you live or die. You can plop down an Ender Chest, load it with goodies, and then break it with a Pickaxe to keep carrying it with you. The items remain in the Ender space between worlds and still appear when you put the chest down anywhere else.

RECIPE

INGREDIENTS	CRAFTING RECIPE	RESULT
Obsidian (8), Eye of Ender		Ender Chest

Eye of Ender

LOCATION	GATHERED WITH	USES
Crafted item	Crafting	Finding strongholds and activating The End Portal

Craft Eyes of Ender when you're ready to face *Minecraft*'s late game. Use these items to find Strongholds (massive dungeons located in the Overworld). These dungeons are quite hard to find on their own, and following Eyes of Ender makes locating them so much easier. Trace the steps of the Eyes of Ender, pick them up when you can, and reuse them until you get to the Stronghold.

Within each Stronghold is a room with a Portal to The End. Use Eyes of Ender to activate these Portals; completing a Portal requires many Eyes of Ender, so bring as many as possible. Afterward, the Portal allows travel between the Overworld and The End. Until you kill the Ender Dragon, it's a one-way trip, so watch out.

RECIPE

INGREDIENTS	CRAFTING RECIPE	RESULT
Blaze Powder, Ender Pearl		Eye of Ender

Fence

LOCATION	GATHERED WITH	USES
Crafted item	Crafting	Blocking movement but not sight

Fences corral animals and monsters so they can't move around or jump over your barricade. Though Fences look like they're one block high, they're a tiny bit taller than that. This prevents normal jumps from clearing them.

Like Doors, you can change the visual appearance of a Fence by using different wood in its creation.

RECIPE

INGREDIENTS	CRAFTING RECIPE		RESULT
Stick (6)		→	Fence (2)

Fence Gate

LOCATION	GATHERED WITH	USES
Crafted item	Crafting	Allowing movement into Fenced areas

Use Fence Gates to act as Doors into Fenced-off areas. These open and close just like Wooden Doors, so they're easy to use. Try different types of wood when crafting a Fence Gate to change its visual appearance.

RECIPE

INGREDIENTS	CRAFTING RECIPE		RESULT
Stick (4), Wood Plank (2)		→	Fence Gate

Fermented Spider Eye

LOCATION	GATHERED WITH	USES
Crafted item	Crafting	Brewing

Craft Spider Eyes into this enhanced brewing item. Fermented Spider Eyes are used in a variety of potions, with Potions of Harming and Invisibility being two of the most fun. Potions of Slowness, combined with a well-trapped area, wreak havoc on enemy players.

RECIPE

INGREDIENTS	CRAFTING RECIPE		RESULT
Brown Mushroom, Sugar, Spider Eye		→	Fermented Spider Eye

Flower Pot

LOCATION	GATHERED WITH	USES
Crafted item	Crafting	Decoration

Flower Pots act like decorative tiles for flowers, trees, and other plant life. Though these items have no functional value, they're nice looking when you want to create a homey look to your outdoor or indoor areas.

RECIPE

INGREDIENTS	CRAFTING RECIPE		RESULT
Brick (3)		→	Flower Pot

Furnace

LOCATION	GATHERED WITH	USES
Crafted item	Crafting	Cooking

Furnaces are easy to make because they require only Cobblestone. Make one or two of them for your base as soon as you can, and bake Wood and Sticks to make Charcoal. Use the Charcoal as a superior fuel to burn more Wood until you accumulate an ample supply of Charcoal.

Use your Furnace to prepare food and smelt raw ore from the mines. Furnaces that are burning items also provide light if you're out of Torches and need to see what you're doing.

RECIPE

INGREDIENTS	CRAFTING RECIPE		RESULT
Cobblestone (8)		→	Furnace

Glass Bottle

LOCATION	GATHERED WITH	USES
Crafted item	Crafting	Brewing

Craft Glass Bottles to use with your Brewing Stand. They're required for every base potion. Use a Glass Bottle while you're facing a supply of Water to transform the item into a Water Bottle.

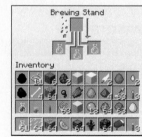

RECIPE

INGREDIENTS	CRAFTING RECIPE		RESULT
Glass (3)		→	Glass Bottle (3)

TOOLS, RESOURCES, AND CONSUMABLES

Glass Pane

LOCATION	GATHERED WITH	USES
Crafted item	Crafting	Decoration and light

You don't have to use Glass Blocks to make windows in your home. Instead, craft Glass into Glass Panes. You get more bang for your buck this way, because you get 16 items to work with instead of six. Cut holes in your wall and install the Glass Panes to make windows.

RECIPE

INGREDIENTS	CRAFTING RECIPE	RESULT
Glass (6)	→	Glass Pane (16)

Glistering Melon

LOCATION	GATHERED WITH	USES
Crafted item	Crafting	Brewing

Use nuggets of gold to turn regular Melon into Glistering Melon. The final product is a major ingredient in Mundane Potions and Potions of Healing.

RECIPE

INGREDIENTS	CRAFTING RECIPE	RESULT
Gold Nugget (8), Melon	→	Glistering Melon

Glowstone

LOCATION	GATHERED WITH	USES
Crafted item	Crafting	Light, broken into Glowstone Dust

Glowstone forms in the Nether, near that world's massive ceiling. Create pillars to climb, and cut down the Glowstone. When you break a Glowstone block, it shatters and drops Glowstone Dust, a useful brewing ingredient.

For a powerful light source that even works underwater, use Glowstone and Redstone to make a Redstone Lamp. It's even brighter than a Torch.

Gold Ingot

LOCATION	GATHERED WITH	USES
Crafted item	Crafting	Making tools, equipment, decorations, and more

Smelt Gold Ore in a Furnace to make Gold Ingots. These ingots are used for crafting golden tools, armor, and weapons. They're also required for Clocks, Powered Rails, Weighted Pressure Plates, and Golden Apples.

In general, golden tools aren't very good. They're fast to use but break much too quickly to be practical.

RECIPE

INGREDIENTS	CRAFTING RECIPE	RESULT
Gold Nugget (9)		Gold Ingot

Gold Nugget

LOCATION	GATHERED WITH	USES
Carried by Zombie Pigmen	Kill Zombie Pigmen	Create Gold Ingots, Crafting

Gold Nuggets are either made by breaking Gold Ingots or hunting groups of Zombie Pigmen. The nuggets are used when crafting Firework Stars, Glistering Melon, and Golden Carrots.

If you have more Gold Nuggets than you need, combine them back into Gold Ingots for more compact storage!

RECIPE

INGREDIENTS	CRAFTING RECIPE	RESULT
Gold Ingot		Gold Nugget (9)

Granite

LOCATION	GATHERED WITH	USES
Anywhere that Stone forms	Pickaxe	Decoration

Granite is naturally occurring rock harvested like normal Stone—it just looks different. Use Granite to make a stone building or floor look brownish in color, for a southwestern feel.

RECIPE

INGREDIENTS	CRAFTING RECIPE	RESULT
Diorite, Nether Quartz		Granite
Granite (4)		Polished Granite (4)

Gray Dye

LOCATION	GATHERED WITH	USES
Crafted item	Crafting	Stain items gray

Use this dye to stain Wool, Stained Glass, Stained Clay, Leather armor, and other items a grim gray color.

RECIPE

INGREDIENTS	CRAFTING RECIPE	RESULT
Ink Sac, Bone Meal		Gray Dye (2)

Hay Bale

LOCATION	GATHERED WITH	USES
Crafted item	Crafting	Feeding Horses, Donkeys, and Mules

A full Crafting Table of Wheat makes a single Hay Bale. Feed these bales to your Horses, Donkeys, or Mules to heal them from injuries. Or break the Hay Bale in a crafting window to make it back into nine Wheat. Store large amounts of excess Wheat in a compact space by leaving it in Hay Bales.

RECIPE

INGREDIENTS	CRAFTING RECIPE	RESULT
Wheat (9)		Hay Bale

Hopper

LOCATION	GATHERED WITH	USES
Crafted item	Crafting	Moving items

Hoppers pull items from containers above them and push the items down into anything below them. Put a Hopper under a Furnace to immediately have cooked/smelted items fall into your Hopper. Similarly, Hoppers above a Chest or Furnace fill those objects with whatever you put into the Hopper.

Brewing Stands and Furnaces can also be fed from their sides. A Hopper beside these objects loads their fuel/ingredient slots. It's pretty neat.

RECIPE

INGREDIENTS	CRAFTING RECIPE	RESULT
Iron Ingot (5), Chest		Hopper

Iron Bars

LOCATION	GATHERED WITH	USES
Crafted item	Crafting	Barriers

Iron Bars let you wall off an area without restricting your view. They're nice when you need to secure a compound and give the appearance of a jail or fortress.

RECIPE

INGREDIENTS	CRAFTING RECIPE	RESULT
Iron Ingot (6)		Iron Bars (16)

Item Frame

LOCATION	GATHERED WITH	USES
Crafted item	Crafting	Decoration

An Item Frame stores an object inside it. Make the frame and place it somewhere in your home. This locks the Item Frame onto a wall, Fence, tree, or whatever else is appropriate. Then slot one of your items and interact with the empty Item Frame to put the object inside it.

There, you have something nice hung in your house. Use this with Clocks to see the time when you're walking around your home. Maps and weapons are fun, too. To get your item back, attack the Item Frame to knock the object out of it.

RECIPE

INGREDIENTS	CRAFTING RECIPE	RESULT
Stick (8), Leather		Item Frame

Jack-o-Lantern

LOCATION	GATHERED WITH	USES
Crafted item	Crafting	Light and decoration

Use spare Pumpkins as bright light sources by adding a Torch to them. These blocks make your home safer yet add a spooky air when you're in a holiday mood. Perfect for Halloween.

RECIPE

INGREDIENTS	CRAFTING RECIPE	RESULT
Pumpkin, Torch		Jack-o-Lantern

Jukebox

LOCATION	GATHERED WITH	USES
Crafted item	Crafting	Play music

Jukeboxes play Music Discs to add fun ambient music to your home. Music Discs are found in special Chests, or are gained by causing Skeletons to shoot Creepers to death. Once you have these discs, hold them in your hand and interact with the Jukebox to turn it on.

RECIPE

INGREDIENTS	CRAFTING RECIPE	RESULT
Wood Plank (8), Diamond		Jukebox

Ladder

LOCATION	GATHERED WITH	USES
Crafted item	Crafting	Safe climbing

Craft quite a few Ladders when you plan to work on pillars, ravines, mineshafts, and other vertical surfaces. Install Ladders on the sheer walls of these areas so your character can safely climb up or down from them.

If you fall near a Ladder, push toward it. Your character catches the Ladder and stops his or her fall without taking damage. This is a useful trick.

RECIPE

INGREDIENTS	CRAFTING RECIPE	RESULT
Stick (7)		Ladder (3)

Lead

LOCATION	GATHERED WITH	USES
Crafted item	Crafting	Grab and control animals

Leads are great for pulling animals back to your home. Using food to lure creatures is acceptable for the same task, but it takes a very long time to entice the animals. They sometimes lose interest. Leads are much more efficient. Walk up to the animal that you want to guide, and use the Lead on it. Once you're tethered, walk back toward home. Use additional Leads to gather even more animals as you go.

Leads can be attached to Fences to tether your animals while you're away.

RECIPE

INGREDIENTS	CRAFTING RECIPE	RESULT
String (4), Slimeball		Lead (2)

Lever

LOCATION	GATHERED WITH	USES
Crafted item	Crafting	Creating on/off switches

Levers create power as an on or off switch. Pull them to activate their power and channel it through nearby machines or Redstone Dust, and turn off the power with a second flip of the switch.

RECIPE

INGREDIENTS	CRAFTING RECIPE	RESULT
Stick, Cobblestone	→	Lever

Light Blue Dye

LOCATION	GATHERED WITH	USES
Crafted item	Crafting	Stains objects light blue

Stain Leather armor, Sheep, Wool, and various other objects to a sky blue color.

RECIPE

INGREDIENTS	CRAFTING RECIPE	RESULT
Blue Orchid or Bone Meal and Lapis Lazuli	→	Light Blue Dye

Light Gray Dye

LOCATION	GATHERED WITH	USES
Crafted item	Crafting	Stains objects gray

Use this to stain Leather armor, Sheep, Wool, Clay, and Glass a mild gray color.

RECIPE

INGREDIENTS	CRAFTING RECIPE	RESULT
Azure Bluet or Oxeye Daisy or White Tulip	→	Light Gray Dye
Gray Dye, Bone Meal	→	Light Gray Dye (2)
Ink Sac, Bone Meal	→	Light Gray Dye (3)

Lime Dye

LOCATION	GATHERED WITH	USES
Crafted item	Crafting	Stains objects bright green

Use Lime Dye to stain Leather armor, Sheep, Wool, Clay, and Glass a bright green color.

RECIPE

INGREDIENTS	CRAFTING RECIPE	RESULT
Cactus Green, Bone Meal		Lime Dye (2)

Magenta Dye

LOCATION	GATHERED WITH	USES
Crafted item	Crafting	Stains objects a darker pink color

Magenta Dye stains Leather armor, Sheep, Wool, Clay, and Glass a darker, saturated pink color.

RECIPE

INGREDIENTS	CRAFTING RECIPE	RESULT
Allium or Lilac		Magenta Dye

Magma Cream

LOCATION	GATHERED WITH	USES
Crafted item	Crafting	Brewing

Magma Cream is either crafted or found when you kill Magma Cubes in the Nether. It's used as an ingredient in Mundane Potions and Potions of Fire Resistance. The latter is a powerful defensive potion when battling in the Nether.

RECIPE

INGREDIENTS	CRAFTING RECIPE	RESULT
Blaze Powder, Slimeball		Magma Cream

Melon Block

LOCATION	GATHERED WITH	USES
Crafted item	Crafting	Food, brewing

Combine a full set of Melons to make a Melon Block, or break Melon Blocks to get Melons. Either way, these blocks grow from Melon Seeds and are similar to Pumpkins in terms of their farming methods.

RECIPE

INGREDIENTS	CRAFTING RECIPE	RESULT
Melon (9)	→	Melon Block

Minecart

LOCATION	GATHERED WITH	USES
Crafted item	Crafting	Transportation

There are several types of Minecarts in the game, and all of them are useful at different times. The base Minecart is a means of transport that rides along Railways both above ground and underneath it. Use downward slopes or occasional Powered Rails to keep your Minecarts moving at high speed, traveling from one end of the track to the other as quickly as possible.

Minecarts with Chests give you storage options. Place items in the Minecart and send it on its way using a Powered Rail system. Because the cart is full, you can't ride along in it. Either use another Minecart to follow, or use another means of transport.

Minecarts with Hoppers are pretty cool. They grab any items along the Railway as they travel (unless they hit an Activator Rail). Set up areas where monsters are slain and farmed for items, and run your Minecart with Hopper through it to collect your treasure.

Minecarts with TNT are mobile explosives that detonate if they touch an Activator Rail—very nice.

Minecarts with Furnaces push other carts ahead of themselves. Add fuel to make them work, and its full speed ahead for your new train of Minecarts.

RECIPE

INGREDIENTS	CRAFTING RECIPE	RESULT
Iron Ingot (5)	→	Minecart
Minecart, Chest	→	Minecart with Chest
Minecart, TNT	→	Minecart with TNT
Minecart, Furnace	→	Minecart with Furnace
Minecart, Hopper	→	Minecart with Hopper

TOOLS, RESOURCES, AND CONSUMABLES

Note Block

LOCATION	GATHERED WITH	USES
Crafted item	Crafting	Make some noise

Note Blocks make a brief noise when something powers them. Interact with the blocks to change the pitch of their noise and customize how they sound. If arranged carefully, this allows people to make music with them.

The instrument played by a Note Block is actually determined by the type of block underneath it. Wooden blocks produce a bass guitar noise. Sand and Gravel yield a snare drum sound. Stones are for a bass drum. Dirt does a synth piano.

RECIPE

INGREDIENTS	CRAFTING RECIPE	RESULT
Wood Plank (8), Redstone	→	Note Block

Orange Dye

LOCATION	GATHERED WITH	USES
Crafted item	Crafting	Stains items orange

Orange Dye stains Leather armor, Sheep, Wool, Glass, and other items a simple orange color.

RECIPE

INGREDIENTS	CRAFTING RECIPE	RESULT
Orange Tulip	→	Orange Dye
Rose Red, Dandelion Yellow	→	Orange Dye (2)

Painting

LOCATION	GATHERED WITH	USES
Crafted item	Crafting	Decoration

Paintings can improve the look of your home. Place them on walls to make your base impressive. Sometimes people put secret passages behind Paintings because you're allowed to walk through them as long as a solid block isn't on the other side. Experienced players are used to this and often search behind Paintings; this is why you might want to put a pit trap behind a Painting, in case someone runs straight through your Painting.

RECIPE

INGREDIENTS	CRAFTING RECIPE	RESULT
Stick (8), Wool	→	Painting

Paper

LOCATION	GATHERED WITH	USES
Crafted item	Crafting	Enchanting, crafting

Paper is made into Books, Maps, and Fireworks. It's made from Sugar Cane, which you can grow in large quantities as long as you have plenty of Water in the area. Turn Paper into Books once you have enough Leather, and use Books to make an Enchantment Table and tons of Bookshelves.
That's the route to better enchanting and superior equipment.

RECIPE

INGREDIENTS	CRAFTING RECIPE	RESULT
Sugar Cane (3)		Paper (3)

Pillar Quartz Block

LOCATION	GATHERED WITH	USES
Crafted item	Crafting	Decoration

Use two Quartz Blocks to make Pillar Quartz Blocks; they're striated in such a way that they look a bit like marble pillars. If you're making arches or other pieces of architectural flair, Pillar Quartz Blocks are perfect for the task.

RECIPE

INGREDIENTS	CRAFTING RECIPE	RESULT
Block of Quartz (2)		Pillar Quartz Block (2)

Pink Dye

LOCATION	GATHERED WITH	USES
Crafted item	Crafting	Stains items pink

Use Pink Dye to give a gentler appeal to Leather armor, Wool, Sheep, Stained Glass, and other items.

RECIPE

INGREDIENTS	CRAFTING RECIPE	RESULT
Pink Tulip		Pink Dye
Peony		Pink Dye (2)
Rose Red, Bone Meal		Pink Dye (2)

Piston

LOCATION	GATHERED WITH	USES
Crafted item	Crafting	Pushing objects

Pistons that receive power push blocks one space in a single direction. They can move an entire line of blocks up to 12 deep. When Pistons retract, they leave empty air behind. This resets their action, making it possible to push additional blocks forward if something new moves in front of them.

Pistons are often placed in areas when Cobblestone forms (from a Cobblestone Generator) or in spots where enemies get trapped. For the enemy scenario, use Pistons to shove blocks toward the enemies' heads. This begins the suffocation process.

RECIPE

INGREDIENTS	CRAFTING RECIPE	RESULT
Wood Plank (3), Cobblestone (4), Redstone, Iron Ingot	→	Piston

Powered Rail

LOCATION	GATHERED WITH	USES
Crafted item	Crafting	Fast Railways

Regular Rails keep your Minecarts moving quickly only if they lead down a slope. Otherwise, you lose speed over time, especially if you try to ascend an upward slope. Powered Rails are a way to combat this problem. Place a Powered Rail every 32 blocks once a Minecart is up to speed, and use a trio of Powered Rails to start your journey from either end. Add Powered Rails more frequently during steep upward sections of rail.

To provide power, use a Redstone Torch next to the Powered Rails. This provides constant energy to them.

RECIPE

INGREDIENTS	CRAFTING RECIPE	RESULT
Gold Ingot (6), Stick, Redstone	→	Powered Railway (6)

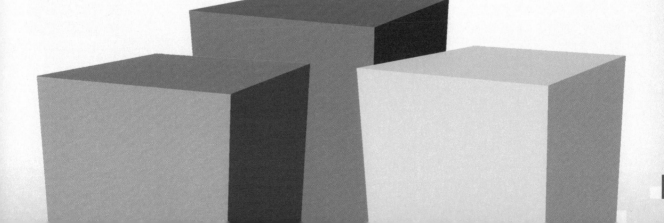

Pressure Plate

LOCATION	GATHERED WITH	USES
Crafted item	Crafting	Triggering power

Put Pressure Plates on the ground when you need to trigger a mechanism based on a monster or person's position. Use them in front of internal Doors to let people run outside without having to stop and open the Door. In more dangerous areas, use Pressure Plates to trigger traps.

RECIPE

INGREDIENTS	CRAFTING RECIPE		RESULT
Stone (2) or Wood Plank (2)		→	Pressure Plate

Purple Dye

LOCATION	GATHERED WITH	USES
Crafted item	Crafting	Stain objects purple

Purple Dye stains Leather armor, Sheep, Wool, Stained Glass, and so forth a pretty purple color.

RECIPE

INGREDIENTS	CRAFTING RECIPE		RESULT
Lapis Lazuli, Rose Red		→	Purple Dye (2)

Rail

LOCATION	GATHERED WITH	USES
Crafted item	Crafting	Minecart transportation

Rails create a path for Minecarts. You have to make these yourself most of the time, but you can find them naturally in abandoned mineshafts in the Overworld. Once you lay a line of Rails between two points, Minecarts with Furnaces can ride between them without much trouble.

Add Powered Rails to a system, give them power, and you won't have to rely on Minecarts with Furnaces or their fuel. Powered Rails accelerate Minecarts as long as they're supplied with power, as from a Redstone Torch.

RECIPE

INGREDIENTS	CRAFTING RECIPE		RESULT
Iron Ingot (6), Stick		→	Rail (16)

Redstone Comparator

LOCATION	GATHERED WITH	USES
Crafted item	Crafting	Making more complex power transmission systems

Redstone Dust carries power from a source, such as a Lever or Pressure Plate, to a machine that needs that power to operate. Redstone Comparators are more complex. They take power from the rear of the unit and transmit it to the front of the unit. Any power that comes in from the sides of the Comparator is used to either stop the back-to-front power entirely or to diminish it.

Use a Redstone Comparator in comparison mode to stop power if the side input is higher than the rear input. Otherwise, comparison mode does not affect power that comes out of the unit.

Use a Redstone Comparator in subtraction mode to reduce power output by the level of power coming in from the sides of the unit.

RECIPE

INGREDIENTS	CRAFTING RECIPE	RESULT
Redstone Torch (3), Nether Quartz, Stone (3)	→	Redstone Comparator

Redstone Lamp

LOCATION	GATHERED WITH	USES
Crafted item	Crafting	Light

Redstone Lamps require power to operate, but they produce light that is stronger than a Torch. They'll function all day and night, provided power isn't interrupted. Fiddle with Daylight Sensors if you'd like to have lamps that turn on only at night.

RECIPE

INGREDIENTS	CRAFTING RECIPE	RESULT
Redstone (4), Glowstone	→	Redstone Lamp

Redstone Repeater

LOCATION	GATHERED WITH	USES
Crafted item	Crafting	Strengthen Redstone signals

Redstone Repeaters let you transmit Redstone power across greater distances. They take the signal coming into the rear of their unit and spit it out the front with greater strength. This causes a brief delay in signal propagation, which is sometimes useful for making complex machine timings, as with Note Blocks and timed music.

RECIPE

INGREDIENTS	CRAFTING RECIPE	RESULT
Redstone Torch (2), Redstone, Stone (3)	→	Redstone Repeater

Redstone Torch

LOCATION	GATHERED WITH	USES
Crafted item	Crafting	Power source, power inversion

Redstone Torches don't yield much light, so they're great for vision only if you put them in an intentionally shady area, like a Mushroom garden. Otherwise, they're good for providing power. A Redstone Torch next to any machine gives that device continuous power. This is useful when you want to ensure that something is always functioning.

In other cases, you might want to invert a signal, and that's where Redstone Torches get exciting. If you supply external power to a Redstone Torch, it turns off! This is known as an inverter, because it turns off with power instead of turning on.

Complex machines are possible thanks to interactions like this. You can have a device that gets power only under certain circumstances. The classic example is a Daylight Sensor that spits out power during the day. Draw a line of Redstone Dust from the Sensor over to a block with a Redstone Torch and a Redstone Lamp on the other side of it. The Redstone Dust carries power to the Redstone Torch during the day, and that disables the power. When the light level falls, the signal does as well, and the Redstone Torch resumes its normal function. This turns the Redstone Lamp back on.

RECIPE

INGREDIENTS	CRAFTING RECIPE		RESULT
Redstone, Stick		→	Redstone Torch

Rose Red

LOCATION	GATHERED WITH	USES
Crafted item	Crafting	Stain items red

Rose Red turns Leather armor, Sheep, Wool, Stained Glass, and other items a deep red color.

RECIPE

INGREDIENTS	CRAFTING RECIPE		RESULT
Poppy or Red Tulip (or Beetroot in the Pocket Edition)		→	Rose Red
Rose Bush (or Rose on Consoles)		→	Rose Red (2)

Sandstone

LOCATION	GATHERED WITH	USES
Deserts, sandy areas	Pickaxe	Decoration

Sandstone forms beneath sandy areas. Use a Shovel to dig through the upper sandy layers and search for the harder Sandstone below. This material is quick to harvest with a Pickaxe, and it looks very nice. For color differentiation, use red sand to create the same types of blocks but in a much deeper color.

RECIPE

INGREDIENTS	CRAFTING RECIPE	RESULT	
Sand (4)		→	Sandstone
Sandstone (4)		→	Smooth Sandstone (4)

Sea Lantern

LOCATION	GATHERED WITH	USES
Crafted item	Crafting	Underwater Light Source

You rarely find Sea Lanterns when exploring the deep oceans of the Overworld. Limited only to ocean temples, these items are only seen on extremely rare occasions. They'll be destroyed if you try to mine them normally; only use items with Silk Touch if you're trying to harvest your own Sea Lanterns.

Lacking that enchantment, you can get enough Prismarine Crystals by breaking a couple of Sea Lanterns to craft one of your own. Though inefficient, this is still effective enough if you can't otherwise get these nifty underwater lamps for yourself.

RECIPE

INGREDIENTS	CRAFTING RECIPE	RESULT	
Prismarine Crystal (5), Prismarine Shard (4)		→	Sea Lantern

Sign

LOCATION	GATHERED WITH	USES
Crafted item	Crafting	Leaving messages

Signs are normally used to alert or remind players about areas that they're moving through. "This Chest has food." "This Chest has metal." "Lava ahead!" You can write several lines on each Sign, conveying a fair amount of information. Use arrows in the text to indicate directions.

```
    <--- Home
    Village --->
```

Your characters can walk through Signs without any problems, but Lava and Water won't flow through them. Use this trick to create air pockets underwater.

RECIPE

INGREDIENTS	CRAFTING RECIPE	RESULT
Wood Plank (6), Stick		→ Sign (3)

Slab

LOCATION	GATHERED WITH	USES
Crafted item	Crafting	Decoration

Slabs of material create half blocks that can be placed on an area's ground or ceiling. Though you don't have to jump to get onto Slabs, they still restrict movement if there isn't enough room overhead, so it's *almost* like you're walking on top of a full block even if it doesn't look that way.

You can place Redstone Dust trails underneath Slabs, allowing you to obscure your traps and machinery in subtle ways. Lay your power lines, test them, and then bury as much of their length as possible under a single layer of Slabs so it looks like nothing is there.

RECIPE

INGREDIENTS	CRAFTING RECIPE	RESULT
Three blocks of the following items: Stone, Sandstone, Cobblestone, Bricks, Wood Planks, Nether Brick, Quartz, Granite, Diorite, Andesite, or Polished Stones		Slab (6)

Snow

LOCATION	GATHERED WITH	USES
Crafted item	Crafting	Decoration

Use groups of Snowballs to craft entire blocks of Snow. Place these in and around your home to add a wintery appeal. Because Snow is packed nice and tight, it won't melt—even in the sun, and regardless of biome.

RECIPE

INGREDIENTS	CRAFTING RECIPE	RESULT
Snowball (4)		Snow

Snowball

LOCATION	GATHERED WITH	USES
Crafted item	Crafting	Crafting or thrown for fun

Break Snow blocks or ground cover to gather Snowballs. These items are crafted into Snow Blocks or can be equipped and thrown at targets for fun. They don't hurt most targets, but Blazes and the Ender Dragon are an exception to this; both of them are vulnerable to Snowball attacks.

Stained Clay

LOCATION	GATHERED WITH	USES
Crafted item	Crafting	Decoration

Go to a Crafting Table with eight blocks of Hardened Clay, which is made by cooking regular Clay Blocks in a Furnace. Craft Stained Clay by adding any dye you like to this batch of Hardened Clay. The result can be any color in the game, determined by the dye used.

Decorate your house any way you like with this method of coloring.

RECIPE

INGREDIENTS	CRAFTING RECIPE	RESULT
Hardened Clay (8), any dye		Stained Clay (8)

Stained Glass

LOCATION	GATHERED WITH	USES
Crafted item	Crafting	Decoration

Combine eight normal blocks of Glass with any dye to produce blocks of Stained Glass. Make a chapel, get some privacy, or just set up neat windows for fun.

RECIPE

INGREDIENTS	CRAFTING RECIPE	RESULT
Glass (8), any dye		Stained Glass (8)

Stained Glass Panes

LOCATION	GATHERED WITH	USES
Crafted item	Crafting	Decoration

Stain your Glass any color, and then craft the results into Glass Panes. They retain their color. Now you have even more decorating options.

RECIPE

INGREDIENTS	CRAFTING RECIPE	RESULT
Stained Glass (6)		Stained Glass Panes (16)

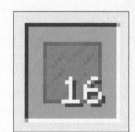

Stairs

LOCATION	GATHERED WITH	USES
Crafted item	Crafting	Saving energy when climbing

You can craft Stairs out of a variety of materials. Create a crude set of blocks going up one block and then over one block. Repeat this until you have a series of "steps" allowing characters to jump until they reach the top. Then descend these natural steps and place your Stairs on the lower side of each block. If you try to place the Stairs too high, they come in upside-down and aren't useful for climbing.

A real set of Stairs reduces jumping and saves a huge amount of energy when climbing a long flight. Jumping burns through your hunger meter, so this is a worthwhile endeavor. Stairs look nice, too, so there's an aesthetic consideration as well.

RECIPE

INGREDIENTS	CRAFTING RECIPE	RESULT
Any six blocks of the following: Wood Planks, Cobblestone, Bricks, Stone Bricks, Nether Bricks, Sandstone, or Quartz		Stairs (4)

Stick

LOCATION	GATHERED WITH	USES
Crafted item	Crafting	Crafting

Divide Wood Planks into Sticks for a wide range of crafting options. Sticks are required for Swords, almost all tools, Rails, Fences, Gates, Signs, Ladders, Item Frames, and more. They're invaluable. Unless your inventory is filling up very quickly, having Sticks on hand is a nice timesaver for replacing broken tools or making new Torches without taking extra steps.

RECIPE

INGREDIENTS	CRAFTING RECIPE	RESULT
Wood Plank (2)		Stick (4)

Sticky Piston

LOCATION	GATHERED WITH	USES
Crafted item	Crafting	Pushing and pulling objects

Sticky Pistons have the same general function as Pistons in that they push blocks one space forward. However, Sticky Pistons pull back the block to which they're attached. They're fun for making doors out of solid blocks. Trigger a Sticky Piston, let it open the makeshift door, and then cut the power to put the wall back in place. How cool is that for a secret lair?

RECIPE

INGREDIENTS	CRAFTING RECIPE	RESULT
Piston, Slimeball		Sticky Piston

TNT

LOCATION	GATHERED WITH	USES
Crafted item	Crafting	Blowing stuff up

Craft blocks of TNT to use in traps, mining, or simply to have fun. The ingredients are easy to come by when hunting Creepers. Carry TNT to a room you want to demolish, and place the block of explosives in the middle. Ignite TNT with a power source or something that creates fire (e.g., Flint and Steel), but make sure you don't stand nearby for the blast. TNT delivers a huge amount of damage.

RECIPE

INGREDIENTS	CRAFTING RECIPE	RESULT
Gunpowder (5), Sand (4)		TNT

Torch

LOCATION	GATHERED WITH	USES
Crafted item	Crafting	Light

Get a supply of Coal and Wood, and you can make Torches by the bundle. They're great for lighting your house, keeping your property clear of monster spawns, and for lighting tunnels while mining and exploring. Put Torches on the walls or the ground to create light. They aren't the strongest light source in the game, but they're close—and they're inexpensive.

RECIPE

INGREDIENTS	CRAFTING RECIPE	RESULT
Stick, Coal/Charcoal		Torch (4)

Trapdoor

LOCATION	GATHERED WITH	USES
Crafted item	Crafting	Covering shafts

Use Trapdoors to conceal pits and prevent creatures from falling into them. Trapdoors open manually but can also be opened or closed with Redstone power. Use trails of Redstone Dust to activate Trapdoors from safety to drop monsters into deadly pits. You can craft Trapdoors with either Wood or Iron Ingots, depending on the visual look of the item you're interested in making.

RECIPE

INGREDIENTS	CRAFTING RECIPE	RESULT
Wood Plank or Iron Ingot (6)		Trapdoor (2) or Iron Trapdoor (1)

Trapped Chest

LOCATION	GATHERED WITH	USES
Crafted item	Crafting	Interesting traps and secrets

Trapped Chests produce Redstone power when they're opened. They have a red tinge around their lock, so careful players spot them before they open the chests. Signals from Trapped Chests are used to activate TNT, pits, and other defenses.

RECIPE

INGREDIENTS	CRAFTING RECIPE		RESULT
Chest, Tripwire Hook		→	Trapped Chest

Tripwire Hook

LOCATION	GATHERED WITH	USES
Crafted item	Crafting	Trap activation

Place two Tripwire Hooks across from each other in a passage; use a piece of String to connect them. This arms your trap, producing a pulse of energy if anything walks over the String or cuts it without using Shears.

Attach your Tripwire Hooks to a Redstone trail and devise a nasty device to punish intruders: Lava from the ceiling, pits below, Pistons to close the corridor around someone, etc.

RECIPE

INGREDIENTS	CRAFTING RECIPE		RESULT
Iron Ingot, Stick, Wood Plank		→	Tripwire Hook (2)

Wall

LOCATION	GATHERED WITH	USES
Crafted item	Crafting	Decoration and defense

Walls protect areas from ingress by monsters, animals, and players. They can't be jumped over, so people have to break them or go around. They still allow a line of sight over the top edge, so you can see the areas outside your defensive perimeter. Shoot over your Wall to safely kill monsters when they approach.

RECIPE

INGREDIENTS	CRAFTING RECIPE		RESULT
Cobblestone (6) or Mossy Cobblestone (6)		→	Wall (6)

Weighted Pressure Plate

LOCATION	GATHERED WITH	USES
Crafted item	Crafting	Sends a variable Redstone signal when used

Weighted Pressure Plates don't send a maximum-strength Redstone signal unless a certain amount of weight is placed upon them. Gold makes plates that trigger more easily and send a full-strength signal if there are 15 entities on top of it. Iron plates require much more weight to give off a strong signal; it takes over 140 items and creatures to fully trigger these plates.

RECIPE

INGREDIENTS	CRAFTING RECIPE	RESULT
Iron Ingot (2) or Gold Ingot (2)		Weighted Pressure Plate

Wood Plank

LOCATION	GATHERED WITH	USES
Crafted item	Crafting	Crafting, construction

Create Wood Planks by crafting any type of Wood in your inventory. You can then break down the resulting Planks even further into Sticks, or use the Planks to make a wide range of Wood-based items. Wood Planks are critical for wooden tools and equipment, the first accessible tier of these implements.

Wood Planks are also used to make a vast range of furniture. At no point in the game do you stop using Wood or Wood Planks. Always keep a large supply in your Chests, and carry a full stack when leaving home.

RECIPE

INGREDIENTS	CRAFTING RECIPE	RESULT
Wood		Wood Plank (4)

Wool

LOCATION	GATHERED WITH	USES
Worn by Sheep	Shears	Crafting

Gather Wool by using Shears on Sheep. Killing them yields less Wool, and live Sheep can regrow their Wool as long as they have access to yummy grass.

Wool is one of the most easily customized items in the game. Use dyes to change the color of your Wool, and then make custom blocks of Wool or craft colored Carpet. Wool is used to craft Beds and Paintings as well.

Written Book

LOCATION	GATHERED WITH	USES
Crafted item	Use a Book and Quill to write in it	Convey information

Craft a Book and Quill, and then use this item from your hotbar. This lets you edit the text in the Book and Quill and turn it into a Written Book. Villagers trade Emeralds for these when you're lucky, and they're also good for writing down stories for other players.

To copy a Written Book that you've edited, craft your existing one with another Book and Quill.

RECIPE

INGREDIENTS	CRAFTING RECIPE	RESULT
Written Book, Book and Quill	→	Written Book (2)

FOOD AND FOOD INGREDIENTS

Apple

LOCATION	GATHERED WITH	USES
Grow on trees	Anything	Food

Apples sometimes drop when you drop Leaves, either by breaking them manually or when you destroy the Wood that the Leaves are associated with. After the Leaves break or decay naturally, an Apple is sometimes left behind. This happens only when working with Oak Leaves; other trees don't leave Apples.

Apples are an adequate food for the early game, when you're looking for something—anything—to eat. Their rarity makes them a poor choice for long-term hunger management. Breed animals or farm to provide for your feeding needs.

You can also craft Apples into Golden Apples or Enchanted Golden Apples when you want to get powerful effects for your character, but both of these items are costly.

Baked Potato

LOCATION	GATHERED WITH	USES
Cooked item	Cook Potatoes in a Furnace	Food

Throw a Potato into a Furnace and cook it. The result is a Baked Potato. Potatoes are extremely renewable because they're easy to grow.

Bowl

LOCATION	GATHERED WITH	USES
Crafted item	Crafting	Make Mushroom Stew

Bowls are used to carry Mushroom Stew. It takes only a few Planks to make your Bowl, so they're fairly easy to craft even out in the wilderness, though you need a Crafting Table as well.

If you're playing the Pocket Edition, Beetroots are also used with Bowls to make Beetroot Soup, a healing food.

RECIPE

INGREDIENTS	CRAFTING RECIPE	RESULT
Wooden Planks (3)		Bowl (4)

Bread

LOCATION	GATHERED WITH	USES
Crafted item	Crafting	Food

Combine three Wheat in order to craft a loaf of Bread. It's not an ideal food item, because it doesn't fill your hunger bar as much as cooked meat. However, Bread is extremely easy to make, and Wheat is renewable on a large scale. Make large Wheat farms to ensure you have food at your fingertips, regardless of the occasion.

RECIPE

INGREDIENTS	CRAFTING RECIPE	RESULT
Wheat (3)		Bread

Brown Mushroom

LOCATION	GATHERED WITH	USES
Swamps, shaded areas, the Nether	Anything	Food

Brown and Red Mushrooms combine to make Mushroom Stew. Carry a wooden Bowl around to make Mushroom Stew while exploring Swamps and various underground areas, including the Nether.

Cake

LOCATION	GATHERED WITH	USES
Crafted item	Crafting	Food

Cake isn't a very powerful food item, but it's fun to eat because you can share it with friends. Once crafted, Cake becomes a block that you must place somewhere before it can be eaten. Stack the Cake on top of a higher block so it's easy to see, and to keep it off the ground. Then up to six people can take a bite out of it. Each bite restores only a tiny amount of hunger.

Baking your first Cake earns an achievement!

RECIPE

INGREDIENTS	CRAFTING RECIPE		RESULT
Milk (3), Sugar (2), Egg, Wheat (3)		→	Cake

Carrot

LOCATION	GATHERED WITH	USES
Carried by Zombies	Anything	Food, Pig breeding

Zombies drop Carrots on rare occasions. You sometimes find them in villages as well. They're a useful crop to farm, and don't require any new locations or methods compared to Potatoes or Wheat. Develop farmland, irrigate it, and start growing Carrots as soon as you find one of them.

When holding Carrots, you can lure Pigs and Rabbits. Carrots are also used to breed Pigs once you have a few of them.

In crafting, Carrots make Carrots on a Stick and Golden Carrots.

Clownfish

LOCATION	GATHERED WITH	USES
Water blocks	A Fishing Rod	Food and Ocelot taming

Clownfish isn't very tasty. There isn't any way to cook it properly, and it doesn't restore much health. Save these until you find Ocelots, and then use them to tame kitties. Ocelots like them as well as any other raw variety of fish.

Cooked Chicken

LOCATION	GATHERED WITH	USES
Cooked item	Cook Raw Chicken in a Furnace	Food

Kill Chickens with fire or cook Raw Chicken in a Furnace to produce Cooked Chicken. This eliminates the chance of food poisoning that Raw Chicken poses.

Cooked Porkchop

LOCATION	GATHERED WITH	USES
Cooked item	Cook Raw Porkchops in a Furnace	Food

Cook Raw Porkchops in a Furnace, or use fire to kill Pigs. Either of these methods produces Cooked Porkchops. They restore a fair amount of hunger.

Cooked Salmon

LOCATION	GATHERED WITH	USES
Cooked item	Cook Raw Salmon in a Furnace	Food

Take Raw Salmon and cook it in a Furnace. That's it; you now have some yummy food to eat.

Cookie

LOCATION	GATHERED WITH	USES
Crafted item	Crafting	Food

Cookies are made from Wheat and Cocoa Beans. They're made in large batches, and it takes quite a few to fill you up. They don't leave you satisfied for long, but having large stacks of them makes it easy to eat only as much as you need so nothing gets wasted.

All in all, Cookies are useful if you have Cocoa Beans and Wheat. They're a reliable food source, despite several minor drawbacks, such as long eating time for the amount of hunger restored.

RECIPE

INGREDIENTS	CRAFTING RECIPE		RESULT
Cocoa Bean, Wheat (2)		→	Cookie (8)

Egg

LOCATION	GATHERED WITH	USES
Near Chickens	Pick them up	Baking

Chickens lay eggs once or twice every 10 minutes. They pop out, making a sound when it happens, and you can grab the Egg any time after that. Eggs are ingredients for Cakes and Pumpkin Pie.

It's also possible to throw Eggs. Equip them on your hotbar and use the Eggs as projectile weapons. They don't inflict any substantial damage, but they sometimes spawn a baby Chicken when they hit something.

Enchanted Golden Apple

LOCATION	GATHERED WITH	USES
Crafted item	Crafting	Special food

Enchanted Golden Apples require nine times more Gold to create than a Golden Apple. They're brutal to craft. However, they add 30 seconds of Regeneration V, the same amount of Absorption as a Golden Apple, and five minutes of Resistance and Fire Resistance. You become almost an un-killable god after eating one. Save Enchanted Golden Apples for boss fights against the Wither or Ender Dragon. Otherwise, you're spending too much Gold to be worthwhile.

RECIPE

INGREDIENTS	CRAFTING RECIPE	RESULT
Apple, Gold Block (8)		Enchanted Golden Apple

Gold Block

LOCATION	GATHERED WITH	USES
Crafted item	Crafting	Decoration or crafting an Enchanted Golden Apple

Put together a full set of nine Gold Ingots to craft a Gold Block. It looks nice, but it's very expensive. You won't use them to decorate your house unless you've been playing for a long time or are working in Creative Mode.

Gold Blocks are ingredients for Enchanted Golden Apples, the most expensive and most useful food in the game.

RECIPE

INGREDIENTS	CRAFTING RECIPE	RESULT
Gold Ingot (9)		Gold Block

Golden Apple

LOCATION	GATHERED WITH	USES
Crafted item	Crafting	Special food

Golden Apples are sometimes found in Chests, but you often have to craft them yourself. Golden Apples act as food items that also provide beneficial effects to your character. Golden Apples give you Regeneration II for several seconds, and add Absorption for a couple minutes. For major battles, Golden Apples are worthwhile items to use.

RECIPE

INGREDIENTS	CRAFTING RECIPE	RESULT
Apple, Gold Ingot (8)		Golden Apple

Golden Carrot

LOCATION	GATHERED WITH	USES
Crafted item	Crafting	Brewing or eating

Golden Carrots are expensive. Get a Carrot from a Zombie and start a Carrot garden. Then craft one of your Carrots with eight Gold Nuggets to make one Golden Carrot. Golden Carrots are used in Potions of Night Vision, or they're eaten to restore a large amount of hunger.

RECIPE

INGREDIENTS	CRAFTING RECIPE		RESULT
Carrot, Gold Nugget (8)		→	Golden Carrot

Melon

LOCATION	GATHERED WITH	USES
Jungle biomes	Anything	Brewing or eating

Melons are naturally found in jungles, though they're also available for trade in some villages. Once you find Melons or Melon Seeds, create a garden at your base. A steady supply of Melons is extremely handy because of their use in brewing.

Combine Gold Nuggets and Melon to make Glistering Melon. This is a major brewing ingredient thanks to its use in Potions of Healing!

Milk

LOCATION	GATHERED WITH	USES
Inside Cows	Bucket	Remove poison and other effects

Cows and Mooshrooms provide Milk if you use a Bucket on either of them. This liquid doesn't fill up your hunger bar, but it's useful for removing a variety of effects. Use Milk after eating poisonous foods to negate their negative effects.

When fighting against creatures that cause poison, it's smart to keep a Bucket of Milk on hand. Use it after battle to reduce the damage you've taken.

Mushroom Stew

LOCATION	GATHERED WITH	USES
Crafted item	Crafted in a Bowl	Snacks

Mushroom Stew requires harvesting a Red Mushroom and a Brown Mushroom. Combine these in your inventory with a Bowl to create this stew. Eating the stew frees up your Bowl to be reused as many times as needed. Carry a Bowl when traveling through swamps or the Nether to get free food on the fly without wasting much time.

Use Bowls to "milk" Mooshrooms to receive this stew. Mooshrooms are insanely useful animals to keep around.

RECIPE

INGREDIENTS	CRAFTING RECIPE	RESULT
Red Mushroom, Brown Mushroom, Bowl		Mushroom Stew

Poisonous Potato

LOCATION	GATHERED WITH	USES
Potato Farms	Anything	None

When harvesting Potatoes, you sometimes (rarely) end up with Poisonous Potatoes as well. Don't eat these; they've gone bad. Throw them away, give them to friends you don't like, or leave them in a Chest in case someone ever comes up with a fun use for them.

Potato

LOCATION	GATHERED WITH	USES
Zombie treasures or villages	Kill Zombies or steal from Village Farmers	Food

If you want to get a Carrot or Potato, kill Zombies often. These rare drops provide an entirely new type of crop to plant in your garden. Potatoes are planted directly into farmland and grow in a way that's similar to Wheat. When they fully pop out of the soil, harvest them and cook them in a Furnace to create Baked Potatoes.

Pufferfish

LOCATION	GATHERED WITH	USES
Water blocks	Use a Fishing Rod	Brew Potions of Water Breathing

Fishing Rods occasionally grab Pufferfish from the water. These are not edible in any safe way; they make your character very sick. However, they're the main ingredient for Potions of Water Breathing. Save your Pufferfish in a Chest with brewing ingredients in case you ever wan to perform involved underwater exploration or construction.

Pumpkin

LOCATION	GATHERED WITH	USES
Found rarely throughout the Overworld	Axe	Helmets, cooking, crafting

Pumpkins are hard to find. They grow naturally in a number of biomes, but they're rare enough that you don't always find them within a minute or two of your home. Getting these plants requires a fair amount of exploration unless you're really lucky!

Once you find Pumpkins, chop them down with an Axe and bring them home. Break your Pumpkins into Pumpkin Seeds, and plant those. Let your Pumpkin garden grow on its own for a while, and then use your excess Pumpkins for pies, Pumpkin Helmets (which don't enrage Endermen), or Jack o' Lanterns (good mood lighting).

Pumpkin Pie

LOCATION	GATHERED WITH	USES
In a baker's oven	Crafting	Dessert

Pumpkin Pie is made when an Egg, Sugar, and a Pumpkin are crafted together. If you have a Chicken pen and gardens for Sugar Cane and Pumpkins, this is a very easy item to make. Cooked meats are better at filling up your character, but Pumpkin Pie still fills a satisfying number of bars on your hunger meter. You just end up hungry sooner than if you eat cooked meats.

RECIPE

INGREDIENTS	CRAFTING RECIPE	RESULT
Pumpkin, Sugar, Egg	→	Pumpkin Pie

Raw Beef

LOCATION	GATHERED WITH	USES
On Cows	Kill Cows with a Sword	Cooking

Each Cow can drop up to several pieces of Raw Beef. Cook these in a Furnace to produce Steak, a very nice food item. If you use fire to kill a Cow, they drop Steak instead of Raw Beef.

Raw Chicken

LOCATION	GATHERED WITH	USES
On Chickens	Kill Chickens with a Sword	Cooking

Hunting Chickens earns Raw Chicken. Kill them with a Sword to get raw meat, or use Flint and Steel to get your Chickens cooked immediately. Always cook Raw Chicken in a Furnace; raw meat from these birds has a chance to make your character sick from food poisoning.

Raw Fish

LOCATION	GATHERED WITH	USES
Water blocks	A Fishing Rod	Cooking

Use a Fishing Rod to harvest Fish and other useful items from Water blocks. Pull the Rod out of the Water when you see bubbling, and hope for something good. Raw Fish are cooked in Furnaces to produce Cooked Fish.

If you want a house cat, feed Raw Fish to Ocelots to try to tame them. Bring several pieces of Raw Fish, because you won't always impress them with your first gift!

In the Pocket Edition of *Minecraft*, Red Mushrooms are cooked in Furnaces to produce Rose Red dye.

Raw Porkchop

LOCATION	GATHERED WITH	USES
Pigs	Kill Pigs with Swords	Cooking

Pigs are found in small groups throughout the Overworld. Kill them with your Sword to grab a few pieces of Raw Porkchops. Cook them in your Furnace to turn them into yummy Porkchops.

If you kill Pigs with fire, they'll drop Cooked Porkchops instead.

Raw Salmon

LOCATION	GATHERED WITH	USES
Water blocks	A Fishing Rod	Food

Gather Raw Salmon by using your Fishing Rod on Water blocks. This takes time and patience, so it isn't as efficient as farming. Once you get Raw Salmon or other edible fish, take it to a Furnace and cook it. Eat the Cooked Salmon whenever you get hungry.

Red Mushroom

LOCATION	GATHERED WITH	USES
Dark areas in forests or the Nether	Anything	Food (Mushroom Stew)

Red Mushrooms and Brown Mushrooms are combined with Bowls to make Mushroom Stew. This is a good food source for people working with shade gardens. It's also nice in the Nether, because there aren't many ways to feed your character in that dimension. Mushrooms grow in the Nether's dim light, so they're a renewable food source. Just bring a Bowl and you're good to go.

Rotten Flesh

LOCATION	GATHERED WITH	USES
On Zombies	Kill Zombies	Healing and taming Wolves

Rotten Flesh is often bad for your health. Eating it often gives your character food poisoning, which drains points from your hunger bar. Eat Rotten Flesh only if you're desperate. Even then, save several Rotten Flesh and eat them all at once. Food poisoning doesn't stack, so you won't be any worse off eating five Rotten Flesh than you would be eating just one or two pieces.

It's better to save Rotten Flesh for Wolves. Feed them to earn their trust, and use Rotten Flesh to heal them or get them breeding once they're already tamed.

Spider Eye

LOCATION	GATHERED WITH	USES
Spider's Heads	Kill Spiders with any weapon	Brewing

Spider Eyes are fermented with Brown Mushrooms and Sugar to make Fermented Spider Eyes. These are very useful in high-end brewing. Regular Spider Eyes only help to make Potions of Poison and Weakness, so they're nice but slightly limited.

It is possible to eat Spider Eyes in an act of complete desperation if you're starving. However, they're poisonous. Drink Milk immediately after, or avoid eating them unless you're already at such low health that the poison won't do any additional damage.

Steak

LOCATION	GATHERED WITH	USES
Cooked item	Cook Raw Beef in a Furnace	Dinner

Slay Cows to collect Raw Beef. Put this inside a Furnace and use any type of fuel to cook the beef into Steak. Alternatively, kill Cows with fire to cook their meat instantly and get Steak straight from the source.

Steak is very filling, so it's a great food item to carry around when going far away from home.

Sugar

LOCATION	GATHERED WITH	USES
Crafting item	Crafted from Sugar Cane	Baking, Horse treats

Make Sugar by crafting a single piece of Sugar Cane into raw Sugar. Sugar is then used to bake Cakes or Pumpkin Pie. It's also an ingredient on Potions of Swiftness.

Feed Sugar to Horses to help tame them. It also helps heal injured Horses and helps them grow from foals into adult Horses.

RECIPE

INGREDIENTS	CRAFTING RECIPE	RESULT
Sugar Cane		Sugar

Wheat

LOCATION	GATHERED WITH	USES
Farms	Any tool	Makes Bread, and for animal breeding

Wheat is grown on farmland. Use Hoes to till Dirt or Grass blocks, plant Seeds on them, and ensure a block of Water is within four blocks so the Wheat grows as quickly as possible. Keep light on the area at all times, with sun, Torches, or Redstone Lamps, and harvest your Wheat when it gets tall and turns slightly brownish.

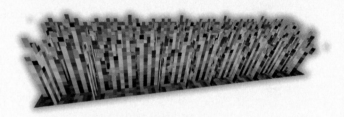

POTIONS

Awkward Potion

LOCATION	GATHERED WITH	USES
Brewing item	Brew a Water Bottle and Nether Wart	This is the core potion that leads to all useful secondary and tertiary potions

Awkward Potions don't do anything neat by themselves, but they're the foundation of brewing. Create a garden of Nether Wart to provide ingredients, and then brew as many Awkward Potions as possible with your surplus Nether Wart.

Awkward Potions are then used as ingredients for more complex potions. The number of effects is impressive: healing, harming, health regeneration, poison, faster movement, resistance to fire, breathing underwater, etc. Everything related to brewing comes from Awkward Potions. Brew them. Love them!

Mundane Potion

LOCATION	GATHERED WITH	USES
Brewing Item	Brew a Water Bottle with almost any common brewing ingredient	Can make a Potion of Weakness

Mundane Potions aren't of any use. They can be brewed again to make a Potion of Weakness, but that's not a great value either. You need to get Nether Wart and make Awkward Potions to get into serious brewing.

Mundane Potion (X)

LOCATION	GATHERED WITH	USES
Brewing item	Brew a Water Bottle and Redstone	Can make an extended Potion of Weakness

This potion doesn't do anything important, but it shows off the core power of Redstone in brewing (i.e., to extend the duration of potions).

Potion of Fire Resistance

LOCATION	GATHERED WITH	USES
Brewing item	Brew an Awkward Potion with Magma Cream	Protects against Lava, fire, and burning damage

If you're working around Lava frequently or fighting monsters in Nether Fortresses, it's great to have a Potion of Fire Resistance around. Blazes are much easier to handle when their attacks don't burn you.

Potion of Harming

LOCATION	GATHERED WITH	USES
Brewing item	Brew a Potion of Healing or Poison with a Fermented Spider Eye	Deals instant damage to a target

Potions of Harming are excellent weapons against heavily armored targets. These potions work great in PvP combat against players with enchanted Diamond Armor!

Potion of Healing

LOCATION	GATHERED WITH	USES
Brewing item	Brew an Awkward Potion with Glistering Melon	Heals targets instantly

Potions of Healing restore health as soon as they are used. Drinking them is fine, but Splash Potions of Healing are even faster because they work as soon as you throw them onto yourself—and they heal friends if you throw them at allies or NPCs. Bring these along when fighting Withers, Ender Dragons, or other players.

Potion of Invisibility

LOCATION	GATHERED WITH	USES
Brewing item	Brew a Potion of Night Vision with a Fermented Spider Eye	Turns you invisible

Potions of Invisibility are fun for sneaking or avoiding conflict. Your weapons and armor are still visible, so remove them if you want to be completely undetectable. Use these potions around other players to sneak into their bases, scout, and cause chaos.

Potion of Leaping

LOCATION	GATHERED WITH	USES
Brewing item	Brew an Awkward Potion with a Rabbit's Foot	Jumping higher than ever before

This potion allows your character to get through rough vertical terrain without having to do as much tunneling and stair construction. It's most useful when exploring places you're not going to return to very often. It's also fun if you're arranging free running races with your friends and want to get an edge (as long as that's allowable by whatever rules you come up with).

Potion of Night Vision

LOCATION	GATHERED WITH	USES
Brewing item	Brew an Awkward Potion with a Golden Carrot	You can see well at any light level

Potions of Night Vision are great when you're underground, in the Nether, or hunting The End. You can see well across long distances, pick out strange areas or buildings, and fight against monsters that would otherwise have a big advantage over you. Your success in battles against Withers depends heavily on these potions, because Withers love to blow up everything around them, including Torches!

Potion of Poison

LOCATION	GATHERED WITH	USES
Brewing item	Brew an Awkward Potion with a Spider Eye	Dealing damage over time

Potions of Poison deal consistent damage over time, regardless of the target's armor. They're nasty to use against other players, especially if your target has enchanted Diamond Armor. Many monsters are immune or resistant to poison damage.

Potion of Regeneration

LOCATION	GATHERED WITH	USES
Brewing item	Brew an Awkward Potion with a Ghast Tear	Restores health over time

Potions of Regeneration don't heal you quickly like a Potion of Healing, but they add a tremendous amount of health to your character over time. Combine this with a full health bar to ensure that you heal quickly from all minor wounds. Save Splash Potions of Healing to restore yourself almost instantly from more severe injuries.

Potion of Slowness

LOCATION	GATHERED WITH	USES
Brewing item	Brew a Potion of Fire Resistance or Swiftness with a Fermented Spider Eye	Slows movement

Make a Splash Potion of Slowness and throw it at enemies that you're trying to avoid. These potions are fairly effective against other characters.

Potion of Strength

LOCATION	GATHERED WITH	USES
Brewing item	Brew an Awkward Potion with Blaze Powder	Dramatically increases melee damage output

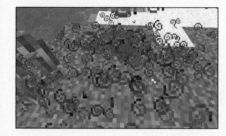

Use these powerful potions any time you deal with dangerous enemies. They're ideal when fighting in Nether Fortresses or when attacking Withers, Iron Golems, or any other scary beasts.

Potion of Swiftness

LOCATION	GATHERED WITH	USES
Brewing item	Brew an Awkward Potion with Sugar	Improves movement and jumping speed

Potions of Swiftness are very useful when exploring on foot, or if you fight fast creatures and need to maintain a speed advantage against them. They're nice for dealing with some of the Nether's dangerous monsters because many possess ranged attacks or high speed.

Potion of Water Breathing

LOCATION	GATHERED WITH	USES
Brewing item	Brew an Awkward Potion with a Pufferfish	You can breathe underwater

Potions of Water Breathing provide several minutes to swim underwater without the fear of drowning. It's nice to have these when exploring deep water, looking through underground caves, or if you want to create interesting structures underwater without having to wall off the area ahead of time.

Potion of Weakness

LOCATION	GATHERED WITH	USES
Brewing item	Brew a Water Bottle with a Fermented Spider Eye	Reduces damage output

Potions of Weakness reduce your damage output for a moderate period. They're useful only if you brew them into Splash Potions of Weakness to use against other targets, and even then they aren't especially important.

Thick Potion

LOCATION	GATHERED WITH	USES
Brewing item	Brew a Water Bottle with Glowstone Dust	Brewing Potions

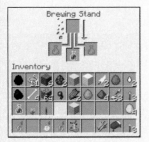

This is just a precursor potion to a Potion of Weakness. To accomplish more powerful brewing, make an Awkward Potion and move up from there.

Water Bottle

LOCATION	GATHERED WITH	USES
Brewing item	Add Water to a Glass Bottle	Brewing potions

Fill a Glass Bottle with Water to create the most basic "potion." Use either a Water source or a Cauldron to put Water into these bottles. These items become the starting point for potions, as explained in the "You Can Do Anything with a Little Practice" chapter.

TOOLS

Axe

LOCATION	GATHERED WITH	USES
Crafted item	Crafted	Harvesting Wood

Trees and other wooden objects can be broken with any tool or object, but Axes carve through these blocks faster than anything. Use Wooden Axes early in the game, but upgrade to Stone as soon as possible. Iron Axes are never required, but they're quick to get the job done, and they look nice too.

In a pinch, Axes are decent weapons. They lose more durability when used to kill monsters but, if you don't have a Sword, these tools offer your best form of defense.

RECIPE

INGREDIENTS	CRAFTING RECIPE		RESULT
Stick (2), Metal (3)		→	Axe

Bucket

LOCATION	GATHERED WITH	USES
Crafted item	Crafted	Carrying Milk, Lava, or Water

Craft a Bucket or two and keep them in your inventory. Use them to carry Water over to farming projects or down into the depths. Use that Water to irrigate farmland, to put out Lava and turn it into Obsidian, or to create traps and waterways that carry creatures or goods from one area to another.

Two Buckets are better than one, because two blocks of Water can form an infinite Water source. Carve out three blocks in the floor to make a trench, and use both Buckets to fill each end of the trench. Now you can gather Water from the middle of the trench without needing additional blocks of Water. This is quite useful underground or in other dry areas.

If you have a Cow, use a Bucket on it to gather Milk. Milk can remove effects from your character, such as Poison!

RECIPE

INGREDIENTS	CRAFTING RECIPE		RESULT
Iron Ingot (3)		→	Bucket

Clock

LOCATION	GATHERED WITH	USES
Crafted item	Crafted	Telling time

Clocks show you the position of either the sun or moon, regardless of where you're standing in the Overworld. This is wonderful if you're worried about getting caught outside in the evening, or if you're underground and still want to stick to a schedule.

RECIPE

INGREDIENTS	CRAFTING RECIPE	RESULT
Gold Ingot (4), Redstone		Clock

Compass

LOCATION	GATHERED WITH	USES
Crafted item	Crafted	Judging direction

A Compass is a basic tool to help you avoid getting lost. It shows the direction you're facing, as long as you stay in the Overworld—Compasses do not work in the Nether or The End.

RECIPE

INGREDIENTS	CRAFTING RECIPE	RESULT
Iron Ingot (4), Redstone		Compass

Empty Map

LOCATION	GATHERED WITH	USES
Crafted item	Crafted	Seeing the world from a bird's eye view

Use Empty Maps to create a picture of the world around your character. Things near the area where you first use the map are visible. It's smart to center these on your starting region. However, Maps don't show very much territory at first. To increase their scope, zoom out—this involves additional crafting. Use more Paper and your existing Map to see a wider area. You can do this up to four times to get maximum coverage.

If you ever need to copy your Map, use your existing one and a new Empty Map. This creates a clone of your old Map to use as a backup. Or you can give these to other players as a way of sharing knowledge.

RECIPE

INGREDIENTS	CRAFTING RECIPE	RESULT
Paper (8), Compass		Empty Map
Paper (8), Map		Zoomed Out Map
Map, Empty Map		Copy of current Map

Fire Charge

LOCATION	GATHERED WITH	USES
Crafted item	Crafted	Ingredient for Firework Stars

Fire Charges are single-use items, so they provide a very costly way to start fires. However, they're often crafted as a precursor to Firework Stars (very fun), or as a way to create dangerous traps. Use Fire Charges and a Dispenser as a way to deal damage to enemies that trigger your trap. This is especially powerful when filling the target area with flammable objects!

RECIPE

INGREDIENTS	CRAFTING RECIPE		RESULT
Blaze Powder, Gunpowder, and Coal/Charcoal		→	Fire Charge

Fishing Rod

LOCATION	GATHERED WITH	USES
Crafted item	Crafted	Gathering materials from Water

Fishing Rods are crafted from simple items. Break Wood into Sticks and kill Spiders to get a couple pieces of String early in the game. Once crafted, your Fishing Rod is a decent source of food or occasional treasure.

- Possible Fish: Fish, Salmon, Clownfish, Pufferfish (don't eat these ones)

- Treasure: Bow, Enchanted Book, Fishing Rod, Lily Pad, Name Tag, Saddle

RECIPE

INGREDIENTS	CRAFTING RECIPE		RESULT
Stick (3), String (2)		→	Fishing Rod

Flint and Steel

LOCATION	GATHERED WITH	USES
Crafted item	Crafted	Starting fires

Flint and Steel is a tool for starting fires without much mess or inconvenience. Carry one of these in your inventory, especially if you're killing livestock for food. Set animals on fire to immediately cook their meat; it's a nice timesaver. Or bring Flint and Steel into the Nether to relight Nether Portals to return home.

Avoid the temptation to set forests on fire. Once started, there's a chance that it can get out of control!

RECIPE

INGREDIENTS	CRAFTING RECIPE		RESULT
Iron Ingot, Flint		→	Flint and Steel

Hoe

LOCATION	GATHERED WITH	USES
Crafted item	Crafted	Gardening

Hoes aren't used too frequently, so you only need them on your quickbar if you're farming. Use Hoes on Dirt or Grass blocks to turn them into farmland. Farmland is used for planting seeds to grow Wheat and other edible crops. Make sure your farmland has access to Water within four blocks to keep it irrigated.

RECIPE

INGREDIENTS	CRAFTING RECIPE	RESULT
Stick (2), Metal (2)		Hoe

Pickaxe

LOCATION	GATHERED WITH	USES
Crafted item	Crafted	Breaking heavy blocks

Pickaxes are possibly the most important tool in *Minecraft*. With these, you can break Stone, Cobblestone, Netherrack, important ores and metals, and so forth. These tools are used constantly when mining, so they always deserve a place on your quickbar.

A certain quality of Pickaxe is needed to mine certain materials. Wood is useful only to harvest your first few pieces of Stone. Stone Pickaxes are faster and stronger, but can't mine better materials, such as Diamond, Redstone, etc. Switch to Iron Pickaxes for most tasks once you're established, and don't look back. Diamond is required only for working on Obsidian blocks.

RECIPE

INGREDIENTS	CRAFTING RECIPE	RESULT
Stick (2), Metal (3)		Pickaxe

Shears

LOCATION	GATHERED WITH	USES
Crafted item	Crafted	Gathering Grasses, Leaves, and Wool

Shears don't get constant use, but they're still nice to have in your inventory. This is especially true when wandering the Overworld's surface. Shears safely collect Wool from Sheep, Red Mushrooms from Mooshrooms, and String or Cobwebs from mine tunnels. And they can hack through Leaves like nobody's business.

RECIPE

INGREDIENTS	CRAFTING RECIPE	RESULT
Iron Ingot (2)		Shears

Shovel

LOCATION	GATHERED WITH	USES
Crafted item	Crafted	Digging through Gravel, Dirt, and Sand

Shovels are essential tools to craft early in the game and never stop creating. A Shovel is the best tool for loose blocks, including Gravel, Dirt, and Sand. Using Axes or Pickaxes for the same tasks damages those tools compared to using them for their normal functions, and it takes much longer.

For this reason, it's smart to keep a Pickaxe, Shovel, and Axe on your quickbar at the same time. Switch between them to always use the correct tool for the job.

RECIPE

INGREDIENTS	CRAFTING RECIPE	RESULT
Stick (2), Metal	→	Shovel

WEAPONS AND ARMOR

Arrow

LOCATION	GATHERED WITH	USES
Crafted item	Skeletons can drop Arrows	Fired from Bows or Dispensers

Arrows are shot from Bows or Dispensers to deal damage to enemies at range. These attacks inflict one to five damage, depending on how well-charged the attack.

Arrows fired into regular blocks can be retrieved if you're quick about it. Use this as a way to recover Arrows used while practicing, or misses from ranged combat.

RECIPE

INGREDIENTS	CRAFTING RECIPE	RESULT
Flint, Stick, Feather	→	Arrows (4)

Boots

LOCATION	GATHERED WITH	USES
Crafted item	Crafted	Damage reduction

Boots are a type of armor. They're made at a Crafting Table by using four pieces of either Leather or metal. Diamond Boots offer the best protection, but Iron Boots are pretty darn good and cost a lot less in terms of time to gather the materials.

Once your Boots are crafted, go into your inventory to put them on. Your character's appearance then changes and damage taken from physical sources is reduced.

RECIPE

INGREDIENTS	CRAFTING RECIPE	RESULT
Leather or Metal (4)	→	Boots

Bow

LOCATION	GATHERED WITH	USES
Crafted item	Crafted	Ranged combat

Bows are either crafted or gathered from defeated Skeletons (as a rare drop). Gather materials for Bow crafting by breaking Wood into Sticks and by killing Spiders to gather extra String.

Once this weapon is complete, equip it and keep Arrows in your inventory for use. You can deal decent damage at long range, as long as you're good at hitting your targets!

RECIPE

INGREDIENTS	CRAFTING RECIPE	RESULT
Stick (3), String (3)		Bow

Chestplate

LOCATION	GATHERED WITH	USES
Crafted item	Crafted	Damage reduction

Craft a Chestplate to dramatically reduce the damage taken from physical sources. This type of armor requires the most Leather or pieces of metal, so it's costly to craft or replace. However, it also offers the most protection out of all your armor pieces.

Once completed, go into your inventory to equip this item and start gaining its benefits. Diamond Chestplates are the best in the game, but Iron Chestplates are suitable for almost all fights.

RECIPE

INGREDIENTS	CRAFTING RECIPE	RESULT
Leather or Metal (8)		Chestplate

Helmet

LOCATION	GATHERED WITH	USES
Crafted item	Crafted	Damage reduction

Helmets are put together with five pieces of Leather or metal. Go into your inventory to equip them. Using armor reduces the damage taken from physical sources, such as melee attacks, Arrows, and explosions.

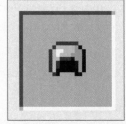

RECIPE

INGREDIENTS	CRAFTING RECIPE	RESULT
Leather or Metal (5)		Helmet

Leggings

LOCATION	GATHERED WITH	USES
Crafted item	Crafting	Damage reduction

Leggings are the fourth type of armor. Put together seven pieces of Leather or metal, and use these to protect your character's legs. Go into your inventory, equip them, and enjoy your increased survivability.

RECIPE

INGREDIENTS	CRAFTING RECIPE		RESULT
Leather or Metal (7)		→	Leggings

Sword

LOCATION	GATHERED WITH	USES
Crafted item	Crafted	Melee attacks

Swords are made with a Stick and two pieces of metal. Early in the game, you're likely to use Stone Swords fairly often, but switch to Iron Swords once you have just a couple pieces of Iron Ingots to spare; these improved blades last a long time and kill enemies quickly. You won't need to switch to Diamond Swords for a good while.

Once you have a Sword, use it in close-range combat to kill enemies. Attack them as you retreat to ensure your character gets in multiple attacks while your opponents suffer from knockback and miss opportunities to counter.

RECIPE

INGREDIENTS	CRAFTING RECIPE		RESULT
Sticks and Metal (2)		→	Sword

CREATURES BiG AND SMALL

This chapter discusses all the monsters, livestock, and anything else you might bump into. We'll show you what items are gathered from *Minecraft*'s beasts and how to safely defeat your enemies. The following list provides basic information for all the creatures in the game. Afterward, we cover each creature in greater depth.

ANIMAL AND MONSTER QUICK LIST

CREATURE	AGGRESSION	SPAWN LOCATION	ITEMS	HEALTH	ATTACK DAMAGE	EXPERIENCE VALUE	TAMEABLE?	RIDEABLE?	NOTES
Bat	Passive	Very low light areas, deep caves	None	6	None	None	No	No	N/A
Blaze	Aggressive	Nether Fortresses	Blaze Rod, Glowstone Dust (not in PC version)	20	5 at range, 6 up close	10	No	No	Can be damaged by Rain, Water, or Snowballs
Cave Spider	Neutral	Abandoned Mine Shafts	String, Spider Eyes	12	1 + Poison	5	No	No	Passive in bright light
Chicken	Passive	Overworld	Feathers, Raw Chicken, Eggs	4	None	1-3	No	No	Produces Eggs over time, and yields Cooked Chicken if slain by fire
Chicken Jockey	Aggressive	Low light areas	Rotten Flesh, Chicken items	20 for Jockey, 4 for Chicken	3-6 depending on Jockey's health	5 for Jockey, 1-3 for Chicken	No	No	Jockeys do more damage when they get hurt
Cow	Passive	Overworld	Leather, Raw Beef, Milk	10	None	1-3	No	No	Yields Steak if killed by fire, and yields Milk with a Bucket
Creeper	Aggressive	Low light areas	Gunpowder, Music Disc	20	49-97	5	No	No	Deals more damage if charged by lightning, and yields Music Discs if slain by Skeleton
Ender Dragon	Aggressive	The End	The Overworld Portal, Dragon Egg	200	10	12,000	No	No	Is healed by Ender Crystals
Enderman	Neutral	The Overworld or The End	Ender Pearls	40	7	5	No	No	Attacks when damaged or if you make eye contact
Endermite	Aggressive	Anywhere	None	8	2	3	No	No	Have a 5% chance of spawning each time you throw an Ender Pearl
Ghast	Aggressive	The Nether, out in the open	Gunpowder, Ghast Tears	10	17	5	No	No	Their shots cause an area-of-effect explosion of fire
Guardian	Aggressive	Underwater	Prismarine Crystals, Prismarine Shards, Raw Fish	30	6	10	No	No	Have a ranged attack and defensive spikes
Horse	Passive	The Overworld	Leather	15	None	1-3	Yes	Yes	Also can drop any equipped item when killed (including Saddles, Horse Armor, and Chests)
Iron Golem	Passive to villagers	Spawn in villages	Iron Ingot, Poppy	100	7	0	No	No	Attacks players that go after them or their villagers
Magma Cube	Aggressive	The Nether	Magma Cream	16	6	4	No	No	Split into smaller and weaker Magma Cubes as they take damage

CREATURE	AGGRESSION	SPAWN LOCATION	ITEMS	HEALTH	ATTACK DAMAGE	EXPERIENCE VALUE	TAMEABLE?	RIDEABLE?	NOTES
Mooshroom	Passive	Mushroom biomes in the Overworld	Red Mushrooms, Leather, Raw Beef, Milk, Mushroom Stew	10	None	1-3	No	No	Very useful creatures, but hard to find
Ocelot	Passive	Jungle biomes of the Overworld	None	10	None	1-3	Yes	No	Creepers are scared of them and will run away if one is nearby
Pig	Passive	The Overworld	Raw Porkchop	10	None	1-3	No	Yes	Can be saddled and ridden; drops Cooked Porkchops if killed by fire
Rabbit	Passive	The Overworld	Rabbit Hide, Raw Rabbit	10	None	1-3	No	No	Can be bred; may appear in an aggressive "Killer Rabbit" variant
Sheep	Passive	The Overworld	Wool	8	None	1-3	No	No	Shearing Sheep yields more Wool than killing them
Silverfish	Aggressive	Spawn inside special blocks or from Monster Spawners	None	8	1	5	No	No	Silverfish blocks take slightly more time to break
Skeleton	Aggressive	Low light areas of Nether Fortresses or the Overworld	Arrow, Bone	20	3 with Bows, 2 with Swords	5	No	No	Sometimes drop their Bows when killed
Slime	Aggressive	Lower areas of the Overworld	Slimeball	16	4	4	No	No	Break into smaller Slimes when damaged
Snow Golem	Passive to players	Created by players	Snowball	4	0 normally	None	No	No	Throws Snowballs that push back targets; these Snowballs can damage Blazes and the Ender Dragon
Spider	Neutral	Low light areas of the Overworld	String, Spider Eye	16	2	5	No	No	Neutral in brighter light; can also climb most blocks
Spider Jockey	Aggressive	Low light areas of the Overworld	Bone, Arrow, String, Spider Eye	20 for Skeleton, 16 for Spider	3 for Skeleton, 2 for Spider	10 total	No	No	These are rare spawns, so you won't see them often
Squid	Passive	Water blocks in the Overworld	Ink Sac	10	None	1-3	No	No	Can't swim up waterfalls
Villager	Passive	Villages in the Overworld	None	20	None	None	No	No	Traders with varied inventories
Witch	Aggressive	Low light areas of the Overworld	Glass Bottle, Glowstone Dust, Gunpowder, Redstone, Spider Eye, Stick, Sugar	26	Potions of Poison and Harming	5	No	No	Rarely drops potions when killed
Wither	Aggressive	Summoned by player	Nether Star	300	8	50	No	No	Created with SoulSand and Wither Skeleton Skulls

CREATURE	AGGRESSION	SPAWN LOCATION	ITEMS	HEALTH	ATTACK DAMAGE	EXPERIENCE VALUE	TAMEABLE?	RIDEABLE?	NOTES
Wither Skeleton	Aggressive	Nether Fortresses	Coal, Bone	20	7	5	No	No	Can drop Wither Skeleton Skulls and Stone Swords
Wolf	Neutral	In Forest and Taiga biomes of the Overworld	None	8 wild, 20 when tamed	2 wild, 4 when tamed	1-3	Yes	No	Tamed with Bones; healed with food
Zombie	Aggressive	Low light areas of the Overworld	Rotten Flesh	20	3-6	5	No	No	Does more damage when wounded
Zombie Pigman	Neutral	The Nether	Rotten Flesh, Gold Nugget, Gold Ingot	20	9	5	No	No	Can drop Golden Swords; attack in packs when provoked
Zombie Villager	Aggressive	Low light areas of the Overworld	Rotten Flesh	20	3-6	5	No	No	Can be cured with a Splash Potion of Weakness

EXPANDED CREATURE ENTRIES
Passive

BAT

AGGRESSION	SPAWN LOCATION	ITEMS	HEALTH	ATTACK DAMAGE	EXPERIENCE VALUE	TAMEABLE?	RIDEABLE?	NOTES
Passive	Very Low Light Areas, Deep Caves	None	6	None	None	No	No	N/A

Bats are spawned in dark caverns of the Overworld. You can hear them flying around in these areas, but they don't have any loot to worry about. It's usually best to leave them alone, because they pose absolutely no threat to your character.

CHICKEN

AGGRESSION	SPAWN LOCATION	ITEMS	HEALTH	ATTACK DAMAGE	EXPERIENCE VALUE	TAMEABLE?	RIDEABLE?	NOTES
Passive	The Overworld	Feathers, Raw Chicken, Eggs	4	None	1-3	No	No	Produces eggs over time, and yields Cooked Chicken if slain by fire

Chickens are very useful to raise for meat and their Feathers. You can breed a fairly large supply of them without much time investment.

Pen in a large group of Chickens and periodically walk through your pen to pick up the Eggs that the Chickens lay. If you carry Wheat Seeds in your hand, Chickens will follow you, making it easier to lead them to your barn/pen area.

Use seeds of any type to get Chickens to breed. Feed the seeds to your Chickens as often as every five minutes, and watch them create a new generation of livestock. Another way to spawn Chickens is to throw their Eggs at any creature or hard surface. When they break, there is a 12.5% chance that a Chicken will appear. In very rare cases, multiple Chickens can spawn from a single egg!

Chicks take 20 minutes to mature and can then be used for breeding, meat, or whatever else you have planned.

By using Hoppers and Dispensers, you can create automated Chicken breeding facilities.

COW

AGGRESSION	SPAWN LOCATION	ITEMS	HEALTH	ATTACK DAMAGE	EXPERIENCE VALUE	TAMEABLE?	RIDEABLE?	NOTES
Passive	The Overworld	Leather, Raw Beef, Milk	10	None	1-3	No	No	Yield Steak if killed by fire, and yield Milk with a Bucket

Cows are valuable additions to your operation, because they are a source of meat, Leather, and Milk (which can be used to cure Poison). It's always good to build a barn for these creatures as soon as you find them and bring them back to your home.

Cows can be found in groups while exploring the Overworld. When you find them, use a Lead or carry Wheat to lure the Cows where you want them to go. Fence them into a safe area, and then bring additional Cows from their herd back to the same place. Once you have a decent group, start your breeding program. Feed Wheat to the Cows to get them to reproduce. You can breed Cows as often as every five minutes. It takes 20 minutes for calves to grow up and become mature Cows.

To save time with adult Cows that are being slaughtered, use fire to cull them and produce Steak instead of Raw Beef. Flint and Steel works well for this purpose.

HORSE

AGGRESSION	SPAWN LOCATION	ITEMS	HEALTH	ATTACK DAMAGE	EXPERIENCE VALUE	TAMEABLE?	RIDEABLE?	NOTES
Passive	The Overworld	Leather	15	None	1-3	Yes	Yes	Also can drop any equipped item when killed (including Saddles, Horse Armor, and Chests)

Several types of Horses inhabit the *Minecraft* universe. Horses, Donkeys, and Mules are the normal varieties of these creatures, but using the PC commands can also spawn Undead and Skeletal Horses.

Search for Horses and Donkeys in areas of plains and savannah. Once you find them, you can tame these useful creatures by riding them a few times and then putting a Saddle on them. Horses can be tethered with a Lead to bring them with your character, or ridden if they are saddled.

Mules are not found in the Overworld on their own. Instead, these are created only when Horses and Donkeys are used in breeding. Mules are sterile and cannot be used for breeding on their own. Though you can't armor Mules or Donkeys, it is possible to load them with Chests for extra carrying capacity.

The taming process for Horses and Donkeys is somewhat involved. Approach these creatures with an open hand and interact with them to ride the creature briefly. They often toss you off pretty soon, but eventually they'll get used to you and get a happy little animation. That's when you can saddle them for long-term use.

Several different foods heal Horses and improve your chances to tame them, as listed here:

FOOD	HEALS	SPEEDS GROWTH BY	IMPROVES TAMING PERCENTAGE BY
Sugar	1	30 sec	3%
Wheat	2	1 min	3%
Apple	3	1 min	3%
Golden Carrot	4	1 min	5%
Bread	7	3 min	3%
Golden Apple	10	4 min	10%
Hay Bale	20	3 min	N/A

Once you have a Horse/Donkey of your own, Shift-click on it to open its inventory. That's where you put the Saddle and either Horse Armor or a Chest. Riding a tamed Horse is very fast, and it can jump higher than your character. Use these creatures to explore the world much more quickly than you otherwise could. Because Saddles and Horse Armor are found in dungeons and temples, you won't often be able to tame Horses early in the game.

To breed Horses, feed two of them Golden Apples as often as every five minutes. Foals take 20 minutes to grow up and gain some of their parents' stats. Because of this, it's smart to choose only your best Horses for breeding purposes. Compare health between Horses, and ride them to get a feel for which Horse is the fastest—there are differences between them!

MOOSHROOM

AGGRESSION	SPAWN LOCATION	ITEMS	HEALTH	ATTACK DAMAGE	EXPERIENCE VALUE	TAMEABLE?	RIDEABLE?	NOTES
Passive	Mushroom biomes in the Overworld	Red Mushrooms, Leather, Raw Beef, Milk, Mushroom Stew	10	None	1-3	No	No	Very useful creatures, but hard to find

Mooshrooms are amazing. They drop and create a wide range of items, making them almost a one-stop-shop for food, poison curing, and crafting goods. The only downside to these beasts is that they're very hard to find. Mooshrooms are a type of cattle that appear only in Mushroom biomes. You can breed them with Wheat and they're easy to take care of, so it's simply a matter of finding a herd.

Shear Mooshrooms to collect Mushrooms from them. Use a Bucket on them to get Milk, or a Bowl to get Mushroom Stew. Cull them for Leather and Raw Beef (or Steak if they're killed by fire). You can't go wrong.

OCELOT

AGGRESSION	SPAWN LOCATION	ITEMS	HEALTH	ATTACK DAMAGE	EXPERIENCE VALUE	TAMEABLE?	RIDEABLE?	NOTES
Passive	Jungle biomes of the Overworld	None	10	None	1-3	Yes	No	Creepers are scared of them and will run away if one is nearby

Ocelots are felines that can be domesticated. Look for Ocelots in jungles around the world. To tame them, use Raw Fish to lure the Ocelot toward your character. Walk until you're roughly ten blocks away from the creature, and then stop moving while holding onto your fish. Give the Ocelot time to notice you and see the fish in your hand.

Be patient to avoid scaring the Ocelot away—let it come to you! Any major movement will likely to scare the Ocelot and reset the taming process. When the Ocelot wanders over, feed the Raw Fish to it. It sometimes takes several feedings to tame your Ocelot. Once the process is complete, the Ocelot changes into a domesticated Cat and gains a new appearance.

Breed Cats by feeding them Raw Fish. As usual, you can breed animals only every 5 minutes, and their offspring take about 20 minutes to grow to maturity. Be careful with your kitties. They aren't terribly tough, they cannot be armored, and they won't last long in the wild if they're attacked or if they wander into a dangerous location. It's safest to leave your Cats at home so they don't get into too much trouble.

PIG

AGGRESSION	SPAWN LOCATION	ITEMS	HEALTH	ATTACK DAMAGE	EXPERIENCE VALUE	TAMEABLE?	RIDEABLE?	NOTES
Passive	The Overworld	Raw Porkchop	10	None	1-3	No	Yes	Can be saddled and ridden; drops Cooked Porkchops if killed by fire

Pigs are another type of livestock that you can breed, slaughter for food, or even ride. Several special attributes make these porcine creatures stand out. Lure Pigs back to your farm with Carrots; you also use Carrots to breed Pigs, so a nice Carrot garden is a must if you want to keep a large number of Pigs. Carrots sometimes drop when you kill Zombies, so hunt the creatures of the night if you want to start your garden.

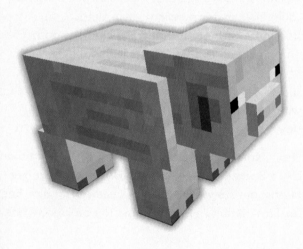

Once you have Pigs in a nice pen, breed them in the standard timing cycle. It takes five minutes before adults can breed again after their feeding, and 20 minutes for Piglets to grow to adulthood. Consider covering your pen with a roof. Pigs that are struck by lightning turn into Zombie Pigmen, and they aren't quite as edible.

If you have a Saddle and want to ride a Pig, craft a Carrot on a Stick and use it to control the Pig while you ride it. Few things in the world offer as much fun as charging around the wilderness with your trusted Pig mount.

RABBIT

AGGRESSION	SPAWN LOCATION	ITEMS	HEALTH	ATTACK DAMAGE	EXPERIENCE VALUE	TAMEABLE?	RIDEABLE?	NOTES
Passive	The Overworld	Rabbit Hide, Raw Rabbit, Rabbit Foot	10	None	1-3	No	No	Can be bred; may appear in an aggressive "Killer Rabbit" variant

Rabbits are normally peaceful animals that hop around meadows. They'll avoid you if attacked, and can be harvested for Hides, food, or sometimes a Rabbit's Foot (useful in potion making). Breed them with Dandelions or Carrots to create a nice population of these animals, and give them about 20 minutes for new Rabbits to grow up.

Killer Rabbits have a more aggressive look; they have different eyes and a bold, white pelt. They'll jump toward your character and attack quite viciously. They have a mean streak a mile wide, but can be fought off if you stay calm, face them, and smack them each time they get close to your character.

SHEEP

AGGRESSION	SPAWN LOCATION	ITEMS	HEALTH	ATTACK DAMAGE	EXPERIENCE VALUE	TAMEABLE?	RIDEABLE?	NOTES
Passive	The Overworld	Wool	8	None	1-3	No	No	Shearing Sheep yields more Wool than killing them

Sheep aren't the most useful livestock in *Minecraft*. They cannot be used for food, so Wool is all you get from them. Sheep drop Wool when slain, but this isn't a very efficient process; you get only one Wool per Sheep this way. Instead of killing the little guys, keep them in a barn and shear them instead. Shears are crafted with Iron, and they let you clip Sheep safely. You get far more Wool per Sheep, even on the first clipping, and their Wool regrows as long as the Sheep have access to grass for food.

You can dye Wool with any dyeing agent, but you can also dye the Sheep itself so that all of the Wool from its next clipping matches the dye's color. Future clippings revert to the Sheep's natural color, which varies between several shades.

SQUID

AGGRESSION	SPAWN LOCATION	ITEMS	HEALTH	ATTACK DAMAGE	EXPERIENCE VALUE	TAMEABLE?	RIDEABLE?	NOTES
Passive	Water Blocks in the Overworld	Ink Sac	10	None	1-3	No	No	Can't swim up waterfalls

Squid appear in large bodies of Water and are peaceful creatures. They happily swim around and don't cause any trouble, despite their dangerous appearance. The only items they drop are Ink Sacs, which are used to create a dark dye. Hunt Squid when you need these items, but otherwise it's fine to leave them alone.

Squid cannot swim up waterfalls, so there are numerous ways to trap them in large groups, where they can be killed later, used as decoration, or whatever else you have in mind.

VILLAGER

AGGRESSION	SPAWN LOCATION	ITEMS	HEALTH	ATTACK DAMAGE	EXPERIENCE VALUE	TAMEABLE?	RIDEABLE?	NOTES
Passive	Villages in the Overworld	None	20	None	None	No	No	Trade with varied inventories

Villagers appear in small towns located in some of the Overworld's plains, savannahs, and deserts. These villages offer exploration and places to trade for characters, and you won't be attacked unless you start any trouble. In that event, Iron Golems often defend Villagers that are under attack.

Interact with Villagers to try to trade with them. They accept Emeralds as payment, but those are rare gems. Most of the time, you'll do well by giving items to Villagers and trading their goods around until you get the items you want. There are several types of Villagers: Farmers, Librarians, Priests, Blacksmiths, Butchers, and regular Villagers. The items each Villager carries are determined by their profession. Interact with Villagers by clicking on them to see what they're carrying and their profession.

To gain Emeralds without mining Extreme Hills for hours at a time, you need to trade Villagers items that they require. Do not purchase generic items that you already have; the cost is very high in terms of time you invest gathering Emeralds. Instead, save your Emeralds and wait for special items to become available, including Diamond tools, Chainmail, Bottles of Enchanting, Pumpkins (only if you haven't found them yet), and so forth.

Villagers have children if their towns start to lose too many people, often to Zombie attacks. If you want a town to have a larger population, add Doors to buildings in the village. The more Doors there are the more people want to live in that town. That's just how Villagers are.

As of version 1.8, Villagers that are struck by lightning turn into Witches. Watch out! They've also learned how to harvest crops, so you can't always rush into town and find an entire field of free goodies to steal (a pity, but I guess Villagers have to eat too!).

SNOW GOLEM

AGGRESSION	SPAWN LOCATION	ITEMS	HEALTH	ATTACK DAMAGE	EXPERIENCE VALUE	TAMEABLE?	RIDEABLE?	NOTES
Passive to players	Created by players	Snowball	4	0 Normally	None	No	No	Throws Snowballs that push back targets; these Snowballs can damage Blazes and the Ender Dragon

Snow Golems are creatures that you create! Stack two Snow blocks and place a Pumpkin on top of the stack. These creatures use Snowballs to defend the area from hostile monsters. Their attacks are ranged but don't do any damage to most targets; they hurt Blazes because Snowballs always damage Blazes. This is also true for the Ender Dragon.

Instead of killing targets, Snow Golems are more of a distraction. They push enemies back and draw their attention. Place them at your property's outer edges so monsters stay near your perimeter instead of coming forward to harass your main buildings.

Snow Golems take damage over time when they're in warmer areas.

IRON GOLEM

AGGRESSION	SPAWN LOCATION	ITEMS	HEALTH	ATTACK DAMAGE	EXPERIENCE VALUE	TAMEABLE?	RIDEABLE?	NOTES
Passive to villagers	Spawn in Villages	Iron Ingot, Poppy	100	7	0	No	No	Attacks players that go after them or their villagers

Iron Golems are defensive creatures, just like Snow Golems. The difference is that these creatures are much tougher, can damage their enemies, and can even hurt your character. If you attack a village that is protected by Iron Golems, you'll get their attention. They'll chase after your character and attack if they get close. Run away to lose their interest, and then return at leisure—Iron Golems have short memories.

To create an Iron Golem, you need either a village or a ton of Iron. To create one directly, forge four Iron blocks and place them in a T-formation: one block on the ground with three blocks horizontally above it. Then add a Pumpkin to the top of the T. This is very expensive but makes a strong guardian that loves to attack monsters. If a village is nearby, simply wait for Iron Golems to appear on their own. This costs you nothing! They can then be farmed for their Iron, making it possible to generate Iron over time without having to mine. That's nifty.

Iron Golems can't be drowned, but regular battle damage and Lava kills them just fine. Or you can suffocate them in Gravel or Sand. This is slower but gets the job done.

Neutral

CAVE SPIDER

AGGRESSION	SPAWN LOCATION	ITEMS	HEALTH	ATTACK DAMAGE	EXPERIENCE VALUE	TAMEABLE?	RIDEABLE?	NOTES
Neutral	Abandoned Mine Shafts	String, Spider Eyes	12	1 + Poison	5	No	No	Passive in bright light

Cave Spiders are tiny monsters that live in the darkness below the Overworld. They fight and move much like regular Spiders, but they have poisonous bites (on most difficulty levels) and can squeeze through any gap in buildings, walls, etc. You have to completely block off an area to ensure they don't get into your safe rooms.

As with both types of Spiders, you should retreat while you fight these creatures. Attack them while backing up to limit their number of attacks against you. Having Milk around is useful in case you get poisoned, and keep yourself well fed so you regenerate health as quickly as possible after the fight.

Lure Cave Spiders away from tight areas, mine shafts with cobwebs, and other difficult places to navigate. Fight them in a place where you can get your back against a wall and force the enemies to come toward you in a straight line. Thus, you won't be overwhelmed by multiple creatures.

ENDERMAN

AGGRESSION	SPAWN LOCATION	ITEMS	HEALTH	ATTACK DAMAGE	EXPERIENCE VALUE	TAMEABLE?	RIDEABLE?	NOTES
Neutral	The Overworld or The End	Ender Pearls	40	7	5	No	No	Attacks when damaged or if you look them in the eyes

Endermen are dark beings from a world beyond our own! They spawn heavily in a place called The End, but they can appear in the Overworld as well. Though they're neutral by default, Endermen are easy to antagonize, and they attack your character viciously if you hit them or even look them in the eyes. Avoid this by staring at Endermen's feet or by wearing a Jack-o-Lantern on your head so Endermen don't know where you're looking.

Ranged attacks don't work against Endermen; they blink out of existence for a moment and reappear somewhere else—behind you as often as not. This, combined with their higher damage and health, makes them incredibly dangerous opponents when you aren't accustomed to fighting them. For the greatest chance of victory, wear armor, stare near the ground, and take consistent swings to chop your Enderman target to ribbons. Attacking an Enderman's legs prevents it from teleporting, so this secures your kill while protecting your character from teleporting attacks to your back.

When they're not being attacked, Endermen wander the world, pick up blocks and move them around, and just kind of act like weirdos. Their ability to teleport allows them to spawn in strange places. You might find them down in your mines, outside, or even within your own home! That's scary stuff. If you hear something moving around indoors, it's probably one of them. Endermen come inside most often when it rains; water hurts them, so they teleport anywhere safe. If your house is nice and dry, it makes a good target.

SPIDER

AGGRESSION	SPAWN LOCATION	ITEMS	HEALTH	ATTACK DAMAGE	EXPERIENCE VALUE	TAMEABLE?	RIDEABLE?	NOTES
Neutral	Low light areas of the Overworld	String, Spider Eye	16	2	5	No	No	Neutral in brighter light; can also climb most blocks

Like many Overworld monsters, Spiders appear during nighttime and thunderstorms, wherever illumination falls to extremely dim levels. Spiders don't burn up in sunlight, though they become more docile and won't attack characters unless provoked. Though they aren't terribly dangerous as single attackers, Spiders are still tricky customers. They fit through single-block openings, can climb over your walls, and make general nuisances of themselves even if they can't get inside. They can also get into your farm field, crush your plants, and must be cleared out manually later on.

Back away from Spiders and fight them while retreating so they can't jump on you as easily. They take only a few hits to kill, so that's a plus. It's easiest to fight these enemies in narrow areas where they can't get around to your side. Make them come through a tunnel or doorway to get to you so it's easier to hit them.

If you're desperate for food early in a game, Spider Eyes are poisonous but edible. Spiders also drop String, which can be used to make a Fishing Pole, allowing you to get more food from any body of Water.

WOLF

AGGRESSION	SPAWN LOCATION	ITEMS	HEALTH	ATTACK DAMAGE	EXPERIENCE VALUE	TAMEABLE?	RIDEABLE?	NOTES
Neutral	In Forest and Taiga biomes of the Overworld	None	8 wild, 20 when tamed	2 wild, 4 when tamed	1-3	Yes	No	Tamed with Bones; healed with food

One can find Wolves in several areas: forests and various taiga biomes. Growling Wolves are hostile and must be treated carefully. Other Wolves may be wild but are friendly enough to approach. Unless attacked, peaceful Wolves will not attack your character.

Hunt Skeletons for Bones if you'd like to tame a Wolf. Feeding Bones to friendly Wolves is how you tame these creatures. Sometimes the first Bone does the trick, but it might take several more to get the Wolf's loyalty. You can tame more than one Wolf, so feel free to try to establish an entire pack for yourself. After they're tamed, Wolves get more health and can deliver more damage, and they won't attack you even if you accidentally hit one of them. They're sweetie pies.

Increase the size of your pack by feeding raw meat to your Wolves. Like most livestock, feeding them causes breeding behavior, as long as two or more Wolves are fed together. Bring spare food to give to the offspring to give them more health. Note that any type of raw meat does the trick, including Rotten Flesh.

ZOMBIE PIGMAN

AGGRESSION	SPAWN LOCATION	ITEMS	HEALTH	ATTACK DAMAGE	EXPERIENCE VALUE	TAMEABLE?	RIDEABLE?	NOTES
Neutral	The Nether	Rotten Flesh, Gold Nugget, Gold Ingot	20	9	5	No	No	Can drop Golden Swords; attack in packs when provoked

In most versions of the game, Zombie Pigmen spawn near Nether Portals or more commonly inside the Nether. They're involved with the Nether Reactor in the Pocket Version. It's possible for lightning to turn a regular Pig into a Zombie Pigman, though this is not a common occurrence.

Zombie Pigmen don't attack your character on sight. They're surprisingly chilled out for rotting, undead monsters. As long as you don't hurt them or stand nearby when they take damage from fire, you'll be okay. Give them some space and avoid trouble. Hurting Zombie Pigmen causes them to become aggressive, and they bring every other Pigman in the area with them. This produces large battles that pose substantial risk to your character unless you retreat to a safe corridor and fight defensively. Be wary! Zombie Pigmen are fast runners, so it's hard to escape from them once they're angry. Sprint toward safety and hope for the best.

Zombie Pigmen drop a variety of golden items when they die, so farming them has value if you need Gold Nuggets, Gold Ingots, or a rare armor drop. Zombie Pigmen can pick up and equip weapons and armor, so don't leave anything useful on the ground unless you want to arm a local militia of undead piggies. For maximum safety, you can kill groups of Zombie Pigmen by walling yourself into a tunnel and shooting outward at enraged targets.

Aggressive

BLAZE

AGGRESSION	SPAWN LOCATION	ITEMS	HEALTH	ATTACK DAMAGE	EXPERIENCE VALUE	TAMEABLE?	RIDEABLE?	NOTES
Aggressive	Nether Fortresses	Blaze Rod, Glowstone Dust (not in PC version)	20	5 at range, 6 up close	10	No	No	Can be damaged by rain, Water, or Snowballs

Blazes are ranged monsters that live in the Nether. Their fire attacks shoot in bursts of three, giving you several seconds afterward to dash between cover or to charge your opponent. Take cover when you see a Blaze, and ready a Bow or some Snowballs to throw at your target. Pop out from cover, shoot, and hide again. Repeat this unless the Blaze gets close to your area, at which point you should switch to your Sword and ambush it for the kill.

Don't trade blows with a Blaze. Their attacks hit extremely hard and deal fire damage to your character. Fire Resistance makes such battles easier, but you still need to be quite careful around these opponents. Put up a barrier of Cobblestone so Blazes can't hit you even if they attack in an open walkway. Make it so Blazes have no choice but to give up their ranged advantage.

Also, watch your sides. Blazes fly, which means they're happy to suspend themselves over large drops so you can't get to them. Block all angles of fire to know where the Blazes will move.

CHICKEN JOCKEY

AGGRESSION	SPAWN LOCATION	ITEMS	HEALTH	ATTACK DAMAGE	EXPERIENCE VALUE	TAMEABLE?	RIDEABLE?	NOTES
Aggressive	Low light areas	Rotten Flesh, and Chicken items	20 for Jockey, 4 for Chicken	3-6 depending on Jockey's health	5 for Jockey, 1-3 for Chicken	No	No	Jockeys do more damage when they get hurt

Tiny Zombies sometimes spawn on top of a Chicken. They ride the Chicken around like a mount and attack your character as aggressively as they can. It's a funny sight, but you still have to be careful and avoid serious damage.

As usual, a fighting retreat is a good response when a Chicken Jockey attacks. They don't have too much health, so you have to hold them back for only a short time. Don't try to flee, because these guys chase you fast and far. Fight it out and get your kill. The good news is that you aren't likely to see any more on their way, because they're so rare in the first place.

CREEPER

AGGRESSION	SPAWN LOCATION	ITEMS	HEALTH	ATTACK DAMAGE	EXPERIENCE VALUE	TAMEABLE?	RIDEABLE?	NOTES
Aggressive	Low light areas	Gunpowder, Music Disc	20	49-97	5	No	No	Deal more damage if charged by lightning; yield Music Discs if slain by a Skeleton

Perhaps the most iconic monster in *Minecraft*, Creepers are nasty pieces of work. They don't attack you directly. Instead, they move toward your character and then explode when they get close enough. You know one is in the area when you hear an occasional kind of grunty noise. Once Creepers start their explosive attack, you hear a distinct hiss. If you hear this noise and can't see the Creeper, *run forward immediately*. The farther you get from the blast, the lower the damage you take.

Creepers are afraid of Ocelots and Cats, so having one around offers some protection against these surprise attackers. Even without that, vigilance is your best friend against Creepers. They're somewhat slow moving, and spotting them at range makes it much easier to avoid the enemies, kill them with Arrows, or set up a very careful melee ambush. If you're extremely careful, hit-and-run methods work well against Creepers. Knock them back with a single attack, and retreat to prevent them from detonating; they stop their explosion if you get far enough away before the point of no return.

Lure Creepers into Lava or bodies of Water to kill or isolate them. Their explosions don't damage blocks if Creepers are submerged, so this makes them much easier and safer to fight, even if your character is still at risk. At a minimum, stay away from your house and fields when Creepers are near, or stay away from the walls at night, even if you don't see a Creeper. One explosion can kill you or obliterate whatever you have nearby. Either of these outcomes is horrible to deal with.

In really special cases, you might see a Creeper with a strange aura around it. This is a Creeper that has been struck by lightning. Charged Creepers produce much deadlier explosions. Don't try to detonate one manually, even on Easy difficulty. Use a Bow and be safe.

ENDER DRAGON

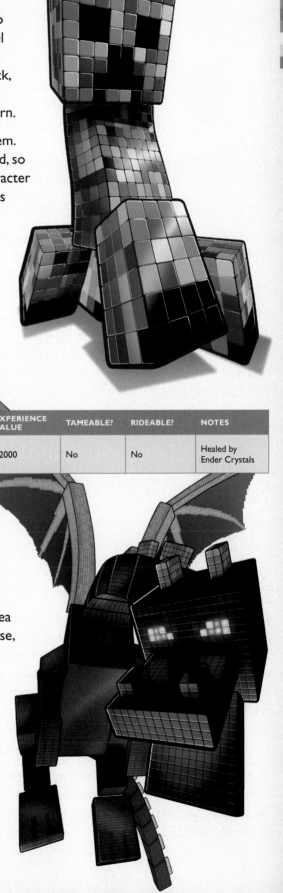

AGGRESSION	SPAWN LOCATION	ITEMS	HEALTH	ATTACK DAMAGE	EXPERIENCE VALUE	TAMEABLE?	RIDEABLE?	NOTES
Aggressive	In The End	The Overworld Portal, Dragon Egg	200	10	12000	No	No	Healed by Ender Crystals

The Ender Dragon is a unique monster that appears only in The End, a special world that can't be accessed until you complete a number of goals. Our explanation for getting to The End appears in the "You Can Do Anything with a Little Practice" chapter.

Fighting the Ender Dragon is difficult. You face an opponent with massive health, mobility, and damage output. Endermen in the area attack if you look at them during the fight. To make matters worse, crystals in The End heal the Ender Dragon, making it practically impossible to kill until you destroy the crystals. Wow.

Avoid the Ender Dragon's charge attack, and know that it can dive through or destroy most blocks. You can't hide from this sucker! Dodge its charges and use the time between them to get to those crystals. Once they're trashed, shoot at the Ender Dragon from behind after it passes you in a charge. Keep your health topped off as best you can. As with the trip to The End, this is covered at greater length in the "You Can Do Anything with a Little Practice" chapter.

ENDERMITE

AGGRESSION	SPAWN LOCATION	ITEMS	HEALTH	ATTACK DAMAGE	EXPERIENCE VALUE	TAMEABLE?	RIDEABLE?	NOTES
Aggressive	Anywhere	None	8	2	3	No	No	Have a 5% chance of appearing after you throw an Ender Pearl

Endermites are a monster that was added in the 1.8 update to *Minecraft*. They're incredibly small but nasty little things. You find them after throwing Ender Pearls, but there isn't a very high chance for them to appear (only 1 in 20). They don't take much damage, so cut them down as soon as possible.

GHAST

AGGRESSION	SPAWN LOCATION	ITEMS	HEALTH	ATTACK DAMAGE	EXPERIENCE VALUE	TAMEABLE?	RIDEABLE?	NOTES
Aggressive	The Nether, out in the open	Gunpowder, Ghast Tears	10	17	5	No	No	Their shots cause an area-of-effect explosion of fire

Ghasts live in the Nether. They're flying, white balls of fluff that fire explosive shots at your character. Their damage output is very good, and their area-of-effect fire blasts set tons of Netherrack on fire, making it hard to move safely when you fight Ghasts.

These monsters also have great vision. They spot you from far away, so sneaking past them isn't easy. You usually have to hit them with Bow attacks instead. Kill them by aiming around their tentacles. If you're really lucky and brave, use a melee attack to bounce Ghasts' fireballs back at them. This is effective but very hard to pull off without substantial practice.

Never get close to Zombie Pigmen while dealing with Ghasts. The explosions from these fire attacks can enrage the Zombie Pigmen, and they'll blame you for their suffering!

GUARDIAN AND ELDER GUARDIAN

AGGRESSION	SPAWN LOCATION	ITEMS	HEALTH	ATTACK DAMAGE	EXPERIENCE VALUE	TAMEABLE?	RIDEABLE?	NOTES
Aggressive	Underwater	Prismarine Crystals, Prismarine Shards, Raw Fish	30	6	10	No	No	Have a ranged attack and defensive spikes
Aggressive	Underwater	Prismarine Crystals, Prismarine Shards, Raw Fish	80	8	10	No	No	Have a ranged attack and defensive spikes

Guardians are aquatic creatures that have a powerful laser attack and vicious spikes that wound anyone who attacks them in melee. The spikes retract when Guardians are swimming, so you can attack them safely at that time, but it's hard to sneak up on them unless you are Invisible. During battle, Guardians look directly at their intended target, charge their laser eyes, and then fire after a few seconds. This attack does strong damage if you don't have any armor, but it's quite survivable as long as you have decent gear.

Water Breathing, enchanted armor, and patience are all useful for killing these pesky targets. They're dangerous to burn down quickly because of the spikes. It's better to fight near obstacles so you can block the laser and come out for free hits afterward.

Guardians can drop a variety of fish, depending on your luck. This is similar to the effects of fishing, so it's random which type of fish you receive.

Elder Guardians have higher stats and inflict Fatigue on players that get too close to them (this has a 50-block range and occurs once per minute to an individual target). Elder Guardians only appear near and within underwater monuments, so if you're hit with the Fatigue, you know that you're getting close to a monument and should find the body of water that it's in. Once you kill the three Elder Guardians that protect each underwater monument, they're gone forever. Bring friends, or use potions and higher-end equipment to kill the Elder Guardians as best you can. They'll be in different sections of the monument, so you won't get rushed by the entire trio. The standard layout is to find an Elder Guardian at the top of each monument and then another in each of the two wings of the temple.

MAGMA CUBE

AGGRESSION	SPAWN LOCATION	ITEMS	HEALTH	ATTACK DAMAGE	EXPERIENCE VALUE	TAMEABLE?	RIDEABLE?	NOTES
Aggressive	The Nether	Magma Cream	16	6	4	No	No	Split into smaller and weaker Magma Cubes as they take damage

Magma Cubes are Slimes from the Nether. They are fairly slow, hopping creatures that do damage by bouncing into you. They split into smaller monsters when they take damage, making it harder to defend against the whole bunch.

Focus on individual, smaller Magma Cubes to weaken their force. Don't try to kill everything at once, or you're forced to fight quite a few smaller Magma Cubes without a break. Bow attacks are much safer against Magma Cubes, and the monsters certainly don't dodge well. However, it is fun to use your Sword on them if you're cautious and a little gutsy. This cuts down on Arrow use dramatically, because Magma Cubes have quite a bit of total health to shoot through.

SILVERFISH

AGGRESSION	SPAWN LOCATION	ITEMS	HEALTH	ATTACK DAMAGE	EXPERIENCE VALUE	TAMEABLE?	RIDEABLE?	NOTES
Aggressive	Spawn inside special blocks or from Monster Spawners	None	8	1	5	No	No	Silverfish blocks take slightly more time to break

Silverfish are hidden monsters that live inside fake blocks. They're found deep inside the Overworld, waiting for you to mine them. Blocks that seem to take longer than usual to mine are actually Silverfish. Once they're uncovered, they attack and cause other Silverfish in the area to break out of their blocks and charge you. This sometimes leads to very large and dangerous battles.

Retreat to a defensive area when a Silverfish appears. You can get onto a two-block pillar and kill the Silverfish safely up there. Or, you can lure them into a spot in a narrow corridor that is somewhat safe. As long as all the Silverfish are on one side of the passage, it's fairly easy to dispatch them. Getting surrounded is the main thing to avoid when you fight these pests.

SKELETON

AGGRESSION	SPAWN LOCATION	ITEMS	HEALTH	ATTACK DAMAGE	EXPERIENCE VALUE	TAMEABLE?	RIDEABLE?	NOTES
Aggressive	Low light areas of Nether Fortresses or the Overworld	Arrow, Bone	20	3 with Bows, 2 with Swords	5	No	No	Sometimes drop their Bows when killed

Skeletons are the biggest annoyances in the Overworld when you're topside, and they're pretty frustrating down in the mines as well. Skeletons have ranged attacks that are fast, accurate, and painful. Their Arrows push you back, making it harder to reach the Skeleton and possibly knocking you off ledges, into Lava, or otherwise causing problems.

Whenever possible, use cover to lure Skeletons toward you. Up close, they're fairly weak and easy to kill. They also drop great treasure; Bones are used to tame Wolves and grow crops, and the free Arrows sure aren't bad either. Sometimes Skeletons even drop their Bows. So, they're valuable enemies to fight, even if they are jerks.

Don't stand on narrow ledges or near dangerous obstacles when facing Skeletons. If you hear their Bows twang, immediately find cover and figure out where the enemy is firing. Use your Bow to counter them if they don't come forward, such as when they're across a chasm. Alternatively, tunnel into the rock, come around to a safe area, and approach them that way. They can't shoot through solid blocks!

The absolutely worst fight with a Skeleton is in Water when you have only a Sword. The Water slows you down, and this, combined with the push back from Skeleton's ranged attacks, can effectively keep you from getting to your enemy. At this point, it's best to retreat and wait for a better situation.

SLIME

AGGRESSION	SPAWN LOCATION	ITEMS	HEALTH	ATTACK DAMAGE	EXPERIENCE VALUE	TAMEABLE?	RIDEABLE?	NOTES
Aggressive	Lower areas of the Overworld	Slimeball	16	4	4	No	No	Breaks into smaller Slimes when damaged

Slimes appear in Swamps (often at night) or in deeper sections of the Overworld. You hear them from great distance because of the telltale squishing noises they make when they jump around. The Slimeballs they drop are pretty useful, so Slime hunting is periodically a worthwhile pursuit. If you find Slimes at a location once, you'll likely bump into them again there in the future. They are somewhat predictable in their spawns. So, mark these areas well and return later for more hunting.

To kill Slimes, use Arrows at range, or approach them carefully with your Sword out. Attack several times in melee, back off, and repeat the assault when you see how the Slime splits apart. Kill smaller Slimes before dealing with larger ones because you don't want to coat the entire area with little hopping menaces; that increases the chance of taking damage.

Slimes spawn even if it's light in the area, so even well-lit Dungeons can have spawns if the conditions are right for Slime growth.

SPIDER JOCKEY

AGGRESSION	SPAWN LOCATION	ITEMS	HEALTH	ATTACK DAMAGE	EXPERIENCE VALUE	TAMEABLE?	RIDEABLE?	NOTES
Aggressive	Low light areas of the Overworld	Bone, Arrow, String, Spider Eye	20 for Skeleton, 16 for Spider	3 for Skeleton, 2 for Spider	10 total	No	No	These are rare spawns, so you don't see them often

Chicken Jockeys are cute and a little dangerous. However, Spider Jockeys aren't cute at all—they're just creepy. You have to deal with a Skeleton that has greater mobility and a Spider that's ready to attack you as well. It's a mean duo.

The Spiders can move on their own, so these Jockeys move like Spiders. The Skeletons only control their ranged attacks, which are as accurate as ever. To play it safe, sprint toward cover and ready your best melee weapon. Eat while you wait if necessary, and then ambush the Spider Jockey when it turns the corner. At close range, you can kill these guys. Still, expect to take damage, so don't even try this fight if your health is low, your armor is poor, or if you're nervous.

WITCH

AGGRESSION	SPAWN LOCATION	ITEMS	HEALTH	ATTACK DAMAGE	EXPERIENCE VALUE	TAMEABLE?	RIDEABLE?	NOTES
Aggressive	Low light areas of the Overworld	Glass Bottle, Glowstone Dust, Gunpowder, Redstone, Spider Eye, Stick, Sugar	26	Potions of Poison and Harming	5	No	No	Rarely drop potions when killed

You don't see Witches as frequently as many monsters in the Overworld, and that's a good thing. These humanoids have potions that can hurt or poison your character, or protect the Witch from harm. Witches can heal themselves and speed their movement, so they have a little bit of everything. Good weapons are very important when you fight a Witch; they have enough health that any damage improvement makes a big difference. Iron Swords are advised!

Because Witches use Harm and Poison attacks, you want to kill them quickly. The longer the fight, the bigger your disadvantage becomes. If you can't eliminate a Witch quickly and become poisoned, mount a sprinting retreat to put cover between your character and the Witch, so additional potions don't hit you.

If you have really good timing, lure a Witch toward a corridor or house with a Door. Keep the Door closed until the Witch is nearby. Open the Door, hit the Witch, and close the Door. Wait a moment and then repeat the process. Witches take a moment to unleash their potion attacks, so this technique is fairly reliable if you have good reflexes.

WITHER

AGGRESSION	SPAWN LOCATION	ITEMS	HEALTH	ATTACK DAMAGE	EXPERIENCE VALUE	TAMEABLE?	RIDEABLE?	NOTES
Aggressive	Summoned by player	Nether Star	300	8	50	No	No	Created with SoulSand and Wither Skeleton Skulls

Withers are major enemies, much like the Ender Dragon. Don't go up against these guys unless you're ready for a serious fight and know what you're doing. For a full strategy on killing these guys, look in our section covering the Nether in the "You Can Do Anything with a Little Practice" chapter.

One can summon Withers by creating an altar of Soul Sand in a T-formation. Place a Wither Skeleton Skull on all three upper blocks of Soul Sand. When you do this, the altar summons a Wither. Make sure to avoid fighting these monsters near your home; they do horrific damage to the land around them. We strongly recommend fighting them deep underground or far away from home.

WITHER SKELETON

AGGRESSION	SPAWN LOCATION	ITEMS	HEALTH	ATTACK DAMAGE	EXPERIENCE VALUE	TAMEABLE?	RIDEABLE?	NOTES
Aggressive	Nether Fortresses	Coal, Bone	20	7	5	No	No	Can drop Wither Skeleton Skulls and Stone Swords

Wither Skeletons guard Nether Fortresses, special areas within the Nether. Unlike generic Skeletons, these undead foes favor melee weapons. They're extremely deadly, dealing high damage up front and causing a damage-over-time effect as well. You need solid armor, full health, and hopefully a full hunger bar to go against Wither Skeletons.

Arches that are only two blocks high are too small for Wither Skeletons to pass through. If you see a Wither Skeleton ahead, place blocks behind you to form a barrier that has just enough room for your character to run through. Shoot at the Wither Skeleton, bring it to the low arch, and then keep hitting it with Arrows. Hit-and-run attacks also work, if you're careful. Another classic move is to attack while backing up. This is effective against many monsters, and it's very good against Wither Skeletons, as long as you don't fall off a ledge or Blazes and/or other Wither Skeletons don't attack you at the same time.

Keep equipment off the ground when you go through Nether Fortresses. Wither Skeletons are quite happy to pick up Bows or Swords, and they're evil when they get their bony hands on either.

ZOMBIES AND ZOMBIE VILLAGERS

AGGRESSION	SPAWN LOCATION	ITEMS	HEALTH	ATTACK DAMAGE	EXPERIENCE VALUE	TAMEABLE?	RIDEABLE?	NOTES
Aggressive	Nether Fortresses	Coal, Bone	20	7	5	No	No	Can drop Wither Skeleton Skulls and Stone Swords
Aggressive	Low light areas of the Overworld	Rotten Flesh	20	1-6	5	No	No	Can be cured with a Splash Potion of Weakness

There are several types of Zombies in *Minecraft*, though the techniques to deal with them are similar. Zombies, Baby Zombies, and Zombie Villagers are all pretty much mindless, undead horrors. They move toward your character, moaning and trying to kill you with slow melee attacks. Baby Zombies have higher walking speed, but that and their short stature is the only significant distinction.

Zombies can spawn with equipment or pick up things they find. Well-equipped Zombies are more dangerous, so watch out for them. Kill those Zombies first when fighting a group. And speaking of groups, it's rare to encounter just a single Zombie. They often appear with several allies, so back off until you see where all your enemies are standing. Lure them into lining up for the fight by retreating until all the Zombies are somewhat close together. Then attack and retreat as you thin their ranks. Zombies with helmets are very lucky; sunlight doesn't cause them to burst into flames (until the helmet itself is destroyed). Pumpkins serve the same role.

Villagers that are killed by Zombies have a chance of turning. If they rise as Zombie Villagers, there is still some hope. A Splash Potion of Weakness leaves the Zombie Villager in a vulnerable state. Feed it a Golden Apple afterward and wait a moderate amount of time; the Zombie Villager will return to life.

BIGGER AND BETTER PROJECTS

Minecraft scales as much as you want. You can build entire countries within it, or you can make a log cabin and live out a hermit's life. Or do both. Whatever you like, do it. In this chapter, we cover more challenging construction projects. Pyramids, cities, massive rail systems, and mountain kingdoms are examples of this style of larger builds.

Searching the Internet, you can find countless examples of works from your favorite fantasy worlds and history alike. Some of these have taken multiple people years to create, and that proves how boundless *Minecraft's* extremes can be.

SAMPLE PROJECT: CHICHEN ITZA

Our first example is a fairly simple project. While still large as a build, we wanted to show something that could be done in a single day with just 4-8 hours of work. That's long enough to give you an idea of the principles of larger builds, without getting too daunting.

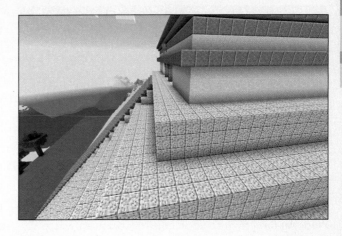

We chose a classic building, El Castillo of Chichen Itza, because it's such a cool and recognizable image. A number of people have created this building in *Minecraft*, so it's kind of a "Hello World" for people who want to try out larger buildings.

HISTORY OF CHICHEN ITZA

In ancient times, Chichen Itza thrived as one of the largest Mayan cities in the Yucatan Peninsula of Mexico. The Mayan civilization was the greatest power of the early Mesoamerican region, and, at their height, the Mayans controlled a third of Mesoamerica. They are known for their calendar system, art, and architecture. They also recorded their history with language on the walls of their cities or temples, upon pottery, and in screenfold books, although most of those were destroyed.

Chichen Itza (translated name "At the mouth of the well of the Itza") was originally settled somewhere between 415 and 455 C.E., but the city grew to prominence around 600 C.E. At this time, much of the Mayan civilization was in decline, but it remains a mystery as to why (although long-term drought certainly played an important role). Nonetheless, people were fleeing their established homes to the south and flooding into Chichen Itza, which boasted a plentiful water source. Because of this influx, Chichen Itza became a huge political and cultural center, with the city-state dominating the local area.

The second settlement of Chichen Itza occurred when it was conquered in the 10th century by the Toltecs, under the King of Tula, Ce Acatl Topiltzin Quetzalcoatl. The Toltecs were not benevolent conquerors; instead, they subjugated the local population with such ferocity that even their ruling descendants regarded it with both awe and terror. The Mayans themselves were not a gentle civilization, so this must have been quite harrowing. As an example, the Toltecs believed in human sacrifice, and although this was probably done by the Mayans occasionally, this was rarely, if ever, practiced by Chichen Itza residents before the Toltecs took them over.

After the conquest of Chichen Itza, the city architecture became a fusion of both Mayan and Toltec elements (called Maya-Yucatec). One of the prime examples of this style is the central pyramid that dominates the city. This pyramid is called El Castillo, and it's a temple dedicated to Kukulkan (a serpent deity closely linked to the Toltec/Aztec god Quetzalcoatl).

We encourage you to examine other monuments in Chichen Itza, most notably the Temple of the Warriors, which is surrounded by a huge number of impressive stone pillars called the Group of a Thousand Columns; El Caracol, which may have been an early astronomic observatory; and the Cenote Sagrado, which is a natural sinkhole filled with water that was used as a sacred pilgrimage site and sacrificial center.

The end of Chichen Itza as a thriving city is unknown. However, by the 13th century, there was no new construction. When the Spanish conquistadors arrived in Chichen Itza, they found a small local population, but certainly no grand metropolis. Most of the city itself had been claimed by the surrounding wilderness. By 1588, Spain had taken all of the Yucatan, and Chichen Itza became a (admittedly impressive) cattle ranch. It wasn't until 1841 that the site was excavated, revealing its archeological importance.

Today, Chichen Itza is owned by the state of Yucatán, and the site's stewardship is maintained by Mexico's Instituto Nacional de Antropología e Historia (National Institute of Anthropology and History). An estimated 1.2 million tourists visit the ruins every year, making it the second most-visited archaeological site in Mexico. Even the pyramid of Chichen Itza conjures fantasies of forgotten ancient ruins buried in the jungle, and we're sure that it will continue to inspire creators for many years to come.

Preparation and Research

The early stages of a build are quite important. Plunging directly into your construction can waste hours because of awkward measurements, poor materials, or myriad other mistakes. Taking an hour or two to figure out what you're doing is well worth the time. The bigger the project, the better your planning needs to be. This is true with single-player builds, and even more accurate when other players join the process. Having multiple people work together can be tricky because someone might not be as careful and end up making your projects with the wrong number or incorrect types of blocks.

So sit down and look at the types of buildings that are inspiring you. In our case, we're doing the classic pyramid of El Castillo. There are tons of pictures of the real building to peruse, so that's where we began. We also read through a wiki about the building to get the proper dimensions of the structure. You don't have to follow the proper scale, but doing so makes it easier to try and recreate a building that exists in the real world. You're less likely to have the dimensions feel off in the final product. While making our building, we left pictures of El Castillo up in our browser, and Alt-Tabbed back and forth to it frequently to make sure things looked decently similar. This helped tremendously while working on the upper temple. Our original looked very bland and didn't approximate some of the outer features at all. With some thought, we found a few ways to create additional elements that came much closer to the real temple. Inverted staircases really made the upper roof pop, and then we used Andesite blocks above the openings to mirror the darker highlights on El Castillo.

We see that El Castillo is 24 meters high and has a 6 meter temple on top of the pyramid. It's also 55.3 meters across on its sides. There are nine tiers on the pyramid. We can't make those measurements perfectly within *Minecraft*, but we can do a decent job of it.

To come close, we're going to make each level three blocks high. That gives us 27 blocks of rise, which is going to feel really close to the 24 meters of the actual building. *Minecraft* blocks take two on top of each other to equal the height of a fully grown person, so saying that they're about a meter high feels adequate. Thus, for reference, we're saying that *Minecraft* blocks are a cubic meter.

Writing your measurements down on paper, or in an electronic document, really helps at this stage. Graph paper is awesome because it's exactly what people use when they're trying to build something with specific dimensions. There are free downloadable pieces of graph paper that you can print, so you won't need a trip to the store unless you want to go out.

After our research, we write down that our levels are three blocks high, with nine total tiers. Then we decide to make the sides 60 blocks each. Again, that isn't exactly the same as El Castillo's 55.3 meter sides, but it's very close and even.

Our foundation will thus be a large square measuring 60x60 blocks of whatever material we'll be using. To do this fully, we'd use 3,600 blocks of material. However, we have options there. It's possible to build over open air in *Minecraft*, so we can create the outer foundation and leave the interior of the pyramid empty. Or we could even make interior rooms, just for fun.

Another option, for people who want to make a building more realistic, is to create the outer sections of your building with special materials (we'll be using Diorite for our exterior), but use Cobblestone or another ultra-common material for non-visual structures. It's a way to save on your best materials if you're building something in Survival Mode.

CREATIVE OR SURVIVAL MODE?

There isn't a right or wrong answer regarding builds in Creative or Survival Mode. It's obviously a more challenging task to work in Survival Mode. You have to contend with monsters, limited resources, and the time it takes to gather the necessary materials. For any build, there is a massive feeling of accomplishment when you finish your work in Survival Mode.

However, Creative Mode has a strong place as well. Though easier to work with (by far), it allows people to come together and experiment with all of the blocks in the game without needing to worry about the hours it takes to mine everything. Make gigantic cathedrals of Diamond and Obsidian. It's just as easy in Creative as making a wall of dirt. But in Survival, that type of undertaking is going to be brutal, even with multiple people working together.

Go with whatever motivates you the most. Almost all of our own work is done in Survival, though recreating El Castillo was done in Creative due to time constraints.

Sticking to Your Measurements

Even with a plan in place, you need to be very rigorous about laying your foundation. Our plan of a pyramid with 60x60 sides is a rather easy one to stick to, but lose count when you're setting things up and suddenly you're lopsided. To help avoid this, use milestones when making runs that are relatively large. Every 10 or 20 blocks, place a torch. This makes it much easier to quickly assess your distances in the future. That comes in handy even after the blocks are on the ground, so leave your markers until the project is entirely done. For example, you can easily put your 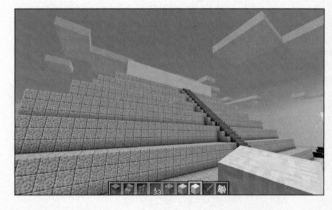 staircases off-center if you don't carefully find the middle point of your walls. Having the torches makes it much faster to figure out where to start placing those elements.

Maybe it goes without saying, but counting is a powerful way to stay on your measurements while putting down blocks. If you're easily distracted, make sure to go back and recount the final product to ensure that you didn't get a bit creative with the math. It's slower this way, but it avoids looking at your finished building and saying, "That wall is three blocks too long. Oh, crud. This will take forever to fix." In tiny builds, a correction takes seconds, so who cares if you do something wrong. But the larger the build, the more time it'll take to correct something.

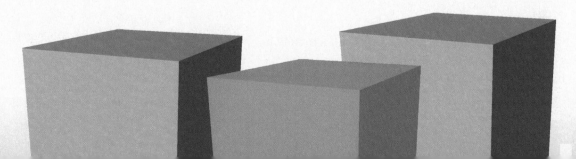

Our Actual Build

We chose Diorite as our primary building material because it gives the closest visual look to El Castillo. The color is very good, and the texture of the rock is closer to the rather smooth stone of the pyramid. The temple on top has a different appearance, so we switched to Chiseled Quartz blocks there. This sets the temple off and gives some variety to the structure. For an Egyptian pyramid, we'd probably go with a traditional Sandstone set, unless you're adding the limestone cap. For those, I'd try Nether Quartz again—it's so nice and bright.

Let's take a moment to talk about the problems that we had, even with a relatively simple project like this. El Castillo was a one-day project, and we'd estimate that almost an hour was still wasted on small mistakes, inefficient construction, and only decent planning. There is always room for improvement.

What did we do right, and what did we do wrong?

One of us (and by that, I mean me) didn't check our torch milestone markers when making a staircase. "This looks like the middle, and it's right next to a torch." Yup. The wrong torch. So one of our staircases is off-center. We decided to leave that in, because it's a great example of what happens when you get fast and free with your measurements.

But all in all, the final product was almost exactly what we wanted to make. The overall appearance of the building is quite nice, the dimensions feel solid, and the pyramid is great to walk around and explore. We were especially happy with the stairs, once we widened them a little.

To keep things uniform, we show all of our screenshots without Resource Packs or shaders installed, but El Castillo looks amazing when you add proper shadows and watch the sunset. So nice.

El Castillo is just one of our projects. Now it's time to talk about another (one that's even more ambitious)!

NEXT UP: A MOUNTAINOUS UNDERTAKING!

Any project in *Minecraft* is all about taking the picture in your head and assembling it bit by bit. It undergoes revisions, runs into unexpected problems, and occasionally requires some creative reworking of the original idea. But in order to create, you must first imagine what you want to do. Anyone can dig a hole in the ground and call it a house (and all of us have at the start!), but when you want to go bigger, you'll need to spend some time getting in touch with your inner dreamer.

Large scale projects take time, and even in Creative Mode you can spend hours (if not days) just working on clearing out an area, or laying the groundwork for a later build. It's not all drudgery, though! In addition to the incredible feeling of accomplishment that comes at the end when your creation is finished, there are small moments of intense satisfaction to be found along the way as you tear apart the landscape and shape it to your needs.

For instance, have you ever wanted to blow up a mountain, and then build a fortress inside? We did! The goal of this build was to carve a space out of the rocky innards of a mountain (using lots of TNT), and then build a large base within the rocky shell.

Demolitions and Groundwork

The first step in hollowing out this mountain was getting a handle on the size. Creative Mode is incredibly useful for a build of massive size. Not only do you get access to all of the necessary building materials, but you can destroy any block without specialized tools or waiting for it to break. You also get access to the single most useful tool in all of *Minecraft*: the ability to fly. This lets you get all sorts of different perspectives on your creation and lets you get to all of the little nooks and crannies speedily. You don't have to use it, but it makes your life a *lot* easier.

Taking to the air provided us a better perspective on the mountain, which influenced the build. In this case, a flyover revealed that while the mountain was tall, it was kind of skinny (for a mountain range).

Any build inside this mountain would need to incorporate a lot of vertical building. The original idea was to hollow it out and then build a fortress inside, but the skinniness of the mountain meant that a sprawling horizontal build would be a lot harder to pull off. However, a build that rose from the bottom of the mountain to the top would have lots of space to work with.

Swinging around to the back of the mountain revealed that it had two large hollows already present. This provided access to the interior and a way to start hollowing it out.

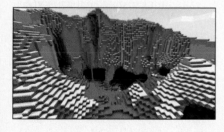

When planning a large build, think about how much the existing landscape needs to be altered. For instance, it is one thing to say, "I'm going to hollow out a mountain," and another to spend hour after hour removing rock and dirt from your build site before you can even lay down a block. Carefully examining the site for potential problems at the start can really save time later.

It didn't look like there were any further geographical complications from the outside. So this is where we decided to begin our work. Let the blasting commence!

Potions of Night Vision are incredibly useful in this sort of work. You'll have to light the area later, but during the build itself, keep that little bottle handy in your hotbar!

Getting an idea of how much stone is actually involved here becomes apparent during the initial drill to the top of the mountain. Widening the initial hole could be accomplished through carefully spiraling outward, or you could use TNT to blast your way to a better, more open future.

As the hole widened, layer by layer, the clock ticked away. People have limited amounts of endurance when it comes to crafting, and during a large scale build, you need to be careful to take breaks and save. It's all about finding that point where you are doing more harm than good! Every build has a point where you want nothing more than to set fire to the whole thing. And when working with TNT, there will absolutely be times when the urge to keep filling a room with more and more TNT becomes overpowering.

Save the game, make a copy of your world, and take a deep breath. Then light the fuse! You have to be able to blow off some steam during a big build, so take some time to revel in destruction. Just make sure to save first in case you end up trashing your own work! Backing up your save files is quite valuable, especially if you reach milestones in the project that are especially successful. "I can always fall back to this later if things don't work out."

Construction Begins

With a large area now successfully carved out of the mountain, construction could begin. It was time to start thinking about building materials and light sources!

I wanted to use the Sea Lanterns for my lighting, as they provide as much light as Glowstone and Redstone Lamps. They don't really work as flooring, though. Glowstone doesn't really look good as a flooring material either (especially with the Sea Lanterns as an additional light source), so I went with Gold Blocks. The solid color and strong contrast really worked well in the end. It gives the place a Hall of the Mountain King feel, and that's pretty cool.

A strong central feature would really unite the build. The mountain has a lot of vertical space, so creating a central feature that everything else could wind around would really pull it all together. We had a lot of options, like a central lava fall, or a central light fixture, or a massive stalactite or stalagmite. However, the Gold Block flooring provided an unforeseen bonus; it allowed for the construction of a Beacon!

Beacons send a column of light into the sky, which would work really well as a central feature for this build. Beacons need to be built on a pyramid of Gold, Diamond, Emerald, or Iron Blocks. With our floor made entirely of Gold Blocks, this won't be an issue.

Beacons need an unobstructed view of the sky in order to turn on, but a quick flight to the top of the mountain removed the last few blocks that were in the way. A few Glass Blocks later, and the Beacon was lit!

Lighting the rest of the interior was a matter of stringing Sea Lanterns on the walls, and building vertical spirals of Sea Lanterns to the ceiling on Dark Oak fence posts.

Setbacks and Problems

Midway through the build, I ran into an unexpected problem. I had *way* too many monsters wandering around my build. Sure, it was Creative Mode, but I wouldn't really feel like the place was mine until I cleared them out and figured out how they were getting in.

As I flew around, I found lots of little nooks and crannies in darkness where the monsters could spawn, as well as several small holes in the retaining walls—during the demolitions I had occasionally gotten too zealous with the TNT and blown holes that were a bit too big for what was needed. In addition, there were several open holes to the outside in the ceiling and the sides that were allowing monsters to just wander in!

Three hours of work later, I had sealed all the outside holes and made sure that anywhere that wasn't lit well was a sheer drop to the floor. So anything that did spawn in the dark places would have nowhere to go but a sheer drop and a sudden stop.

This is one of those instances where a bit more thought ahead of time would have made a difference in the initial demolitions. I was aware that dark areas spawned monsters, and I would need a lot of light to deal with the large open space that I was creating. However, during the actual demolitions, and during the construction, I was using Potions of Night Vision constantly. To me, the area was brightly lit (regardless of the actual light level), and so the whole problem slipped under my radar until late in the build. I also got a little TNT happy during demolitions and broke through the walls a few times. Patching the holes wasn't as much fun as making new ones with TNT, so I put it off until later. Both of these issues were relatively small and could have been dealt with much earlier—putting them off meant I had to stop everything mid-build!

Stairway to Progress

With my Beacon lit, and the lighting poles in place, construction resumed. The next step was to build a spiraling wooden staircase around the Beacon, following the light toward the ceiling. At regular intervals, platforms would be constructed to allow for living spaces. Dark Oak was the best wood for the purpose, as it provided a strong contrast with the Sea Lanterns and Gold floor.

The first platform was going to be the living platform. Every fortress needs a place for the lord of the castle to sleep, so a bed was a foregone conclusion. However, it looked all alone by itself on such a large platform!

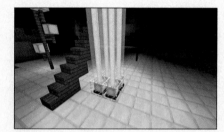

A nice red carpet added a touch of color, and a variety of chests and crafting stations guaranteed that anyone who lived in this fortress would have everything they needed to expand if they wanted to go to Survival Mode later on. It was a touch too dark, so a few more Sea Lanterns completed the platform.

SWITCHING FROM CREATIVE TO SURVIVAL

In the PC version of the game, you can switch a world to LAN Mode to open things to your friends and others. While doing this, you can also change the game's mode. This is a viable way to transition to Survival Mode after a major build is completed.

A few more turns on the staircase and it was time for another platform. This was going to be the library platform, with an Enchanting station and lots of Bookcases. The red carpet worked so well on the previous platform that I kept the theme with this one.

Moving up a few more turns led to the third platform, which was going to be all about potions and brewing. A Brewing station, Cauldron, and plenty of Chests ensured that anyone who wanted to make potions would have all the materials at hand!

None of these platforms took all that long because of all my preparation. I had a strong idea of what I wanted for each one, and all the materials and space that I needed. All I had to do was make a few measurements, to keep the widths consistent, and everything just clicked into place!

The Final Platform

The last platform was going to be a bit different. Initially, it was going to be an observation deck at the very top of the mountain. But as I was building the staircase, I decided it would be the perfect place for a garden. Most gardens end up on the ground level of a build, but there was no real reason why it couldn't be on top. And the proximity to the surface meant it would be extremely easy to knock a hole in the ceiling to let in additional light. Besides, everyone needs fresh vegetables, even people who live inside mountain fortresses!

The platform for the garden was extra-thick, so a water channel could be built (and so it wouldn't leak). Because the top of the mountain was so near at hand, it was a simple matter to create a hole and use glass blocks to provide natural light.

Shortly after finishing the platform, the water blocks started freezing. The top of the mountain was a chilly, snow covered place, and the water was freezing from the cold! The quickest solution was to put Sea Lanterns beneath each water block to make sure that it stayed melted.

With the water flowing and the crops flourishing, the final platform was complete!

Home Sweet Mountain Home

With the platforms complete and the Sea Lanterns pushing back the darkness, everything looked good! If I wanted to expand on the mountain fortress, there were plenty of possibilities—underground railways, secret dungeons, and so forth—but this was the core of the build. Very fun.

OTHER PEOPLE'S COOL PROJECTS

Here are some neat examples of other things that people have made with *Minecraft*. Take a look and see what you think of these larger builds.

All of Denmark Recreated in Minecraft

The Danish Geodata Agency took on an incredibly ambitious project; they made a 1:1 scale of Denmark within *Minecraft*. It's a four-trillion brick build, and the save file for it weighs in at an entire terabyte. Phew. That's one heck of a download.

The project was accomplished using the agency's own elevation model of the region. Here are a few things we asked them about their work!

I've read that you were trying to raise interest and awareness in spatial data. Could you tell me more about that?

On January 1st, 2013, the Danish spatial data became available for everybody. It opens great opportunities, but in order to use them, people need to know they are there. So we made Denmark in *Minecraft*, mainly to raise interest among children and teachers, but also in general—for example among game developers, because *Minecraft* is a good showcase of the opportunities.

Why did you decide on *Minecraft* as a tool to make people more excited about this?

Very many people know *Minecraft*, so it was a good but different way of getting our message out. And it was fun!

Was it a difficult task to create such a massive area in the game? Even the file size for the completed work is huge!

It actually didn't take us that long, because the spatial data that we used had such high quality.

Is there anything that you'd like to say about your project and its reception?

We are still grateful that so many people got excited about this and decided to share our work. We got much more attention than expected, and we are so proud of our Denmark in *Minecraft*. It really was great fun to work on this project!

Minecart Interstate

SirCrest, on YouTube, put out a video of his Minecart Interstate in the early days of the game. This brought attention to the game and to some of the cool things that everyone could work on. We tracked him down to ask a few questions. Take a look at his work in 1440P to really get a smile.

How much time have you put into Minecart Interstate?

For the original V3.0 video (which at the time was just the third video of the same track which had been extended), I think I told most viewers I spent about 24-26 hours on the build itself. This was spread over perhaps two to three months. And I would be playing the game at the time, not solely placing blocks. The video aspect, I couldn't even tell you. It's been nearly five years since I released that video.

As for the V3.0 remake, likely over 100 hours. Even though the track was technically already made, there was a significant amount of work for updating the map file for use in the then-latest version of *Minecraft*. Loading it in Alpha, then Beta for it to convert, then Release for it to convert again. I had to rotate the entire track in some mapping tools so the sun and moon were in the correct position compared to the original video. Then due to certain mods not being updated in years and with how certain mechanics with the engine had changed, I had to use those same mapping tools to replace parts of the track to keep the same speed, and thus the same timing in the video. I'm boiling it down but this process took a week or two to do.

The recording, editing, and processing of the resulting video took another 30-40 hours, chief of which was just waiting for the video to render at various stages. In order to create the very clean, high fidelity visuals, you need to be a very patient person, or own a tablet to watch stuff on.

Was the construction more a matter of time or planning? Inspiration or perspiration?

Construction was purely time. For a portion of the track, the resources were manually gathered believe it or not. I had a huge hole I dug in the first few hours of owning the game in July of 2010. I had chests full of Cobblestone, and I ended up using most of that for the track. You can see this hole in some of my follow-up videos in 2010 where I talk about the project. To finish the track though, I had to start using some inventory editor tools. This was before the days of MCEdit or mods for giving items. You had to use a save file editor, close the game, find the inventory for that item, type in the amount of blocks, save it, and reload the game and keep building. Very tedious, but to the best of my knowledge I didn't have an alternative.

Do you scan through the areas well ahead of time to judge if everything is going to be scenic, or just start tunneling to see what comes up?

I am still adamant that Alpha had the best world generation. Yes, you only had really one biome; however, that one biome was so well generated. At the time I used the term, "highly realistic, but low resolution." So because of that, I didn't plan anything for V3; I just kept building because, to be honest, I knew it would look interesting and would move well past the view.

For V4, I did use a flycam to scout out the track a few times to see where I'd have problems. But eventually I landed on a generation that I liked.

Do you have any suggestions for other large builders out there? Any tips for doing crazy stuff?

Research your tools. There may be something out there which can automatically do what you want to do manually. While I often enjoy the brute force methods in some of my video projects, that is not always the smartest route. And frankly, I use these video projects as an excuse to try out these methods of video creation. Don't be afraid to sit down and browse forums or do some Internet searches for a few hours before starting on a project; you may find some information to inspire a change or you might find someone did something similar and you can learn from their experience. And that applies to anything in life.

Any Closing Comments?

Only thing I think I'd close with is that, as silly as it sounds, the V3.0 Interstate video changed my life. That video got me interviews with websites and some TV networks. I got thousands upon thousands of emails and comments and messages talking about that video. It jumpstarted my "real" YouTube career as well as all the experience in editing and video production that I have now. If that video didn't go viral, video editing and production would still just be a weird hobby I have, rather than my career and passion.

MODIFYING YOUR GAME

Even the best games sometimes need a few updates to remain exciting, especially if you play for years on end. That's why *Minecraft* has implemented quite a few ways to customize your game, how it's played, and how it appears. We'll wrap up this book by discussing some of the ways to keep *Minecraft* new, even after months or years of use.

THE OPTIONS MENU

Before doing anything radical to modify your game, try the basic options available to everyone.

DIFFICULTY

Knowledge Required	None
Potential for Problems	None

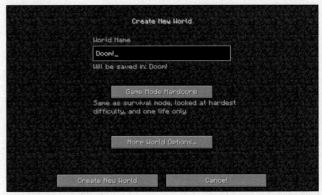

You can modify the game's difficulty at any time, moving it from Peaceful all the way up through Hard. All of the non-Peaceful settings determine the damage output of monsters. It's a fairly impressive spread, but the change between Easy and Hard is very noticeable. If you're into Survival Mode challenges, pushing the difficulty higher and higher is a big way to keep things fun.

Difficulty is set per world, so you can't change the difficulty dynamically. You might want to create several worlds to test different difficulties and challenges under a variety of conditions.

If you find higher difficulty frustrating, it's possible to dial back the settings whenever desired. There is literally no risk or downside to experimenting with this setting—unless you're playing a Hardcore character, in which case you already know what you're getting into. At worst, your character gets killed.

SKINS

Knowledge Required	Low
Potential for Problems	Very Low

Search for "Minecraft Skins" if you'd like to alter the appearance of your character. Sites hosting these skins allow users to download them to a computer or directly upload them to Mojang. Skins can then be added to your account and used in the future.

Skins don't change anything except the look of your character, so they're fairly risk free. There are literally hundreds of skins available, and they can change your character's gender, race, or even species.

BROADCAST SETTINGS

Knowledge Required	You need a Twitch account linked with Mojang
Potential for Problems	Few

Watching other players on Twitch is quite fun, but you don't have to limit yourself to viewing. With online friends or followers, you can stream your gameplay sessions and demonstrate cool building techniques, help others, show off, or whatever else you'd like to do.

To get ideas for what can be done while streaming *Minecraft*, look at other people's channels and see what people like.

RESOURCE PACKS

Knowledge Required	Moderate
Potential for Problems	Moderate

Minecraft gives players the ability to modify the textures, sounds, and functionality of their games through Resource Packs. These are available online at a wide range of sites. Search for "Minecraft and Texture Packs" using your internet browser, and look for places with free content—you can use most of them without cost!

Follow the instructions for installing each pack. Once they're on your system, go into the Options Menu, select the Resource Pack you want to activate, and proceed from there. You can almost completely reinvent *Minecraft* by getting the pack that's right for you.

With Resource Packs installed, it's fairly simple to switch between them. Go with your mood and change the game at your leisure.

Updates to the game engine can sometimes make a Resource Pack non-functional or semi-functional for a while. When this happens, you have to stop using the Resource Pack until it gets an update. This is the most common type of problem.

If you can't run your Resource Pack, go back to regular *Minecraft* (the Default) and stick with that while you check your favorite Resource Pack website for updates. No big deal.

For the maximum effect, use a Resource Pack and a Shader Mod to crank *Minecraft*'s visual beauty to the maximum. The difference is huge. It's like seeing an entirely different game.

GAME MODS

Knowledge Required	High
Potential for Problems	Somewhat High

If you want to go deeper than most Resource Packs, search for "Minecraft mods." People like to push further into the game engine with mods, making it possible to do all sorts of things: mini-maps, engines, pumps, spaceships, more monsters, and so on. There's a lifetime's worth of content to check out.

To use mods, you must download and install them. Each mod should have a guide to help you get it working. You may need to get additional downloads to help with launching mods, so it's not a quick process the first time you try one. Be patient though, and you'll be impressed.

Game mods can be really tricky. They can mess with your game and cause enough disruption that you might not be able to play without reinstalling the game. Be aware of these risks from the outset. If you aren't comfortable enough with computers to back up your *Minecraft* saves, then mods probably aren't for you yet. There's a ton to learn. It's worth the time, but only when you're ready and excited to invest hours getting familiar with everything.

BUILD, DISCOVER, SURVIVE!
MASTERiNG MINECRAFT®
REViSED and EXPANDED

Written by Michael Lummis,
Christopher Burton, and Kathleen Pleet

Illustrations by Daz Tibbles

DK/Prima Games, a division of Penguin Random House LLC.
6081 East 82nd Street, Suite #400
Indianapolis, IN 46250

ISBN: 978-0-7440-1647-5

Printing Code: The rightmost double-digit number is the year of the book's printing; the rightmost single-digit number is the number of the book's printing. For example, 15-1 shows that the first printing of the book occurred in 2015.

18 17 16 15   4 3 2 1

Printed in the USA.

CREDITS

Editor
Matt Buchanan

Book Designer
Jeff Weissenberger

Production Designer
Justin Lucas

PRiMA GAMES STAFF

VP & Publisher
Mike Degler

Editorial Manager
Tim Fitzpatrick

Design and Layout Manager
Tracy Wehmeyer

Licensing
Aaron Lockhart
Christian Sumner

Marketing
Katie Hemlock
Paul Giacomotto

Digital Publishing
Julie Asbury
Tim Cox
Shaida Boroumand

Operations Manager
Stacey Beheler

ACKNOWLEDGEMENTS

Michael Lummis: I'd like to thank the *Minecraft* community for making so much amazing content. *Minecraft*, by itself, is one of the most amazing games I've ever played. Adding the wealth of mods, resource packs, and funny stories from other players has given me more hours of fun than I can count. Keep building neat stuff, everyone, and watch out for those Creepers. Sssssssss. Oops, gotta go!

FREE eGUIDE!

Enter this code at primagames.com/code to unlock your FREE eGuide:

AKV7-74KF-75RY-3337

Mobile Friendly

Access your eGuide on any web-enabled device.

———

Searchable & Sortable

Quickly find the strategies you need.

———

Added Value

Strategy where, when, and how you want it.

Check Out Our Complete eGuide Library
at primagames.com!

www.primagames.com